D1602508

BEYOND
DEATH'S
DOOR

BEYOND DEATH'S DOOR

Understanding Near-Death Experiences in Light of the Restored Gospel

Brent L. Top   Wendy C. Top

BOOKCRAFT
Salt Lake City, Utah

Library of Congress Catalog Card Number: 93–72418

ISBN 0–88494–895–1

Second Printing, 1994

Printed in the United States of America

Dedicated to the memory of
Ralph Palmer Cope, Jr.

Contents

11   The Life Review 197

12   "Welcome Home" 215

13   Eternal Possibilities 228

PART V   Impact on Mortality

14   Changed Lives 251

15   What Does This Mean to Latter-day Saints? 276

      Bibliography 289

      Index 293

Preface

Our fascination with the near-death-experience phenomenon began several years ago after reading Dr. George Ritchie's famous book *Return from Tomorrow* and Dr. Raymond Moody's pioneer work *Life After Life*. We soon became serious students of the subject, reading every book about and examining every account of encounters with the spirit world that we could find, both LDS and others. Through this review of the available literature on near-death experiences we also were introduced to some of the most prominent and highly respected scholars and authors in the field, such as Dr. Kenneth Ring, Dr. Bruce Greyson, Dr. Melvin Morse, Scott Rogo, and many others. From our study we realized that relatively little had been written on the subject from a Latter-day Saint perspective, and those that had been written often lacked the depth and breadth of scholarship that characterized many of the national studies.

As a result of this interest, back in 1989 after the publication of Raymond Moody's third book, *The Light Beyond*, we embarked on serious research with the intent of writing a book for the LDS audience. We were intrigued that in Moody's writings he often referred to Mormon beliefs on death and the spirit world. Hearing him talk on radio and television about the findings in his new book further piqued our interest. We were amazed at the similarities and consistencies between near-death accounts and the doctrines of the restored gospel that pertain to the next life and the plan of salvation. The more we looked into such accounts, the more of these parallels we found. Not only did we find LDS teachings about what the spirit world is like that correlated with the descriptions given by those who have had near-death experiences and other glimpses of the spirit realm, but we also discovered that our doctrines about why such things exist and what it all means were borne out to a remarkable extent in these encounters. We wanted members of the Church to be as thrilled and uplifted as we felt by this. Thus we began what has come to be this book.

In August 1990 Brent, along with Dr. Robert L. Millet, dean of Religious Education at Brigham Young University, attended the annual conference of the International Association for Near-Death Studies. There they met several of the researchers and experiencers cited in this book. When such participants found out that Brent and Dr. Millet were "Mormon" they were very interested, knowing that the Church has a strong belief in and some unique and definitive teachings about death, the afterlife, and the immortality of the soul. They were very encouraging of our research and not at all unwilling to accept religious explanations.

From that experience and their many discussions with NDE researchers and experiencers from around the world, Brent and Dr. Millet became even more convinced than ever that the doctrines of the restored gospel contain most of the answers to life's biggest questions. Explanations for what are perceived by many to be life's inexplicable inequities and death's most troubling dilemmas are to be found in the gospel. Psychologists, medical doctors, social scientists, and others have sought to explain the near-death experience from every possible angle, yet each of their explanations, as thoroughly researched and thought out as it may be, is incomplete and inadequate. The fullest illumination is to be found only in the revelations of God.

Researching and writing this book has not been easy, but it has been rewarding and life-changing. As we would ponder and pray and write, we would be led to find and understand many principles we had missed in previous studies. At those moments we, like those who have glimpsed the spirit world, would marvel at how everything fits together so perfectly and logically. This experience has brought us to a much greater understanding of birth and death, of life and love, of good and evil, of God our Father and his Son, Jesus Christ. We have also gained a greater appreciation for and insight into the magnitude of that "marvelous work and a wonder" we call the Restoration. We often found ourselves in awe of the deep doctrinal teachings and the profound spiritual insight of the prophets and Apostles. And we have come to realize that when it comes to studying and understanding the things of God we have only scratched the surface.

Since most of the experiencers and researchers mentioned in this book are not Mormons, we have chosen the easy course of noting in the text those who *are* of that faith, rather than noting those who are of some other religious persuasion or of none.

We would like to express our gratitude to the staff at Bookcraft for their unwavering support and guidance in the face of some controversy over this subject. Cory Maxwell trusted and believed in us, encouraging us personally and professionally throughout the project. To him we owe a special thanks.

We also wish to extend our appreciation to Dean Robert L. Millet of Brigham Young University for his support and suggestions, as well as to many of Brent's other colleagues in Religious Education at BYU for their willingness to listen to our ideas and serve as "sounding boards" for many of the concepts that are presented here.

This book is dedicated to Wendy's father, who had a brief near-death experience of his own in 1987. He was spared to finish some personal preparations for the world to come; and then he passed on in 1988.

PART I

Introduction

_____

CHAPTER 1

Why Study Death

Death intrigues us; sometimes it terrifies us. Certainly such reactions arise from curiosity about the mysterious and the fear of the unknown. As Latter-day Saints we are often reassured that we need not dread the "grim reaper," as it is so morbidly called; and yet, not seeing or completely understanding what lies beyond and having never experienced anything like it, we may understandably approach death with at least some trepidation.

Some may feel that because death is shrouded in mystery it is frightening and we should never think or talk about it. Others may have the idea that because a veil is drawn over our minds in mortality, we are not to know very much about it. Still others refuse to even mention the subject of death, especially their own, hoping thereby to postpone facing its inevitability. However, the Prophet Joseph Smith importuned the Saints to include this subject in an intense study. "All men know that they must die. And it is important that we should understand the reasons and causes of our exposure to the vicissitudes of life and of death, and the designs and purposes of God in our coming into the world, our sufferings here, and our departure hence. . . . It is but reasonable to suppose that God would reveal something in reference to the matter, and it is a subject we ought to study more than any other. We ought to study it day and night, for the world is ignorant in reference to their true condition and relation. If we have any claim on our Heavenly Father for anything it is for knowledge on this important subject." (*History of the Church*, 6:50.)

Why would the Prophet include the subject of death in such an emphatic and definitive pronouncement? Perhaps it is because the very essence of our mission here on earth is to prepare to die, for if we have properly and faithfully prepared for it, death is our admission to eternal life. Elder Sterling W. Sill once echoed this emphasis on death in LDS theology.

Someone has said that the most important event in life is death. Death is the gateway to immortality. We live to die, and then we die to live. Ordinarily we don't like to think about death because it is associated with unpleasantness.

But death does not cease to exist merely because it is ignored. The ancient Egyptians had a much more logical procedure for handling this situation. On their important festive occasions they kept constantly on display before the revelers a great image of death. They wanted to remind themselves that someday they would die. Now I don't want to frighten anyone unduly here today, but I would just like to point out in passing that someday each one of us is going to die. Someone has said that judging from the past there will be very few of us get out of this world alive, and certainly one of the wisest ways to spend life is in an effective preparation for death. (In Conference Report, April 1964, p. 11.)

Many of the General Authorities of the Church throughout the years have spoken on the importance of preparing for death. President Hugh B. Brown spoke of life as a "pre-natal state" and of death as a form of birth. "Man, in his mortal state," he declared, "is not a being completed and perfect. Rather, mortal life is a prenatal state, awaiting birth. As Franklin so truly said, 'Life is rather a state of embryo, a preparation for life. A man is not completely born until he has passed through death.'" (In Conference Report, April 1967, pp. 48–50.) Elder Delbert L. Stapley contemplated the overriding impact that death and a knowledge of what follows it should rightfully have on mortality.

> It seems strange, but people generally fail to understand these gospel teachings and, living as they do in this mortal world, are prone to think and act in terms of mortal existence, which they only partially understand. As a result, they fail to project themselves into that eternal state of life after the death of the mortal body and to envision their true place in it according to their present manner of living here in mortality. If somehow we could view with clarity the impressive picture of the life hereafter resulting from obeying every gospel principle and ordinance while here, perhaps we would plan our lives in mortality differently and see to it that all our daily actions are motivated by truth and righteousness and good works. Life then would have sincere purpose and would earn rewarding values for the soul. (In Conference Report, April 1961, p. 67.)

President Spencer W. Kimball once pointed out how our understanding of death may affect the whole meaning of our life. "To the unbeliever it [death] is the end of all, associations terminated, relationships ended, memories soon to fade into nothingness. But to those who have knowledge and faith in the promise of the gospel of Jesus Christ, death's meaning is . . . a change of condition into a wider, serener sphere of action; it means the beginning of eternal life, a never-ending existence. It means the continuation of family life, the reuniting of family groups, the perpetuation of friendships, relationships, and associations." (*The Teachings of Spencer W. Kimball*, p. 39.)

Thus, understanding what is important in the next life teaches us what is important in this life, because the foundation of our eternal life is laid in mortality. Death is a "graduation day" for which we are all preparing. This is undoubtedly the most important reason for studying death and is a central thesis of this book. In addition, it should also be noted that acquainting ourselves with the processes and expectations of passing beyond the veil can lessen the anxiety we all have about death. President Joseph F. Smith even taught that we should acquaint our children with the doctrine of death while also teaching them of the Savior's ultimate victory over it.

It is a principle widely accepted that it is not desirable to teach these little ones those things that are horrifying to childish natures. And what may be said of children is equally true in all stages of student life. But death is not an unmixed horror. With it are associated some of the profoundest and most important truths of human life. Although painful in the extreme to those who must suffer the departure of dear ones, death is one of the grandest blessings in divine economy; and we think children should be taught something of its true meaning as early in life as possible.

We are born that we may put on mortality, that is, that we may clothe our spirits with a body. Such a blessing is the first step toward an immortal body, and the second step is death. Death lies along the road of eternal progress; and though hard to bear, no one who believes in the gospel of Jesus Christ, and especially in the resurrection, would have it otherwise. Children should be taught early in life that death is really a necessity as well as a blessing, and that we would not and could not be satisfied and supremely happy without it. Upon the crucifixion and the resurrection of Jesus, one of the grandest principles of the gospel depends. If children were taught this early in life, death would not have the horrifying influence that it does have over many childish minds.

. . . It would be a great relief to the puzzled and perplexed conditions of their minds if some intelligent statements of the reason for death were made to them. No explanation of death to a child's mind can anywhere be found that is more simple and convincing than is the death of our Master, connected as it is and ever must be with the glorious resurrection. (*Gospel Doctrine*, pp. 296–97.)

Indeed, one of the most remarkable things about near-death

experiences is their propensity to completely banish this fear of dying from those who have them. Having once tasted of death, they tend to look forward to passing once again through the veil and entering the spirit world. This should be a source of great comfort to those of us who must live on faith alone. Perhaps these types of experiences are the bestowals of a loving God who desires to teach *all* of his children that death can be a deliverance, not merely a demise.

Why Examine Near-Death Experiences

The reality of near-death experiences (NDEs, as they are called by researchers) and other contacts with the spirit world is nothing new to Latter-day Saints. From the beginning of the Restoration, such events have been faithfully recorded in family and Church histories as deeply spiritual, instructive, and inspiring gifts from God. Other cultures and peoples throughout history have recorded near-death experiences also, but these accounts tend to be rather obscure (see Carol Zaleski, *Otherworld Journeys*). Therefore, they seem to be a relatively new and novel occurrence to much of the rest of the world. Furthermore, it may be that near-death experiences not only are reported more often now that they are becoming more scientifically acceptable but also that they occur more frequently because of modern life-saving technology. Whatever the case may be, those who have immersed themselves in the study of these remarkable experiences overwhelmingly agree that there seems to be some type of divine or spiritual purpose behind them. They believe that a Supreme Being is attempting to communicate an important message to mankind. Dr. Kenneth Ring, whose book *Heading Toward Omega* is subtitled *In Search of the Meaning of the Near-Death Experience*, concluded:

> From the study of the NDE, we have learned to see death in a new way, not as something to be dreaded but, on the contrary, as an encounter with the Beloved. Those who can come to understand death in this way, as NDErs are compelled to, need never fear death again. And liberated

from this primary fear, they too, like NDErs, become free to experience life as the gift it is and to live naturally, as a child does, with delight. Not everyone can have or needs to have an NDE, but everyone can learn to assimilate these lessons of the NDE into his own life if he chooses to.

Beyond this, of course, is the virtual unanimity [that] . . . there is *only* life—life now, and life following what we still presume to call death. This . . . is the message the Light told [one NDEr] to spread—and it is the universal message of hope, . . . from all NDErs. None of these persons brings scientific proof of life after death, of course. They bring something personally more important: subjective proof. They claim to know in a way and from a source that removes all doubt. Each of us must make of this collective testimony what we will, but it is hard—at least for me—to believe that this is a meaningless consolation given to so many for so many more. (*Heading Toward Omega*, pp. 268–69.)

Researchers like Dr. Ring, after witnessing the NDE's incredible ability to transform its percipients to a higher, nobler way of life, also believe that this higher power in the universe is trying to help mankind grow into a kinder, gentler, more ethically and morally advanced society—"the next stage of human evolution, the dazzling ascent toward Omega and the conscious reunion with the Divine" (*Heading Toward Omega*, p. 269).

After careful and extensive review of almost all of the available literature on near-death experiences and studies, we, the authors, tend to agree with these conclusions. We believe that, in general, these types of experiences do come from a loving and merciful Father in Heaven to his children on earth, many of whom are lost, desperate, confused, and afraid. The experiences are, it would seem, a message of hope to the hopeless and love to the loveless. What makes us think they are from God? The Savior taught that "a good tree bringeth not forth corrupt fruit; neither doth a corrupt tree bring forth good fruit. For every tree is known by [its] fruit." (Luke 6:43–44.) The prophet Mormon clarified: "But behold, that which is of God inviteth and enticeth to do good continually; wherefore, every thing which inviteth and enticeth to do good, and to love God, and to serve him, is inspired of God" (Moroni 7:13).

The unquestionably positive overall impact of these near-death experiences and the accompanying spiritual knowledge that comes to those people who have them has led us to believe that they are "virtuous, lovely, . . . of good report . . . [and] praiseworthy," and that we should "seek after" truth by learning from these things (see the thirteenth article of faith). Moreover, we have discovered that they almost always correspond to gospel teachings and can serve to enhance our understanding of the plan of salvation. While near-death studies do not prove the reality of life after death or the existence of God, President Hugh B. Brown taught that scientific and religious inquiry can go hand in hand. "With the tremendous strides that science is making in our day, there is dawning upon this age what might be termed a scientific spirituality—a new type of mind that studies the truths of faith with the care and caution and candor of science, yet keeping the warmth and glow and power of faith. Spiritual insight is as real as scientific insight. Indeed, it is but a higher manifestation of the same thing. The saint as well as the scientist has witnessed the truth of reality. One may deem his knowledge revelation, and the other, intellectual conclusion, but in both cases it is insight—the conviction of reality." (In Conference Report, April 1967, p. 49.)

While there are still many who doubt the actuality of near-death-type experiences, we are certainly not among them. There should be no question in a Latter-day Saint's mind about the reality of a postmortal life or even of a premortal life. There should be no question about the actuality of dreams and visions of the spirit world. We have no doubt that we are spiritual beings inhabiting human bodies; that, when empowered by the Lord to do so, our spirits are able to leave our bodies at death or at other times; and that we are able to discern spiritual things with our spiritual eyes. For these reasons, in this book we will not dwell on proving that NDEs and other spiritual manifestations are a real possibility—are not the result of drugs, hallucinations, psychological phenomena, birth memories, bad dreams, fantasies, or genetically programmed responses to death—as some researchers have sought to do. Neither will we attempt to establish that they are not programmed into us by our religion. There are many other books now available on the national market which attempt to prove, by the scientific method, the validity of near-death experiences as genuine "out-of-body occurrences." These are excellent and fascinating books, and many of them will be cited in this work, but the primary purpose of this book is to strengthen the faith and enhance the doctrinal understanding of those who already believe.

This book is also intended, however, to offer a carefully studied religious explanation for near-death experiences. A whole new academic discipline has grown up around the study of NDEs and similar paranormal phenomena. There is an International Association for Near-Death Studies (IANDS) which encourages and supports the study of these occurrences from every possible angle and even publishes a monthly newsletter (*Vital Signs*) and a quarterly research journal entitled *The Journal of Near-Death Studies*. As mentioned above, researchers have sought every possible explanation from drugs to dreams. We offer this book as an extensive analysis from a religious viewpoint of the restored gospel, which, unlike many other Christian denominations, is rich with doctrines and tenets on the subject of death, the immortality of the soul, the spirit world, and the literal resurrection of all mankind.

Why Use Near-Death Experiences That Are Not LDS

In this study we have primarily used the near-death experiences of people who are not members of The Church of Jesus Christ of Latter-day Saints. There are several reasons for this. First of all, many of the LDS experiences have been published over and over again from the earliest days of the Restoration to the present, and most members of the Church are already well acquainted with them. In addition, several books published recent to the time of this writing have focused exclusively on near-death experiences of Latter-day Saints. While accounts of such experiences, whether LDS or not, are not to be viewed as official doctrine, they tend to support and heighten our comprehension of the world to come. What is most fascinating and gratifying, however, is to study the experiences reported by those outside the Church who either have no preconceived ideas concerning death and the spirit world or have religious beliefs which differ from LDS views, to see how well the reports correspond with and add to our LDS understanding of death and the next life. Such a comparison allows experiencers who are of other faiths to act as a sort of control group in the study of NDEs, since they are not biased toward LDS interpretations of what they have experienced and seen.

Researchers in the field of near-death studies have used similar methodology to determine the validity of the NDE itself. Dr. Melvin Morse conducted a study using children as a control group, because they tend to be "culturally innocent," that is, they haven't absorbed or understood enough of their own culture to understand death and to know what they "should" see or not see in the next life. They usually have no acquaintance with near-death experiences and therefore have no preconceived agenda. For instance, Dr. Morse interviewed one little girl who was revived from death and who described as "doctors" the people in white whom she had seen all about her, because they seemed to be "big and dressed in white and [she] was scared of them" (*Closer to the Light*, pp. 34–35). Despite her strange description, she helped to confirm what many adult NDErs have reported—that they saw beings in human form, dressed in white clothing.

Other researchers have compared different cultures to validate the NDE, deathbed visions, and other out-of-body experiences. One of the more famous cross-cultural studies was conducted by Drs. Karlis Osis and Erlendur Haraldsson, who studied hundreds of NDEs among Christian and Hindu Indians and Christian Americans in an effort to determine the subjective nature of near-death experiences. Their fascinating results were published in a book entitled *At the Hour of Death*. "It became clear to Osis and his co-workers that American deathbed visions had to be compared to those of a culture where the Bible is not part of the population's religious upbringing. [They wanted to] determine whether deathbed visions are a reflection of Bible stories, kind of a playback of what Americans learn through acculturation." (*At the Hour of Death*, p. 20.) They discovered through their studies that while there were definite cultural differences in the perception and description of such experiences, the basic elements of the episodes were the same. Many other near-death researchers have used similar control groups.

Because they often have few or no preconceived ideas about death, most NDErs also tend to describe what they see and experience from a more innocent and basic point of view. Not having learned a religious term for something they might observe or feel, they tend to describe it in detail in order to make it more understandable to those who have never experienced it. For example, LDS teachings set forth the doctrine of a spirit world which is more beautiful and peaceful than this earth. While an LDS person entering the spirit world might take such a thing somewhat for granted because that is what he or she expected to see, other NDErs often give remarkable and enlightening descriptions of this world they unexpectedly encounter after "dying." They portray in detail the buildings, the plant life, the atmosphere, the feelings, the people, the activities, and even the music of that world. We, the authors, have discovered, in reading these delightful and sometimes sobering depictions, that we have much to learn from them. They seem to verify and illustrate many of the things we have always taught and believed. The thrilling and uplifting details provided confirm LDS teachings and beliefs and enlarge our doctrinal understanding.

One example of this is found in the well-known experience of George Ritchie, as detailed by him in his book, *Return from Tomorrow*. He saw beings who had died yet were still desperately but futilely trying to obtain cigarettes and alcohol from those who were still in mortality. He wrote: "Presumably these substance-less creatures had once had solid bodies, as I myself had had. Suppose that when they had been in these bodies they had developed a dependence on alcohol that went beyond the physical. That became mental. Spiritual, even." When they lost that body, he concluded, they would be forever craving the thing they could never have. (See p. 61.) This certainly seems to coincide with doctrinal LDS teachings about one's being possessed by the "same spirit"—that is, attitudes, desires, and so on—that possessed it before death (see Alma 34:34). It would also seem to illustrate graphically and quite literally the teachings of the prophets which indicate that it is much harder to repent or overcome bad habits in the spirit world when we no longer have a body. It reaffirms our belief that *this life*, mortality, is indeed the time to repent and set our hearts upon the things of God—not upon the things of this world.

Countless other examples will be explored and examined in this book. We must always keep in mind, however, that these anecdotal accounts are not proof of the verity of our doctrines and teachings. We can, however, view them as "external evidences"—as somewhat like the many modern discoveries and evidences that have come to light that confirm the teachings and testimony of the Restoration.

Besides adding to our understanding of LDS doctrines, studying the near-death experiences of people not of our faith can provide us with additional insights about how our Heavenly Father deals with *all* of His children. In turn, we can thus learn to see, feel about, and treat them as he does. This insight is important to us because having the blessings and understanding of the gospel may tend to cause some of us to unwittingly fall into the trap of assuming we are somehow superior to or more loved than others, especially those who seem to be sinful or who otherwise don't measure up to our expectations of gospel living. For instance, consider the following experience that Scott Rogo, an NDE researcher, had, as recorded in his book, *The Return from Silence*. While it may raise many questions for us as members of the Church, it also gives us much food for thought.

> I stopped by my neighborhood bar while I was running some errands. . . . The establishment usually caters to those of us in the area, so I was somewhat unnerved to see two rough-looking men sitting together drinking beer. Because of their dress and demeanor, it didn't take long to realize that they were members of a motorcycle gang—i.e., people here in California who like to live nomadically and often tussle with the law. I became more uneasy when a third patron walked up to them and began pointing at me!
>
> The tension mounted when the heavier of the two bikers looked over at me silently. Then he offered an almost

imperceptible smile and cocked his head in the direction of the other patron.

"Do you know anything about people who die and come back?" he finally asked.

The third patron spoke at this moment. "Yeah, he does. Go ahead and ask him."

The biker then asked me what I knew about people resuscitated from death, so I briefly explained what psychology had learned about the near-death experience. The man then opened up completely, since he felt he really had to talk to somebody. It seemed that, a few months previously, a friend and fellow gang member had been involved in a motorcycle crash. The rider had nearly been killed, but his life was saved by the emergency team at a local hospital. When he finally recovered, his left leg remained paralysed and the doctors didn't know whether he would ever regain control of it. Despite this threat to his mobility and life-style (it was doubtful whether he would ever ride a motorcycle again), he seemed unusually serene when his friend visited him. The patient finally explained why he wasn't bothered by his obviously serious predicament.

While still confined to bed, the partially paralysed man told his friend that when the accident occurred, he found himself floating down a bright tunnel. The tunnel seemed endless and the light illuminating it became brighter and brighter until it engulfed him. While he couldn't see anyone near him, he sensed that he was in the presence of God. It was a kindly presence, a presence that loved him and accepted him completely and without judgment. Much to his surprise, the crash victim wasn't intimidated by the being, even though totally awed by it. Then the presence spoke to him and explained that everything would be all right and he would live. They also apparently discussed his life experiences and what changes he would make upon his recovery.

"They just talked," the biker said to me. "Just like you and me, like friends. It was really great."

At this point in the conversation, the biker's companion spoke for the first time. "Yeah," he said while sipping from his beer bottle. "He said that God was really cool." . . .

The reason for the crash victim's serenity became clear later, when the two bikers talked further. The patient explained that the presence warned him that some paralysis would be left in his leg, but gave the exact date when it would lift. The experience was so real that the injured man didn't question the information and was casually waiting for the healing. From what my informant said, the paralysis did spontaneously heal right on schedule and his friend recovered completely. (*The Return from Silence*, pp. 11–13.)

It might seem puzzling to Latter-day Saints and even people of other Christian sects that one who engaged in this kind of life-style could have such a positive near-death experience—that he would feel so completely loved and accepted in the "presence of God." Surely he had not been very "religious." How could he be loved and treated in the same way in which the "faithful" would hope to be received? Obviously, we have something to learn and understand from such experiences about God's perfect and divine love for all his children. This is one of the most important topics we will discuss in this book. We will see how the Lord reveals his light, love, and understanding to all mankind—both in and out of the Church. This understanding of God's dealings with us and all our spirit brothers and sisters should have a lasting impact on how we perceive our fellowman.

God Enlightens All People

We know and are taught by our own scriptures and latter-day prophets and Apostles that the Lord gives to all of his children some level of light and understanding commensurate with their faith and their willingness to receive it. The prophet Alma confirmed this long ago. "For behold, the Lord doth grant unto all nations, of their own nation and tongue, to teach his word, yea, in wisdom, all that he seeth fit that they should have" (Alma 29:8). In our day, the First Presidency also affirmed this principle in an official statement issued February 15, 1978. "The great religious leaders of the world such as

Mohammed, Confucius, and the Reformers, as well as philosophers including Socrates, Plato, and others, received a portion of God's light. Moral truths were given to them by God to enlighten whole nations and to bring a higher level of understanding to individuals. . . . Consistent with these truths, we believe that God has given and will give to all peoples sufficient knowledge to help them on their way to eternal salvation, either in this life or in the life to come."

More recently, as President of the Quorum of the Twelve Apostles, Elder Howard W. Hunter reiterated this principle.

We believe there is a spiritual influence that emanates from the presence of God to fill the immensity of space. (See D&C 88:12.) All men share an inheritance of divine light. God operates among his children in all nations, and those who seek God are entitled to further light and knowledge, regardless of their race, nationality, or cultural traditions.

Elder Orson F. Whitney . . . explained that . . . "[God] is using not only his covenant people, but other peoples as well, to consummate a work, stupendous, magnificent, and altogether too arduous for this little handful of Saints to accomplish by and of themselves." (As quoted by Elder Joseph B. Wirthlin, in *Ensign*, March, 1993, p. 72.)

One of these enlightened individuals whose experiences will be discussed later in this chapter and throughout the book was Emanuel Swedenborg, an eighteenth-century Swedish scientist, engineer, and religious philosopher who was also a faithful, lifelong member of the Lutheran church. He likewise propounded this precept of universal light, even though his church taught the necessity of baptism and conformity to Lutheran beliefs in order to gain entrance into heaven. He reasoned: "Anyone who thinks with some enlightened rationality can see that no one is born for hell. The Lord is actually Love itself, and His love is a desire to save everyone. So He provides that everyone may have a religion, and through it may have a recognition of something Divine and a more inward life. . . . He [the person] therefore moves away from a worldly life, which is a more outward life." Swedenborg also seemed to imply that the whole world is blessed and lifted by the "Lord's church" and that each enlightened person is, in his or her own way, an extension of His church. "It may be seen . . . that the Lord's church is distributed over the whole world—it is universal—that it includes all people who live in the good of charity in accord with their own religious persuasion; that the church where the Word is known and the Lord is known through it, is to those outside that church like the heart and lungs in a person, from which all the members of the body live—differently in keeping with their forms, locations, and connections." (*Heaven and Hell*, pp. 240, 248–49.)

As Latter-day Saints we should be continually striving to acquire light and truth wherever it may be found. The Prophet Joseph Smith proclaimed that the Saints are not circumscribed by a rigid and unchanging creed or a prescribed set of beliefs, as were some of the churches of his day. He said, "We believe that we have a right to embrace all, and every item of truth, . . . when that truth is clearly demonstrated to our minds, and we have the highest degree of evidence of the same" (*The Personal Writings of Joseph Smith*, p. 420). Brigham Young addressed the all-encompassing nature of the gospel more specifically. " 'Mormonism,' so-called, embraces every principle pertaining to life and salvation, for time and eternity. No matter who has it. If the infidel has got truth it belongs to 'Mormonism.' The truth and sound doctrine possessed by the sectarian world, and they have a great deal, all belong to this Church. . . . All that is good, lovely, and praiseworthy belongs to this Church and Kingdom. 'Mormonism' includes all truth." (*Discourses of Brigham Young*, p. 3.)

Thus the Lord has bestowed portions of his truth upon good men and women everywhere. When we couple it with the doctrines of the Restoration and the enlightenment of the Holy Spirit, we can glean truth from many other sources, including people who have had their own glimpses of eternity.

How to Discern Truth in Near-Death and Spirit World Experiences

Such individuals, including some who experience near-death visions, not only have revealed to them a portion of what we are already blessed to know but they may also have some light and understanding to reveal to us. We can be greatly blessed by their insights and experiences, just as we hope someday to bless their lives with our knowledge. And just as we would want them to ascertain the truth of our teachings by the witness of the Holy Ghost, we can distill truth from their experiences by the same means; for "by the power of the Holy Ghost ye may know the truth of all things" (Moroni 10:5). Furthermore we have the added guidelines found in scriptural and other prophetic statements. Hence we will endeavor in this book to examine the knowledge gained from NDEs, using these standards of measurement and following the pattern proposed by the Lord for those who would study the Apocrypha. "Verily, thus saith the Lord unto you concerning the Apocrypha—there are many things contained therein that are true, and it is mostly translated correctly; there are many things contained therein that are not true, which are interpolations by the hands of men. . . . Therefore, whoso readeth it, let him understand, for the Spirit manifesteth truth; and whoso is enlightened by the Spirit shall obtain benefit therefrom; and whoso receiveth not by the Spirit, cannot be benefited." (D&C 91:1–2, 4–6.)

Furthermore, we have additional guidelines given by modern prophets. Presidents Joseph Fielding Smith and Harold B. Lee offered the following standards for discerning truth and the spirit of inspiration. It is essential that near-death and other spiritual accounts, both LDS and others, be measured against these touchstones. President Smith spoke of things which contradict revealed doctrine. "It makes no difference what is written or what anyone has said, if what has been said is in conflict with what the Lord has revealed, we can set it aside. My words, and the teachings of any other member of the Church, high or low, if they do not square with the revelations, we need not accept them. Let us have this matter clear. We have accepted the four standard works as the measuring yardsticks, or balances, by which we measure every man's doctrine." (*Doctrines of Salvation*, 3:203.)

President Lee addressed the subject of ideas which do not necessarily conflict with doctrine but which would add to what is revealed. "I don't care what his position is, if he writes something or speaks something that goes beyond anything that you can find in the standard Church works, unless that one be the prophet, seer, and revelator—please note that one exception—you may immediately say, 'Well, that is his own idea' " (*Stand Ye in Holy Places*, pp. 162–63).

As members of the Church we are greatly blessed to have these guidelines, although some feel restricted and balk at them. Without these markers we would be open to no end of chaos and confusion in the Church. If these moorings were taken away, the Church could drift from the truth.

It is therefore very important that we measure all spirit world experiences against the fixed standards of the Church rather than measure the Church against the somewhat subjective and less reliable content of the reported experience itself. Elder Boyd K. Packer taught this principle in relation to academic disciplines and other pursuits in which we may be engaged. While near-death studies have become an academic discipline in their own right, most of us will never approach it from that point of view and involvement, but the same principle still applies. "Rather than judge the Church and its program against the principles of our profession, we would do well to set the Church and its accepted program as the rule, then judge our academic training against this rule" ("A Dedication—To Faith," p. 6).

Finally, we are fully aware that the interest in near-death experiences that is current at the time of this writing may be a passing phenomenon, especially if they become sensationalized. While they may be inspiring and enlightening, we must remember that these encounters are not the source of eternal gospel principles. They are interesting, but not imperative. They can be witnesses of the truth, but not the source of it. Thus, Elder Bruce R. McConkie warned the Saints, "Do not put too much stock in some of the current views and vagaries that are afloat, but rather, turn to the revealed word, get a sound understanding of the doctrines, and keep yourselves in the mainstream of the Church" ("Our Relationship with the Lord," p. 97).

Emanuel Swedenborg

These principles will be particularly applicable in the case of Emanuel Swedenborg, who was mentioned earlier and who is quoted frequently in this book because of the length, depth, and breadth of his experience. Swedenborg claimed to have been allowed to visit what we would call the "spirit world" (he called it "heaven and hell") on a regular and prolonged basis. He himself explained the purpose for this in his classic work, *Heaven and Hell*, which was first published in Latin in 1758 and in English in 1812.

> Today's churchman knows almost nothing about heaven, hell, or his own life after death, even though this is all described in the Word. It has gone so far that even many people born in the church deny these things and ask in their hearts, "Has anyone come back and told us?"
>
> To prevent so negative an attitude (which is particularly prevalent among people with much worldly wisdom) from infecting and corrupting people of simple heart and simple faith, it has been made possible for me to be right with angels and to talk with them person to person. I have also been allowed to see what heaven is like and then what hell is like; this has been going on for thirteen years. So now I may describe heaven and hell from what I have seen and heard, hoping for the enlightenment of ignorance and the dispersion of disbelief by this means. (*Heaven and Hell*, p. 27.)

Because of these assertions, many both in his day and ours have labeled Swedenborg a "kook." This reaction, however, tends to come from those who have not carefully studied his voluminous works. Ralph Waldo Emerson wrote of him: "One of the . . . mastodons of literature he is not to be measured by whole colleges of ordinary scholars. . . . Our books are false by being fragmentary. . . . But Swedenborg is systematic and respective of the world in every sentence . . . his faculties work with astronomic punctuality, and this admirable writing is pure from all pertness or egoism." (*Heaven and Hell*, p. 10.) Other admiring writers and philosophers who have studied his works but who refused to believe that his experiences were literal claimed that he spoke in parables, or that he was tapping a previously unknown level of his own mind or perhaps of what Carl Jung might have called the "collective unconsciousness."

Though these worldly wise men tried to rationalize away the theological explanation that Swedenborg gives for his visits to this other world, they considered his works otherwise to be eminently reasonable and profound.

Yet Swedenborg insisted that "he was not exaggerating or telling lies, or speaking in parables." Those who met him "agreed that he was a polite, logical man with a kindly manner and a sense of humor." (Pp. 11–12.) For our—the authors'— part, in studying his book *Heaven and Hell* we too have found the preponderance of his work to be consistent, rational, genuine, and filled with true principles and doctrines, many of which are consistent with doctrines unique to Mormonism and which must have seemed heretical in his day. We believe that he actually did experience the things he attempts to describe. However, while he may have been blessed to receive more enlightenment than most who lack the restored gospel, he was still limited in what he was allowed to see or comprehend. Also, he saw some things that he subsequently interpreted incorrectly. For instance, he was not allowed to see, or at least perceive, that there are resurrected beings other than Jesus Christ. He thought the spirit world, divided as it was between the righteous and the wicked, was the final destiny of its inhabitants—heaven and hell. Because he was not allowed to understand the existence of a premortal life, he mistakenly believed that there was no actual being who was called the "devil" or "Satan," reasoning that God would never purposely create such a being. These are probably the most serious fallacies we discovered, and readers will need to keep them in mind as we study his descriptions of the spirit world.

Another important point to remember as we read Swedenborg is that he was trying to describe a world for which we have very inadequate vocabulary and only limited comprehension, even within the gospel framework. Elder Parley P. Pratt acknowledged the limitations of those outside the Church in explaining eternal truths and the limitations of those who have not reached the spirit world in understanding that realm.

> Take another class of spirits—pious, well-disposed men; for instance, the honest Quaker, Presbyterian, or other

sectarian, who, although honest, and well disposed, had not, while in the flesh, the privilege of the Priesthood and Gospel. They believed in Jesus Christ, but died in ignorance of his ordinances, and had not clear conceptions of his doctrine, and of the resurrection. They expected to go to that place called heaven, as soon as they were dead, and that their doom would then and there be fixed, without any further alteration or preparation. Suppose they should come back, with liberty to tell all they know? How much light could we get from them? They could only tell you about the nature of things in the world in which they live. And even that world you could not comprehend, by their description thereof, any more than you can describe colours to a man born blind, or sounds to those who have never heard. (In *Journal of Discourses*, 1:12.)

Understanding this "human handicap" is very important, not only in relation to Swedenborg but also in reference to all of the experiences cited in this book. While this inability to find mortal words to describe immortality is a hallmark of those who have had near-death experiences, it also becomes a source of great frustration. One experiencer explained: "From the near-death experience I can tell you that we humans are attempting to explain a phenomenon, a concept, a super being which simply is beyond our explanation. . . It really is somewhat of a Catch-22. . . . The closest analogy might be a fruit fly trying to explain a nuclear submarine to a fellow bug. Our understanding, our comprehension, is quite inadequate." (Raymond C. Babb, Ph.D., in *Vital Signs*, August–September 1992, p. 12.)

Perhaps this is why Emerson, quoted earlier, went on to warn that understanding Swedenborg "requires almost a genius equal to his own" (*Heaven and Hell*, p. 10). Undoubtedly Swedenborg was somewhat of a genius in his own right, and some of his writing does require careful pondering, as with that of any great philosopher. Through the clarifying lenses of the restored gospel, however, many of the writings that are mysterious and strange to others are quite discernible and logical to Latter-day Saints. His testimony and teachings can even help us to better understand the meaning and implications of some of our own beliefs.

Faith Is Still Required

Scott Rogo asserted that near-death experiences "have been used to 'validate' everything from Fundamentalist Christianity to New Age spirituality—strange bed (or deathbed) fellows, indeed!" (*The Return from Silence,* p. 44.) As Latter-day Saints, we must never fall into the trap of touting these phenomena as "proof" that the Church is true. Such "proof" must come internally—from the witness of the Holy Ghost. We can identify completely in this with the previous statement by Dr. Kenneth Ring about those who have had NDEs: "They bring something personally more important: subjective proof. They claim to know in a way and from a source that removes all doubt." We would never desire anyone to believe merely on the basis of these external supports. Without the firm inner conviction of the truthfulness of the gospel these "evidences" can become mere coincidences, interesting but easily reasoned away.

Further, we have always taught that knowing the gospel is true, in and of itself, is not enough. The devils know and tremble (see James 2:19). Many mortals have received signs, or seen visions, or had great knowledge revealed to them, but not "unto salvation" (see D&C 63:7). Faith in Christ is still required. Knowledge absent of righteousness has no redeeming power. Knowing that there is life after death is not sufficient to save us. Knowing that near-death experiences may seem to agree with Mormon teachings will not exalt us. Leaders in other religions have also recognized this drawback to the study of NDEs. Monseigneur Corrado Balducci, a Catholic official, addressed this concern in a popular news magazine which featured an article on near-death experiences. "These 'postmortem visions' can be looked upon as good," Balducci said. "But we can't go beyond that. They cannot be considered proof of the hereafter because proof of the hereafter comes to us only from the word of God. We might consider them the grace of God. But we should not look for them. God wants faith from us. If someone believes in an afterlife simply because he had such an experience, he is making a big mistake." (As quoted in "At the Edge of Eternity," by Verlyn Klinkenborg, *Life*, March 1992, p. 71.) Moreover, the Savior seemed to imply that those who must exercise faith are even more blessed in some ways than those who have certain knowledge. As he told his once-skeptical Apostle, Thomas, "Because thou hast seen me, thou hast believed: blessed are they that have not seen, and yet have believed" (John 20:29; see also 3 Nephi 12:2).

Thus this book has not been written to try to persuade anyone outside the Church to convert to the restored gospel. To the world, we can only offer this information as another possible explanation for the NDE phenomena that are being investigated and interpreted in numerous ways. Those members of the Church who are already inwardly converted do not need anecdotal evidence or "proof" of the gospel to help them believe or motivate them to greater righteousness.

There is limited value in a mere recitation of people's "encounters" with death. Such stories may be popular and fascinating, but by themselves they do not provide the depth of motivation for real gospel living which can only be found in the scriptures and the words of the living prophets. We, the authors, however, find the bulk of these experiences, when studied within a doctrinal context, to be so uplifting and enlightening that we wish to offer them to the LDS audience through a systematic, gospel-oriented study of our own. We hope this presentation will stimulate the reader to a further search for truth through the scriptures, the words of the prophets, and the guidance of the Holy Ghost. Above all, we pray that an understanding of mortal death and of what lies past its portal will help us see and treasure life both here and hereafter as the incredible gift it is.

An Overview

While all near-death and other "spiritual" experiences share many basic, identifying elements, they are as varied as the people who have them. Indeed, it will be noted over and over again that each person perceives and describes this experience according to his or her own understanding, background, and culture. Dr. Raymond A. Moody, the well-known author and the "father" of the modern study of near-death experiences, dealt with the problem of differing descriptions in his book *The Light Beyond*.

> But still the basic question remains: Shouldn't everybody who nearly dies have the same experience?
>
> My answer to that is "No." Think of it this way. If ten people visited France, I doubt that any of them would have the same experience. Three of them might say that they saw this big building. Five might say they had wonderful food, and two of them might say that they had floated down a river. Everybody who came back from France would have a slightly different story, although there would be areas of overlap.
>
> Similarly, in NDEs, while overlapping traits are reported within a common framework, no two experiences are exactly alike. (Pp. 185–86.)

In fact, the variety of viewpoints provided in these diverse accounts is one of the things that makes them so helpful. Moreover, the type and extent of the experience itself seems to vary among individuals, perhaps according to the Lord's purposes. We know that the Lord is merciful and gentle in teaching his children and allows them to receive knowledge "line upon line, precept upon precept" (2 Nephi 28:30), according to their ability to comprehend and in the way most suited to them. This principle must always be kept in mind in considering near-death accounts, because it will recur in every aspect of the experience. A prime example of this is Peter's vision of the animals which the Jews considered unclean and which he was commanded to "kill and eat." The Lord was teaching the President of his church that the time had come for the gospel to be taken to the Gentiles, whose association the Jews had previously been taught to shun. (See Acts 10.) It instructed Peter in a way that may have little meaning in our culture but was graphic and unforgettable to him.

Thus, while the experiences we will examine are varied in

their content and extent, we have attempted to organize them according to some of the elements they have in common. This organization corresponds more or less to the general order or sequence of the near-death experience, although not every NDEr experiences all of these elements or undergoes them in this order. One writer has suggested the following general stages of the experience:

1 Lifting out of one's body and being able to look at the resuscitative efforts going on.
2 Being in a dark void.
3 Floating through a tunnel at a very rapid rate.
4 Seeing and communicating with deceased relatives or others (this stage can occur at various points).
5 Moving toward a bright light, which gets larger until the person becomes engulfed in it.
6 Encountering a being of light of overwhelming, total love and absolute knowledge.
7 Being asked by the Light how one has lived one's life.
8 Undergoing a life review in which events of one's life are presented and in which one empathically experiences the effects of one's action on others.
9 Being engulfed by and feeling total love and knowledge.
10 Going through the Light and seeing populated cities of crystal or other dazzling brilliance.
11 Being given a choice whether or not to return, with the Light emphasizing that the experiencer has unfinished tasks or is needed by loved ones.
12 Returning, either through a rapid reversal of the experience or finding oneself back in one's body. (*After the Beyond*, p. 10.)

In this book some aspects are classified according to their nature rather than their sequence because they seem to fit in with the discussion better in that way. Furthermore, we will evaluate only those elements of the NDE which are of doctrinal importance and impact. We have chosen to begin with attributes and abilities of the spirit body, because the first thing

NDErs tend to notice is that they exist outside the physical body, having a form that is still human yet has heightened and increased capacities. Second, we will discuss the conditions in the spirit world that NDEers observe as they leave their mortality behind. In the third section of the book, dealing with experiences in the spirit world, we will examine some of the things that happen to individuals while they are in that realm. Next, we will look at the impact on mortality of the near-death experience, noting the common transformations which seem to permeate the lives of these "survivors." Finally, we will ask, What does this mean to Latter-day Saints? In this chapter we will suggest some applications for this insightful information in the everyday and overall lives of members of the Church. It is our hope that the experiences and doctrines examined in this book will strengthen and encourage the Saints as they have done for so many of Heavenly Father's children.

A Final Caution

Since we, the authors, began our extensive research of near-death experiences in 1988, there has been an explosion of interest in the subject among both Latter-day Saints and others alike. We have witnessed some positive and negative aspects of this new awareness. The positive results have reinforced what we hope to teach in this book. The negative side of the equation has caused us great concern. This concern covers two areas: 1) the tendency to make the sacred common or, even worse, sensational; and 2) the inclination among some Saints to seek after these things as a substitute or easy and tantalizing alternative to seeking truth from the scriptures and the words of the living prophets—creating, in essence, a kind of "pop" gospel.

First, while most publications of such stories may be intended to inspire and edify, and they often fill that intent, the way some are marketed or publicized seem exploitative; intentionally or unintentionally, the stories become sensationalized. What is sacred may be held out to titillate and pique interest and thereby be taken out of its spiritual context and made common before those who would receive it with only idle curiosity at best and with disdain at worst. This may be an example of what Jesus characterized as "casting pearls before swine" (see 3 Nephi 14:6). To the extent that such books have been successful among members of the Church, one hopes that this is because they are good and true and helpful and they stimulate the Saints to search the scriptures, and not because they offer an easier or more exciting and engaging version of the gospel than our simple, basic doctrinal teachings about the afterlife. In this book we hope to avoid this pitfall by emphasizing the doctrine as the center of interest and using excerpts of spiritual experiences only as illustrations and witnesses of the truth.

This leads to our second area of concern. In this age of audio-visual stimulation we may fall into the trap of wanting a "gospel according to Hollywood" or "drive-through religion." Some Saints seem to be attempting to learn and teach the gospel in a way that is quick, entertaining, and effortless. While these stories may be interesting and even inspiring to a certain extent, they must never become a substitute for the imperative study and application of the scriptures and prophetic counsel which are essential to our testimonies and our salvation. They cannot change lives and build strength to resist temptation with the same power and certainty as the word of God (see Alma 31:5). "Many things are only interesting and enticing," Elder William R. Bradford pointed out in general conference, "while other things are important" (in *Ensign*, November 1987, p. 75).

Furthermore, while we can always rely on the scriptures and the words of the prophets, some of these NDE stories and accounts may inadvertently or even knowingly set forth mistaken or false doctrines that could lead Church members astray and mislead others about our beliefs. That is why NDEs may be used only as a side dish—so long as they bear witness of the truth—but never as the main course. They are never a source of doctrine or a replacement for the teaching or study of doctrine and the exercise of faith. Relying only on such fare for one's spiritual nourishment will inevitably cause spiritual starvation.

PART II

Attributes and Abilities of the Spirit Body

CHAPTER 2

The Immortal Spirit

Through modern prophets and restored scripture, Latter-day Saints have been blessed with knowledge of the eternal existence of man. In the King Follett discourse Joseph Smith said: "I want to reason more on the spirit of man; for I am dwelling on the body and spirit of man—on the subject of the dead. I take my ring from my finger and liken it unto the mind of man—the immortal part, because it has no beginning. Suppose you cut it in two; then it has a beginning and an end; but join it again, and it continues one eternal round. So with the spirit of man." (*Teachings of the Prophet Joseph Smith*, p. 354; hereafter cited as *Teachings*.)

There are many people in the world, however, who were quite surprised to discover during their near-death experience that life goes on after death. Many had fully expected to cease to exist at death. Some believed they would sleep until there is some type of resurrection (usually spiritual, not physical). Others imagined that they would continue on in some altered form of consciousness. Undoubtedly there are countless opinions and philosophies about what does or does not happen at death, but the overwhelming conclusion of those who have glimpses of the next life, either through personal experience or through revelation, is that the spirit never dies.

There seem to be differing levels of perception among NDErs about their own state in this existence beyond death. Some experience themselves merely as a "mind," some sort of consciousness—a "soul" capable of thought but without senses. Those who experience a fuller perception of their existence report not only having thoughts but also having the use of their senses—seeing, feeling, hearing, and even smelling—though they do not perceive themselves as actually having a body. Still others experience some sort of body that thinks, senses, and moves, but they seem at a loss to describe it other than as a cloud, an illumination of "colors," or as having roughly the same shape as the physical body. Finally, there are those who experience themselves in a real, "spiritual" body which is somewhat a duplicate of their mortal body. (For an interesting discussion on the possible reason for the divergent levels of perception of the spirit body, see Dr. Kenneth Ring's *Life at Death*, pp. 224–33.)

In her work *Otherworld Journeys*, Dr. Carol Zaleski summarized some of the research on this point. "In a study conducted by Bruce Greyson and Ian Stevenson, 58 percent of those who reported near-death experience said that they sensed themselves in a new body, the same size and age as its physical counterpart, but lighter in weight. Most of Moody's informants also felt that they had a body of some sort, taking shape as a mist, cloud, or sphere, or mimicking the contours of the physical form. For Elisabeth Kubler-Ross, the spiritual body is an exact replica of the physical body, lacking only its defects." (P. 116.)

Through modern revelation, LDS theology confirms the actuality of a spirit body in the human form. "That which is spiritual being in the likeness of that which is temporal; and that which is temporal in the likeness of that which is spiritual," the Lord explained to the Prophet Joseph Smith, "the spirit of man in the likeness of his person" (D&C 77:2). Michael Sabom, a medical doctor, reported that some NDErs "described their 'separated self' as if it had features consistent with their original physical body" (*Recollections of Death*, p. 21). One experience illustrates this: "To my surprise I found that I still had hands, and feet, and a body, for I had always regarded the soul as a something without shape and void. In those days I had read no Spiritualistic books on after death conditions, and to find, that though I was 'dead' I still had form, was new to me." (*The Return from Silence*, p. 162.)

Emanuel Swedenborg taught that spirits have human form, even though such a concept was not widely accepted in his day and was even viewed as heretical by most churchmen of his generation.

> I have often told angels how people in Christendom are in such blind ignorance about angels and spirits that they believe them to be minds without form, or nothing but thoughts, which could not be conceptualized except the way one might conceptualize an ether containing something living. And since they predicate of angels nothing human but thought, they believe they cannot see because they have no eyes, cannot hear because they have no ears, and cannot talk because they have no mouth or tongue. . . .
>
> On the basis of all my experience, covering to date many years, I can say, I can insist that angels are completely people in form. They do have faces, eyes, ears, chests, arms, hands, and feet. They do see each other, hear each other, and talk with each other. In short, nothing proper to man whatever is missing, except that they are not clothed with a material body. (*Heaven and Hell*, pp. 70–71.)

Several other NDErs agree that their spirit bodies were whole and healthy even though their physical bodies were not. "In a near-death experience, the body becomes perfect again," Dr. Elisabeth Kubler-Ross observed. "Quadriplegics are no longer paralyzed, multiple sclerosis patients who have been in wheelchairs for years say that when they were out of their bodies, they were able to sing and dance." (Quoted by Carol Zaleski in *Otherworld Journeys*, pp. 116–17.) Dr. Moody also recounted an interesting observation of a patient who had lost a large portion of his leg in an accident. In his near-death experience, the man saw the doctors working on his maimed body. "I could feel my body, and it was whole," he later said. "I know that. I felt whole, and I felt that all of me was there, though it wasn't." (*Life After Life*, p. 53.)

This surely harmonizes with the Church's teachings concerning the eternal nature of the spirit body. The First Presidency of the Church, in an official statement entitled "The Origin of Man," declared: "'God created man in His own image.' This is just as true of the spirit as it is of the body, which is only the clothing of the spirit, its complement; the two together constituting the soul. The spirit of man is in the form of man, and the spirits of all creatures are in the likeness of their bodies." (*Improvement Era*, November 1909, p. 77. This First Presidency statement is also in *Encyclopedia of Mormonism*, 4:1665–69.)

Elder Orson Pratt, a member of the Quorum of the Twelve Apostles and one of the Church's leading theologians, also testified of the eternal nature of the spirit and its freedom from earthly handicaps and physical limitations. "We, as Latter-day Saints, believe that the spirits that occupy these tabernacles have form and likeness similar to the human tabernacle. Of course there may be deformities existing in connection with the outward tabernacle which do not exist in connection with the spirit that inhabits it. These tabernacles become deformed by accident in various ways, sometimes at birth, but this may not altogether or in any degree deform the spirits that dwell within them, therefore we believe that the spirits which occupy the bodies of the human family are more or less in the resemblance of the tabernacles." (In *Journal of Discourses*, 15:242–43.)

There are those who don't remember having a human-like body in the NDE experience but who report functioning as if they were in that type of body. As previously mentioned, they speak of seeing, feeling, hearing, thinking, smelling, and even crawling, walking, running, and jumping. (See Melvin Morse, M.D., with Paul Perry, *Closer to the Light*, p. 36.) Swedenborg further affirmed the completeness of the spirit body. "I have even talked with some people a couple of days after their death, telling them that now their funeral services and arrangements were being organized for their burial. They responded that it was good to cast off the thing that had served them for a body and for bodily functions in the world. They wanted me to state that they were not dead, that they were alive, just as human as ever, that they had only journeyed from one world to another; also that they were unaware of any loss, since they were in a body and its sensations just as before, involved in understanding and intention just as before, having similar thoughts and affections, similar sensations, and similar desires, to those they had had in the world." (*Heaven and Hell*, pp. 235–36.)

The Empty Glove

Having cast off the "thing that had served them for a body and for bodily functions in the world," some NDErs don't even recognize that body. Perhaps it is because they didn't expect to exist outside of their physical body, thinking it was all that constituted their being. Dr. George Ritchie, in his own extensive near-death experience recounted in his book *Return from Tomorrow*, stated that he did not recognize the body in the bed he had just left.

> Someone was lying in that bed.
> I took a step closer. He was quite a young man, with short brown hair, lying very still. But . . . the thing was impossible! I myself had just gotten out of that bed! For a moment I wrestled with the mystery of it. (P. 37.)

Once Ritchie recognized his body and realized that he might be "dead," he was incredulous that he could exist apart from it.

> But I wasn't dead! How could I be dead and still be awake? Thinking. Experiencing. Death was different. Death was . . . I didn't know. Blanking out. Nothingness. I was me, wide awake, only without a physical body to function in. (Pp. 47–48.)

Besides the difficulty some experience in recognizing their mortal body, some have a feeling of detachment and almost disinterest toward the physical body once they experience the existence outside of it. One experiencer made just such an observation even before his spirit had completely left his body. "I was still in the body, but the body and I had no longer any interests in common. I looked in astonishment and joy for the first time upon myself—the me, the real Ego, while the not me closed in upon all sides like a sepulchre of clay. . . . I beheld the wonders of my bodily anatomy, intimately interwoven with which, even tissue for tissue, was I, the living soul of that dead body. I learned that the epidermis was the outside boundary of the ultimate tissues, so to speak, of the soul." (As quoted in D. Scott Rogo, *The Return from Silence*, p. 59.)

Other such reports are quite common in near-death accounts. Dr. Zaleski relates that "survivors of near-death experience often say that it has made them less preoccupied with their bodies and with material things." She then goes on to quote one of these survivors: "After this, my mind was the main point of attraction, and the body was second—it was only something to encase my mind. I didn't care if I had a body or not. It didn't matter because for all I cared my mind was what was important." (*Otherworld Journeys*, p. 116.)

Perhaps the teachings of the gospel can shed some light on the reason for this strange reaction. As Latter-day Saints, we know that before we had physical bodies we lived as spirit beings begotten in the image of God. We realize that at birth we entered into a body, created by our earthly parents, that generally resembles our spirit body in form and function. We understand that we will leave it behind again at death until the resurrection day. Elder Boyd K. Packer, of the Quorum of the Twelve Apostles, has illustrated death as a separation of the immortal spirit from the physical body with an excellent analogy of the hand in the glove, the glove being lifeless and unable to function without the hand inside it. (See Boyd K. Packer, *Teach Ye Diligently*, pp. 230–36.) "Take the spirit from the body," President Brigham Young declared, "and the body is lifeless" (in *Journal of Discourses*, 9:287). Once these individuals realize this concept—that their body is not the real "them" but only the house they lived in on earth—it is easy to understand why they no longer feel any strong attachment to it. Ironically, those who return from NDEs do not become careless and cavalier with their physical bodies; rather, they tend to take better care of themselves than before. They seem to have grasped the purpose of their earthly body as a temple for a divine, immortal spirit.

We might also postulate from this phenomenon that perhaps the spirit is what constitutes our recognition of ourselves and others. Those who have lost a friend or loved one often have the sensation when viewing the body of the deceased that it no longer closely resembles the living person they once knew, or what's more, they may simply feel, "It's not him," or "It's not her." George Ritchie reported a similar sensation concerning his own body. "I had never seen myself. Not really. Not the way I saw other people. From my chest down I had seen myself 'in the round' of course, but from the shoulders up, I now realized, I had seen only a two-dimensional mirror-image staring at me from a piece of glass. And occasionally a snapshot, equally two-dimensional. That was all. The roundedness, the living, space-filling presence of myself, I did not know at all. And that, I now discovered, is the way we recognize each other. Not by the shape of the nose or the color of the eyes, but by the whole three-dimensional impact of all the features at once." (*Return from To-morrow*, p. 43.)

Surely this three-dimensional view includes the animation which comes only from the spirit. NDErs often recognize friends and loved ones in the spirit world, and yet we understand that a person's spirit does not necessarily look exactly like his or her body. The appearance of our earthly bodies is governed, to a large extent, by natural laws of genetics, while our spirit already had a certain appearance of its own before entering those bodies.

It may be that we recognize ourselves and others as much by what we are like spiritually as how we look physically. "For the face of a person's spirit differs markedly from his physical face," wrote Swedenborg in *Heaven and Hell*. "His physical face comes from his parents, while his spirit's face stems from his affection, being its image." (P. 355.) Maybe this helps to explain why some people recognize the spirits of those who have died as babies or small children, even though those beings often appear to them as full-grown adults. Still others report that they did not actually see the relative or person they knew on earth, but simply sensed his or her presence. Thus it seems that, at least to some degree, there is a recognition of spirits rather than bodies.

Spirit Substance

Our spirits, however, are composed of more than just our inward personality traits, our intellectual capacities, and our attitudes and desires. A spirit body is actually composed of a form of matter. The Prophet Joseph taught: "There is no such thing as immaterial matter. All spirit is matter, but it is more fine or pure, and can only be discerned by purer eyes; we cannot see it; but when our bodies are purified we shall see that it is all matter." (D&C 131:7–8.) Elder Parley P. Pratt later also elaborated on the nature of spirits.

> Why, they are organized intelligences. What are they made of? They are made of the element which we call spirit, which is as much an element of material existence, as earth, air, electricity, or any other tangible substance recognized by man; but so subtle, so refined is its nature, that it is not tangible to our gross organs. It is invisible to us, unless we are quickened by a portion of the same element; . . .
>
> Now let us apply this philosophy to all the degrees of spiritual element, from electricity, which may be assumed to be one of the lowest or more gross elements of spiritual matter, up through all the gradations of the invisible fluids, till we arrive at a substance so holy, so pure, so endowed with intellectual attributes and sympathetic affections that it may be said to be on a par, or level, in its attributes, with man. (In *Journal of Discourses*, 1:8.)

Many NDErs describe their spirit bodies in terms which seem to coincide with this statement. "Some sense themselves as an 'energy pattern' or 'wave length,' resembling the body in form, but composed of finer or faster 'vibrations'" (*Otherworld Journeys*, p. 117). Dr. Moody reports that one person had "studied his hands while he was in this state and saw them to be composed of light with tiny structures in them. He could see the delicate whorls of his fingerprints and tubes of light up his arms." (*The Light Beyond*, p. 10.) In his first book, *Life After Life*, Moody provides us with an account of one NDEr who explained: "[My 'being'] felt as if it had a *density* to it, almost, but not a physical density—kind of like, I don't know, waves or something, I guess: Nothing really physical, almost as if it were charged, if you'd like to call it that. But it felt as if it had something to it." (P. 48.)

Another experiencer described his "second" body as "very thin, very delicate. Very light. Very, very light." Spiritualists of the nineteenth and early twentieth centuries also believed in a physical and a spiritual body in man. "Underlying this conception of the relation between body and spirit was an assumption that matter and spirit exist on a continuum, differing in degree rather than in kind" (*Otherworld Journeys*, p. 117). As one remembers the inadequacy of human language and the varying depths of perception among NDErs, all of these characterizations of the spirit as purified matter and energy seem to correspond with Elder Pratt's allusions to pure and refined matter, of which electricity is a grosser "element"—an earthly manifestation of more sophisticated, "invisible fluids."

At first reading, it might seem that Elder Pratt, lacking the benefits of modern science, is mistaken in referring to electricity as a form of matter. However, the Apostle may have known something through revelation that modern scientific methods are only beginning to uncover. In his book, *Transformed by the Light* (p. 135), Dr. Melvin Morse notes the following discovery. "That has been the accepted view of matter [atoms composed of electrons, neutrons, and protons]—until about fifty years ago. Then science discovered an even smaller world than the electron. They call this tiny world wave/particle duality. According to astrophysicist Stephen Hawking, it works like this: As physicists have split the atom into smaller and smaller particles, they have discovered to their surprise that there is no final 'tiniest part' of nature. Rather, there are forces best described as wavelengths of electromagnetism, or light. These pieces of light serve as the fundamental building blocks for everything. What this theory tells us is that everything we consider to be real actually breaks down into simple light, in all of its various wavelengths."

President Brigham Young also spoke of the earthly tabernacle as "this coarser organization" (*Discourses of Brigham Young*, p. 379), and on another occasion he interestingly referred to electricity in lightning as "a fine illustration of the ability and power of the Almighty," in portraying the power and speed with which we will be able to travel in the next life because we will "possess a measure of this power" (in *Journal of Discourses*, 14:231). Conceivably, then, the spirit body is made up not only of rarified matter but also of an element which embodies some higher form of energy, perhaps something akin to the Light of Christ, which gives life to all things (see D&C 88:6–13). "Its [the Light of Christ] inherent properties embrace all the attributes of intelligence and affection," declared Elder Parley P. Pratt. "It is endowed with wisdom, knowledge, truth, love, charity, justice, mercy, in all their ramifications. In short, it is the attributes of the eternal power and Godhead." (*Key to the Science of Theology*, 1855 edition, pp. 43–45, cited in *The Life Before*, p. 44.)

The Prophet Joseph Smith made another statement in regard to the material nature of the spirit, adding one interesting characteristic—elasticity. He reasoned: "In tracing the thing to the foundation and looking at it philosophically, we shall find a very material difference between the body and the spirit; the body is supposed to be organized matter, and the spirit, by many, is thought to be immaterial, without substance. With this latter statement we should beg leave to differ, and state the spirit is a substance; that it is material, but that it is more pure, *elastic* and refined matter than the body; that it existed before the body, can exist in the body; and will exist separate from the body, when the body will be mouldering in the dust; and will in the resurrection, be again united with it. (*Teachings*, p. 207, italics added.)

While they do not directly mention the elastic nature of the spirit body, several near-death accounts contain some intriguing allusions to this attribute. The following was related by a late-nineteenth century physician, Dr. A. Wiltse, who "died" of typhoid fever. This account was first published in 1889 in the *St. Louis Medical and Surgical Journal*. "I watched the interesting process of the separation of soul and body. By some power, apparently not my own, the Ego was rocked to and fro, laterally, as a cradle is rocked, by which process its connection with the tissues of the body was broken up. After a little time the lateral motion ceased, and along the soles of the feet beginning at the toes, passing rapidly to the heels, I felt and heard, as it seemed, the snapping of innumerable small cords. When this was accomplished I began slowly to retreat from the feet, toward the head, as a *rubber cord shortens.*" (As quoted in *The Return from Silence*, p. 59, italics added.)

The same doctor went on to explain what happened after his spirit left his body: "As I turned, my left elbow came in contact with the arm of one of two gentlemen, who were standing at the door. To my surprise, his arm passed through mine without apparent resistance, *the severed parts closing again without pain, as air re-unites.*" (As quoted in *Life at Death*, p. 230, italics added.)

Another gentleman who had suffered a cardiac arrest revealed: "Almost instantly I saw myself leave my body, coming out through my head and shoulders (I did not see my lower limbs). The 'body' leaving me was not exactly in vapour form, yet it seemed to *expand very slightly* once it was clear of me. It was somewhat transparent, for I could see my 'other' body through it." (As quoted in *The Return from Silence*, p. 71, italics added.)

Two other interesting accounts also allude to the pliant nature of the spirit body. "Though the light was above her, she became fascinated by a strange sensation in her hands. They were expanding, painlessly, beyond their normal size." (*Full Circle*, p. 20.) "Again, I reentered through the top of the head, feeling the need to shrink and then squeeze back into the tight form [my] body offered" (*Coming Back to Life*, p. 37).

Finally, Swedenborg, who claimed that he was allowed to experience death, wrote of his own experience, "Especially, I was allowed to perceive and feel that there was a pulling, a kind of drawing of the more inward elements of my mind—hence of my spirit—out of my body" (*Heaven and Hell*, pp. 346–47). While these recollections do not prove the elasticity of the spirit substance, they are interesting anecdotal references to Joseph Smith's inspired words.

Spirit Sight

As noted by the dying doctor whose spirit arm passed through the arm of the living gentleman, the matter composing the spirit body is so refined and pure that it can move through temporal matter. Many NDErs relate this same phenomenon. Dr. George G. Ritchie noticed this "problem" during his experience. "I could walk through the bed and walls. I could not pick up the sheet when I wanted to pull back the covers to look at the face to make sure it was my body. I could, by a manner of thinking, manage to sit on the bed beside the body." (*My Life After Dying*, p. 15.)

Dr. Raymond Moody told of a woman he was trying to resuscitate after a cardiac arrest. He reported what she later told him: "She was standing behind me, trying to tell me to stop, that she was fine where she was. When I didn't hear her, she tried to grab my arm to keep me from inserting a needle in her arm for injecting intravenous fluid. Her hand passed right through my arm. But when she did that, she later claimed that she felt something that was the consistency of 'very rarified gelatin' that seemed to have an electric current running through it." (*The Light Beyond*, p. 9.)

These experiences do not seem bizarre or totally without substance to Latter-day Saints. Doctrinal teachings by leaders of the Church, both in the early days and in our time, seem to confirm the notion that the spirit world is in a different "dimension" and is populated by spirits made of more refined matter than our earthly bodies. Elder Charles W. Penrose spoke of this condition of the spirit body. "Spirit is a substance, it is not immaterial; it may have some properties that are different from that which we see and handle, which we call matter, but it is a reality, a substantial reality. And spirit can understand spirit and grasp spirit. A spiritual person can take the hand of another spiritual person and it is substantial. A person in body could not grasp a spirit, for that spirit has different properties to those of our bodies, and it is governed by different laws to those that govern us in this sphere of mortality. A spiritual substance, organized into form, occupies room and space just as much in its sphere as these natural particles occupy in this sphere." (In *Journal of Discourses*, 26:22.)

In addition to the concept of spirit substance, we have also been taught that there is another world occupying the same sphere in which we mortals live—a world with beings and objects composed of this finer matter which we cannot see. President Brigham Young instructed the Saints that "spirits are just as familiar with spirits as bodies are with bodies, though spirits are composed of matter so refined as not to be tangible to this coarser organization" (in *Journal of Discourses*, 3:371–72). From the doctrines of the Restoration we have come to understand that we can only view this spirit world when our spirit leaves our body or when our eyes are "quickened" by the power of the Lord. On that point President Young further taught: "Can you see spirits in this room? No. Suppose the Lord should touch your eyes that you might see, could you then see the spirits? Yes, as plainly as you now see bodies, as did the servant of Elijah. If the Lord would permit it, and it was His will that it should be done, you could see the spirits that have departed from this world, as plainly as you now see bodies with your natural eyes." (In *Journal of Discourses*, 3:368.)

Several instances recorded in scripture also testify to this doctrine. The prophet Moses alluded to the same principle with regard to his own remarkable vision, though with reference to the glory of God, the highest of all spiritual states: "But now mine own eyes have beheld God; but not my natural, but my spiritual eyes, for my natural eyes could not have beheld; for I should have withered and died in his presence; but his glory was upon me; and I beheld his face, for I was transfigured before him" (Moses 1:11). The Prophet Joseph Smith several times had this type of experience. With reference to his vision of the three degrees of glory, he wrote: "By the power of the Spirit our eyes were opened and our understandings were enlightened, so as to see and understand the things of God" (D&C 76:12). President Joseph F. Smith described a similar experience, as recorded in his vision of the spirit world and the work of the spiritual redemption of those who had died. "On the third of October, in the year nineteen hundred and eighteen, I sat in my room pondering over the scriptures," he testified. ". . . As I pondered over these things which are written, the eyes of my understanding were opened, and the Spirit of the Lord rested upon me, and I saw the hosts of the dead, both small and great." (D&C 138:1, 11.)

Many NDErs come to understand this principle through practical experience in their new spiritual environment, especially when they cannot make contact with mortals, who neither see nor hear them. In the account of a death-bed vision, published in 1864 in booklet form, a mother related that her dying daughter was able to view her brother who had died seven months previously, while she, herself, could not. "I was sitting beside her bed, her hand clasped in mine. Looking up so wistfully at me, she said, 'Dear Momma, I do wish you could see Allie; he's standing beside you.' Involuntarily I looked around, but Daisy thereupon continued, 'He says you cannot see him because your spirit eyes are closed, but that I can, because my body only holds my spirit, as it were, by a thread of life.'" (As quoted in *The Return from Silence*, p. 48.)

Emanuel Swedenborg elaborated on this same principle several times in *Heaven and Hell*. His words seem to add a unique, second witness to the prophetic statements quoted earlier.

> It should however be noted that angels are not visible to men through men's physical senses, only rather through the eyes of the spirit within man. . . . Like sees like because it is made of like material. Further, the body's organ of sight, the eye, is so crude that it cannot even see the smaller elements of nature except through a lens, as everyone knows. So it is still less able to see things above the realm of nature like the things in the spiritual world. However, these things are visible to man when he is withdrawn from physical sight and his spirit's sight is opened. This happens in a moment if it is the Lord's good pleasure that they be visible. At such times, it seems to the person exactly as though he were seeing these things with his physical eyes. (P. 72.)

While not all near-death experiences bring their subject into full contact with the spirit world, including the full perception of the person's own spirit body, all seem to be brought to a common understanding—that life goes on after death. As Latter-day Saints we are thrilled to have many in the world begin to comprehend this momentous truth, and our faith is rewarded when we see many of our own doctrines borne out by independent witnesses. Some may say that we are only picking and choosing those experiences which affirm our own beliefs. However, after careful examination of these accounts we are convinced that even where an aspect of an account seems not to square with LDS concepts the difference is almost always one of perception or of depth of the experience. The deeper the NDE, the more it tends to correlate with LDS teachings.

Further, we are endowed with the blessed knowledge that forever we are more than a mind or a spot of consciousness. We know that we will continue to function in the next life as we do in this life, but without some of the limitations of mortality. As we read and ponder NDE accounts and relevant prophetic statements we may begin to understand the wonders of the spirit body, its remarkable composition and capacities. And as we continue here to discuss some of the qualities of that body, we have reason to rejoice once more at the wondrous gifts that Heavenly Father has to bestow upon his spirit children.

CHAPTER 3

The Beautiful
Appearance of Spirits

Although some NDErs don't comprehend the human-like shape of their own spirits, they often speak of seeing other beings whom they describe in human terms. They may see deceased relatives, "guardian angels," or other people they don't know. "Beyond the mist, I could see people, and their forms were just like they are on the earth" (as quoted in *The Return from Silence*, p. 74). However, these people almost always appear to be more beautiful and more perfected than mortal beings. Often their clothing is described in terms of whiteness beyond earthly comprehension. For the Latter-day Saints, this concept usually brings to mind the descriptions set forth in some of the visions of the Prophet Joseph Smith. Although generally these visitors were not spirits but flesh-and-bone, resurrected, glorified beings, the Prophet's description of the angelic messenger, Moroni, for example, may be instructive in the present context.

> A personage appeared at my bedside, standing in the air, for his feet did not touch the floor.

He had on a loose robe of most exquisite whiteness. It was a whiteness beyond anything earthly I had ever seen; nor do I believe that any earthly thing could be made to appear so exceedingly white and brilliant. His hands were naked, and his arms also, a little above the wrist; so, also, were his feet naked, as were his legs, a little above the ankles. His head and neck were also bare. I could discover that he had no other clothing on but his robe, as it was open, so that I could see into his bosom.

Not only was his robe exceedingly white, but his whole person was glorious beyond description, and his countenance truly like lightning. The room was exceedingly light, but not so very bright as immediately around his person. (Joseph Smith—History 1:30–32.)

Radiant White Clothing

It is interesting and important to our study to point out the Prophet's description of the loose, white robe worn by Moroni. In *Closer to the Light*, Dr. Melvin Morse identifies seeing people clad in radiant white as a "core element" of the NDE (p. 35). Interestingly, one NDEr, while not explicitly mentioning color, described the clothing on his spirit body in some of the same terms used by the Prophet in describing the angel, Moroni. "All I felt—I had a piece of clothing on; it was very, very loose. And I remember [having bare feet]." (*Life at Death*, p. 52.) Some describe a "being of light" who meets them during their experience as being dressed in shining white clothing, though some only perceive him as a "presence" or a brilliant light without a body. (The "being of light" will be more thoroughly discussed in a subsequent chapter.)

Dr. Carol Zaleski confirmed that many, but seemingly not all, beings in the spirit world are dressed in white. "In near-death reports, as in medieval visions, the other world is inhabited by throngs of white-clad or etheric beings whose rank is lower than the being of light, but whose company seems just as welcome. Unlike the angelic or divine presence whose boundaries as an individual tend to blur into a bright cosmic mist, these spirits are recognizably human; most are deceased relatives or friends." Zaleski goes on to quote one experience: "I came to some place and there were all my relatives, . . . My grandparents were dressed . . . all in white and they had a hood over their heads. . . . " She then summarizes, "The white robes . . . are standard issue for spirits; some, moreover, appear in familiar street clothes, as if to assure the newcomer that normal social life continues on the other side." (*Otherworld Journeys*, pp. 134–35.)

There may be other possible reasons why NDErs see beings dressed in something other than white clothing (aside from the possibility that in some parts of the spirit world white clothing is indeed not "standard issue"). It may be that in some cases mortal clothing would make an individual more recognizable to an experiencer. We find a possible example of this in the recorded near-death experience of Ella Jensen, a young Latter-day Saint woman. She gave the following account: "The people were all dressed in white or cream, excepting Uncle Hans Jensen, who had on his dark clothes and long rubber boots, the things he wore when he was drowned in the Snake River." Since her uncle's body had never been found, he had only been presumed drowned before Ella's visit to the spirit world. After her experience, the family considered the mystery solved. (See *Life Everlasting*, p. 81.) In addition, perhaps different roles or responsibilities require different apparel in the spirit world as they do on earth.

While we may not fully understand in this life the significance of white clothing in the spirit world or the reasons for other types of attire, there seems to be some spiritual meaning associated with whiteness. According to Emanuel Swedenborg, the reason for the diverse appearance in clothing can be found in the varying degrees of intelligence of individuals. As we will see in a later chapter, his definition of "intelligence" closely resembles the Lord's designation of the same as "light and truth" (see D&C 93:36). "All the people in heaven are seen dressed in accord with their intelligence; and since one person surpasses another in intelligence . . . one will have more outstanding clothes than another. The most intelligence [sic] have clothes that gleam as if aflame, some radiant as if alight. The less intelligent have shining white clothes without radiance, and those still less intelligent have clothes of various colors." (*Heaven and Hell*, p. 137.)

This would certainly account for the resplendence of the white robe worn by the resurrected prophet Moroni in his appearances to Joseph Smith. In addition, John the Revelator also taught that in celestial glory the righteous will be arrayed in white. "They shall walk with me in white: for they are worthy. He that overcometh, the same shall be clothed in white raiment." (Revelation 3:4–5.) He later delineated other aspects of those who will be worthy to wear white. "What are these which are arrayed in white robes? and whence came they? . . . And he said to me, These are they which came out of great tribulation, and have washed their robes, and made them white in the blood of the Lamb." (Revelation 7:13–14.)

"Clothed with Light"

Indeed the magnificent, indescribably white clothing of the righteous may not only emanate light; it may actually be completely or at least partially composed of light in some way incomprehensible to mortals. Consider the following experience, from which we have previously quoted.

> "Dear Momma, I do wish you could see Allie [a son who had died seven months previously]; he's standing beside you." . . . I then asked her further, "Daisy, how does Allie appear to you? Does he seem to wear clothes?" She answered, "Oh, no, not clothes such as we wear. There seems to be about him a white, beautiful something, so fine and thin and glistening, and oh, so white, and yet there is not a fold, or a sign of a thread in it, so it cannot be cloth. But it makes him look so lovely." Her father then quoted from the Psalmist: "He is clothed with light as a garment." "Oh yes, that's it," she replied. (As quoted in *The Return from Silence*, p. 48.)

In modern revelation the Lord has also referred to such a condition. He spoke of one "clothed with light for a covering" (D&C 85:7). Referring to his second coming, he spoke of being "clothed with power and great glory" (D&C 45:44) and "clothed in the brightness of his glory" (D&C 65:5). Power, glory, and brightness are properties of the Light of Christ. Whether the clothing of the righteous is fashioned of light we do not know for sure, but we do know that "that which is of God is light; and he that receiveth light, and continueth in God, receiveth more light; and that light groweth brighter and brighter until the perfect day" (D&C 50:24). In other words, the righteous are those who are the most receptive to the Light of Christ, in a literal sense. We know that everything about these beings radiates light, including their white clothing.

Bodies of Light

In fact, aside from the matter of clothing, those NDErs who saw friends, relatives, or other beings usually speak of them as having been in the same "luminescent" body in which they found themselves (see *The Light Beyond*, p. 13). Moreover, they often remark that these people looked younger, happier, and more beautiful than on earth. Andrew Jackson Davis was able to witness the spirit of one of his patients as it departed from her body. He noted the better condition of her spiritual constitution as compared with her physical one.

And now I saw that she was in the possession of exterior and physical proportions, which were identical, in every possible particular—improved and beautified—with those proportions which characterized her earthly organization. That is to say, she possessed a heart, a stomach, a liver, lungs, etc., just as her natural body did previous to . . . its death. This is a wonderful and consoling truth! But I saw that the improvements . . . were not so particular and thorough as to destroy or transcend her personality; nor did they materially alter her natural appearance or earthly characteristics. So much like her former self was she, that, had her friends beheld her (as I did) they certainly would have exclaimed . . . "Why how well you look! How improved you are!" (As quoted in *Otherworld Journeys*, p. 118.)

Since the composition of the spirit body is more refined and purified and probably possesses an element of the Light of Christ, it would be reasonable to believe that these bodies are indeed finer and more delicate and exquisite than our mortal makeup. Many near-death experiences contain depictions of these spirit beings that seem to bear this out. "Everyone who came looked as they had when last I saw them, only they seemed more vibrant and healthier than before, brighter" (Atwater, *Coming Back to Life*, p. 35). Another NDEr provided this encouraging perception: "My grandmother had been ninety-six. She never did look old, she looked perhaps forty or forty-five. My mother was sixty when she died and way overweight, and she looked trim and a good general-health look, happy and healthy [during the NDE]. Everybody looked healthy, real, real healthy." (As quoted in Sabom, *Recollections of Death*, pp. 48–49.)

This characterization of those in the spirit world as youthful or ageless also appears often. Dr. George Ritchie commented on this as he recalled his experience many years later in his book *My Life After Dying*. "It also seemed the longer a being was in any of these realms, the closer they came in appearance to being around 30 to 35 years of age" (p. 24). Another NDEr made this same observation about the dear friends he met after his "death." "They did have a physical shape; it's hard to describe, but it somehow combined the youth and vigour of twenty-one-year-olds, with a sense of perfect maturity" (*Return from Death*, p. 53). One woman told of seeing another person who had also died recently. "She did not know who this person was, but made the very interesting remark that 'I did not see this person, this spirit, as having any particular *age*, at all'" (*Life After Life*, p. 57).

In light of all these experiences, it is interesting to note Swedenborg's eighteenth-century teachings. He maintained that the more spirits grow in light and truth, the more beautiful and youthful they look. "People who are in heaven progress steadily toward the springtime of life, and the more thousands of years they live, the more pleasant and happy the springtime. This goes on forever, with the increase keeping pace with the growth and level of their love, charity and faith. As the years go by, women who have died aged, debilitated by age, who have lived in faith in the Lord, charity toward the neighbor, and happy true marriage love with their husbands, come more and more into the flower of youth and young womanhood—into a beauty that outstrips every concept of beauty that sight can possibly perceive." (*Heaven and Hell*, p. 320.)

Brigham Young seemed to confirm this when he implied that this principle also has application in this life. "'Mormonism' keeps men and women young and handsome;" he reasoned, "and when they are full of the Spirit of God, there are none of them but what will have a glow upon their countenances; and that is what makes you and me young, for the Spirit of God is with us and within us" (*Discourses of Brigham Young*, p. 455).

"As He Thinketh in His Heart, So Is He"

Indeed, it seems that as both a spirit and a resurrected being a person's righteousness affects the quality of his or her appearance, just as in those realms the whiteness and brightness of one's clothing is affected by the amount of light and truth the person possesses. Almost without exception, NDErs speak of having their thoughts immediately known in that spiritual realm. They tell of being able to read the thoughts of others, sometimes even those of mortals they have left behind. We will discuss this phenomenon more thoroughly in the next chapter, but we must note here that while it is a more perfect manner of communicating, it could also be a drawback for those of us who seek to hide our innermost thoughts, motives, and true identity. If indeed this thought communication operates throughout the spirit world, there will be no place for hypocrites to hide in the next life. We will immediately be exposed for what we are deep down in our hearts, where our ideas and desires originate. If we are loving and good at heart, that will be immediately evident in our thoughts and appearance. If we secretly desire evil, that will also be manifest in our thoughts and countenance. Dr. Ritchie, after seeing spirit beings who were addicted to the habits they had formed during earth life, received "the impression they were more a product of their thoughts than are humans in our realm" (*My Life After Dying*, p. 23). He later related that he was actually taught this lesson by the Savior himself, whom he claims to have met during his NDE. "There was another lesson The Christ had tried to teach me by taking me through part of the Astral Realm and it is, *We bring into existence what we think,* or, as He quoted from Proverbs, *'For as he thinketh in his heart, so is he' "* (p. 32).

Emanuel Swedenborg propounded this same principle repeatedly in his writings. It seems as though he felt he couldn't emphasize it enough. "All the more inward affections are visible and radiate from a person's face, faces there being the very outward form and picture of these affections. In heaven, there is no way to have a face different from one's affections." (*Heaven and Hell*, p. 52.)

Perhaps Joseph Smith was referring to this concept of literally being what we think in our hearts when he spoke of those who receive the ultimate reward, whose hearts will be the most pure and whose vision will be the most clear. "They who dwell in his presence are the church of the Firstborn; and they see as they are seen, and know as they are known" (D&C 76:94).

The principle of having an appearance completely commensurate with and indicative of the inward creature would explain Joseph's description of that great and righteous servant of the Lord, Moroni. As with clothing, so with the immortal body: "Not only was his robe exceedingly white, but his whole person was glorious beyond description, and his countenance truly like lightning. The room was exceedingly light, but not so very bright as immediately around his person." (Joseph Smith—History 1:32.) The Prophet Joseph affirmed later in his life that there are two kinds of righteous beings in heaven— spirits, or just men made perfect, and resurrected persons (see D&C 129:1–3) who are further along in their progression. "Spirits can only be revealed in flaming fire and glory," he taught. "Angels have advanced further, their light and glory being tabernacled; and hence they appear in bodily shape. . . . Angels have advanced higher in knowledge and power than spirits." (*Teachings*, p. 325.)

Being a resurrected personage and therefore more advanced

and perfected would cause Moroni to appear even more beautiful and filled with light than righteous spirits. "We will have our bodies glorified, made free from every sickness and distress, and rendered most beautiful," President Lorenzo Snow confirmed. "There is nothing more beautiful to look upon than a resurrected man or woman." (*The Teachings of Lorenzo Snow*, p. 99.)

A man provided a description of a magnificent being of that spirit realm that could also be representative of a resurrected being. "I have never, before or since, seen anything as beautiful, loving, and perfectly pleasant as this being. An immense, radiant love poured from it. An incredible light shone through every single pore of its face. The colors of the light were magnificent, vibrant and alive." (As quoted in *Heading Toward Omega*, p. 65.)

Few who have near-death experiences give a description of beings in the next world as extensive as that of Emanuel Swedenborg. However, because he did not or was not allowed to perceive that the spirit state is not man's final state, he did not realize that all men would be resurrected and enter a final kingdom of glory. He spoke of three different levels in "heaven," the inner or highest realm having the most inwardly righteous inhabitants. This sounds very familiar to Latter-day Saints and will be discussed in detail later. For our purposes here, it is important to understand that, in the following excerpt, Swedenborg may be describing the spirits of just men made perfect or he may be describing resurrected beings, in the case of those in the "inmost heaven." Either way, the principle is the same.

It is worth knowing that the more inwardly a person has loved Divine truths and has lived by them, the more beautiful is his human form after death. . . .

This is why angels who are in the inmost heaven are the most beautiful—because they are forms of celestial love. People who have loved Divine truths more outwardly and hence have lived them more outwardly are less beautiful. . . .

In a word, all perfection increases toward more inward levels and decreases toward more outward levels. As perfection rises and falls, so does beauty.

I have seen angelic faces of the third heaven, whose quality was such that no artist, with all his skill, could impart enough of that kind of light to his colors to capture a thousandth part of the light and life you can see in their faces. But the faces of angels of the lowest heaven can be captured to some extent. (*Heaven and Hell*, pp. 356–57.)

And again, he gave this moving description.

I have seen them in their own light, many times brighter than earth's noon, and everything about their faces was crisper and clearer in that light than the faces of people on earth appear. I have even been given to see an angel of the inmost heaven. He had a more brilliant and radiant face than the angels of lower heavens. I looked at him carefully, and he had a human form in all perfection. (*Heaven and Hell*, pp. 71–72.)

"We Shall Be Like Him"

We can reasonably draw the conclusion, then, that the more Christlike a person becomes, the more he looks like Christ, the ideal. We even notice this effect to some extent in mortality. Who has not observed a certain aura of light or brightness that surrounds a very Christlike person? Indeed, the prophet Alma admonished us to have God's image engraven in our countenances (see Alma 5:19). How much more true this is in the next life, then, when the light within is not muffled by the coarser elements of the physical body, but that light is the embodiment or manifestation of our individual righteousness and, through the grace of God, may grow and increase until we actually appear to be like Christ, having his image engraven in our countenance! "And if your eye be single to my glory, your whole bodies shall be filled with light, and there shall be no darkness in you; and that body which is filled with light comprehendeth all things" (D&C 88:67). That light is the Light of Christ. Further, the Apostle Paul assured the Philippians that the redeemed will one day have a glorified body "like unto" their Savior's. "For our conversation is in heaven; from whence also we look for the Saviour, the Lord Jesus Christ: who shall change our vile body, that it may be fashioned like unto his glorious body, according to the working whereby he is able even to subdue all things unto himself" (Philippians 3:20–21).

George Ritchie, who saw many different types of beings in his NDE, confirmed that he saw people in the highest realm that personified this principle.

> And then I saw, infinitely far off, . . . a city. A glowing, seemingly endless city, bright enough to be seen over all the unimaginable distance between. The brightness seemed to shine from the very walls and streets of this place, and from beings which I could now discern moving about within it. In fact, the city and everything in it seemed to be made of light, even as the Figure at my side was made of light.
>
> . . . I could only gape in awe at this faraway spectacle, wondering how bright each building, each inhabitant, must be to be seen over so many light-years of distance. Could these radiant beings, I wondered, amazed, be those who had indeed kept Jesus the focus of their lives? Was I seeing at last ones who had looked for Him in everything? Looked so well and so closely that they had been changed into His very likeness? (*Return from Tomorrow*, pp. 72–73.)

Undoubtedly, we will not lose our own personal identity in future lives, yet we hope that in some manner we will become so like him and become "one" with him to such an extent that we "shall be like him" (1 John 3:2–3). At least in the sense of righteousness and light, this seems to be a quite literal change.

Eternal Beauty Is Earned

And so we see that there are all levels of beauty and brilliance in the appearance and clothing of beings who inhabit the spirit world, just as there are variations and gradations here on earth. However, in that realm where inward desires cannot be hidden by a mortal body, the distribution of true beauty is far more just, fair, and meaningful than on earth, where it is often a random and unearned gift. There, goodness and love are beauty itself, and one is comely to the extent that he or she possesses them. Even a magnificence like Christ's may be obtained by anyone willing to pay the price.

> Wherefore, my beloved brethren, pray unto the Father with all the energy of heart, that ye may be filled with this love, which he hath bestowed upon all who are true followers of his Son, Jesus Christ; that ye may become the sons of God; that when he shall appear we shall be like him, for we shall see him as he is; that we may have this hope; that we may be purified even as he is pure. Amen. (Moroni 7:48.)

CHAPTER 4

Capacities
of the Spirit Body

Those whose spirits actually leave their bodies soon discover that they are limited in their ability to communicate with and function in the physical world they have left behind. However, they also quickly comprehend that their spirit being operates with greatly enhanced and advanced capacities in the spirit realms, where communication, travel, and learning all take place in ways of which human beings can only dream.

Communication

As discussed in chapter 3, almost all those who encounter spirit beings during their near-death episodes speak of communicating with them instantly—primarily through thought transferral or some form of telepathy rather than through the spoken word. They report that not only thoughts were transmitted but also every feeling, desire, and nuance associated with those thoughts. This suggests a lack of misunderstandings or "communication gaps" in at least some part or parts of the spirit world. It suggests too that genuine loving expressions can be fuller, richer, and more meaningful there than on earth.

Of his experience one NDEr reported: "There is no miscommunication. There is no room for hiding anything. It is instantaneous, absolute, and without even the hint of flaw." (Raymond C. Babb, in *Vital Signs*, August–September, 1992, p. 11.) (This being said, we must point out that there have been times when an NDEr was not allowed to completely perceive or remember everything he or she saw and experienced, this presumably being according to the Lord's purposes. In addition we must not construe this to mean that all thoughts can be read at all times by all spirits.)

While there is no official Church doctrine concerning the presence or absence of this perfect pattern of communication in the spirit world and in the eternal kingdoms of glory, some of the early Brethren addressed the idea of such a language. We also find some evidence of this type of divine communication in mortality. We know that much of our earthly correspondence with the spirit world and other personal revelation comes from the Spirit of the Lord to our minds and hearts. In granting Oliver Cowdery permission to attempt to translate, the Lord instructed him, "Yea, behold, I will tell you in your mind and in your heart, by the Holy Ghost, which shall come upon you and which shall dwell in your heart. Now, behold, this is the spirit of revelation." (D&C 8:2.) We note too that the Prophet Joseph taught, "All things whatsoever God in his infinite wisdom has seen fit and proper to reveal to us, while we are dwelling in mortality, in regard to our mortal bodies, are revealed to us in the abstract, and independent of affinity of this mortal tabernacle, but are revealed to our spirits precisely as though we had no bodies at all" (*Teachings*, p. 355).

Orson Pratt reasoned that our interaction with the Lord may be an example of the kind of correspondence we will enjoy with all beings in the immortal world.

> For instance, how does God perceive the thoughts of our hearts? Is there not here a language by which He can discover and discern the thoughts and intents of the heart? Are we not told in many of the revelations how that God

can perceive the thoughts of man, and that for every idle thought we are to be brought into judgment? Yes, He discerns the thoughts, and the intents of the hearts of the children of men. Suppose we had some of that power resting upon us, would not that be a different kind of a language from sound, or from a written language? It would. If spirits could commune with spirits, and one higher intelligence commune with another, by the same principle through which God sees the thoughts and intents of the heart, it would be nothing more than what has already existed here in this world, according to that which is revealed. (In *Journal of Discourses,* 3:102.)

In a general conference of the Church, Elder Eldred G. Smith, then Patriarch to the Church, provided an appropriate analogy for spiritual reception of the Holy Ghost, which may be a type of all spiritual communication.

Now, I think if we will apply some of the laws of electronics, that is, radio and television, we will be aided in a possible understanding of how we can receive a message from the Holy Ghost. We have a spirit mind and a mortal mind. Our spirit mind can receive messages from the Holy Ghost, who is a spirit.

In this room now there are many waves going by of sound, of pictures, and even of colored pictures. We cannot detect them with our mortal eyes or ears, but if we set up a receiving set and put it in tune, then we pick up the sound or pictures by the mortal ears or eyes. Similarly, the Holy Ghost may be constantly sending out messages like a broadcasting station. If you put yourself in tune, that is, knock or ask or seek, you may receive the message. It may be as if you were to open an imaginary window or door between your spirit mind and your physical mind and permit the message to come through. Spirit can talk to spirit, and you are part spirit—just open that imaginary door and let the mortal mind receive. (In Conference Report, October 1964, pp. 10–11.)

Furthermore, Joseph Smith reminded us that the spirits of the just who have passed beyond the veil "know and understand our thoughts, feelings and motions" (*Teachings*, p. 326). In light of these teachings and our understanding of the advanced abilities of spirit and resurrected beings, the mode of communication often described by NDErs makes perfect sense. We can comfortably accept the consistent witness of those who have visited the spirit world. It is interesting to note the observations and insights of NDErs regarding this remarkably complete method of communication.

> I could see people all around, and I could understand what they were saying. I didn't hear them, audibly. . . . It was more like knowing what they were thinking, exactly what they were thinking, but only in my mind, not in their actual vocabulary. I would catch it the second before they opened their mouths to speak. (*Life After Life*, p. 52.)

> I saw people that I knew had died. There were no words spoken, but it was as if I knew what they were thinking and at the same time I knew that they knew what I was thinking. (*Return from Death*, p. 50.)

> I was seated by the tree of life . . . there I saw many thousand spirits clothed in white. . . . They did not converse by sound, but each knew the other's thoughts at the instant, and conversation was carried on in that way, also with me. (*The Return from Silence*, p. 62.)

> "Dear Momma, I do wish you could see Allie [a son who had died seven months previously]; he's standing beside you." . . . Then wondering how she could be conversing with her brother when I saw not the least sign of conversation, I said, "Daisy, how do you speak to Allie? I do not hear you or see your lips move." She smilingly replied, "We just talk with our think." (*The Return from Silence*, p. 48.)

It was Swedenborg's claim that he was allowed to experience death and that his spirit was ready to leave his body only when he was able to communicate by thought with those spirits who were sent to escort and guide him in the spirit realm. "The angels who sat by my head were silent, only their thoughts communicating with mine. When these thoughts are accepted, the angels know that the person's spirit is in a state to be led out of his body. The communication of their thoughts was accomplished by their looking at my face, this being in fact how communication of thoughts takes place in heaven." (*Heaven and Hell*, p. 346.)

Swedenborg maintained that angels can also speak with their mouths and hear with their ears by virtue of their human-like spirit bodies. "Angelic speech, like human speech, . . . is just as much spoken aloud and heard aloud, for angels have mouths, tongues, and ears." However, he asserts that though they may speak out loud to mortals, their words are still communicated primarily through the thought processes. "The speech of angels or spirits with man sounds just as 'audible' as the speech of one person with another. However, it is not audible to people nearby, only to the individual himself. This is because the speech of an angel or spirit flows into the person's thought first, and comes by an inner path to his physical ear; it thus activates it from within." (*Heaven and Hell*, pp. 170, 178–79.) Dr. George Ritchie alluded to this same condition in his depiction of the conversation he felt he had with Christ. "When He spoke, I heard Him in a way different from anyone else. I heard Him from deep within in my own mind." (*My Life After Dying*, p. 18.)

Languages in the Spirit World

Not only is communication in this realm literally from spirit to spirit—heart to heart, and mind to mind—but also it seems to transcend typical language barriers. A few NDErs have reported hearing languages other than their own spoken on the other side of the veil, and yet in many cases it seems they understood what was being said. "I could hear *languages*," related one woman. "All languages. Languages that I had never heard before and I could understand them." (*Heading Toward Omega*, p. 74.)

It seems logical, knowing that we take all that we have learned and all that we are into the spirit world with us, that we could still retain our native tongue and customs. However, it also seems reasonable that, while these languages persist, communication would not be hindered by them, as on earth. One NDEr believes that "in an instant telekinesis your thought waves are read, regardless of language" (as quoted in *Return from Death*, p. 53). Swedenborg averred that since the language of heaven stems from inward thoughts and desires, it is natural to all its inhabitants. "The language is not learned there—it is native to everyone. It actually flows from their affection and thought." He later elaborated on this idea: "A language like that of the spiritual world is instinctive in every individual, but it is in the realm of his more inward understanding. However, since this [earthly] realm does not, in man's case, find its way into words that parallel affections the way it does with angels, man is unaware that the language is there. Still, this is why man is at home with this language of angels and spirits when he enters the other life, and knows how to speak it without being taught." (*Heaven and Hell*, pp. 170, 175.)

Perhaps the explanation is that spirits are able to speak or even think in their own mortally acquired tongue, but these words and thoughts transcend the earthly differences in language and are communicated perfectly to the listener or receiver. Dr. Raymond Moody reported that some NDErs perceive a dialogue of this type that takes place between themselves and the "being of light." "This unimpeded exchange," he summarizes, "does not even take place in the native language of the person. Yet, he understands perfectly and is instantaneously aware." (*Life After Life*, p. 60.)

Whatever else we know or do not know, it is clear that the Lord deigns to teach his children in the manner most suited to each of them individually. "For the Lord God giveth light unto the understanding;" wrote Nephi, "for he speaketh unto men according to their language, unto their understanding" (2 Nephi 31:3). The Prophet Joseph reasoned, "We may come to Jesus and ask Him; He will know all about it; if He comes to a little child, he will adapt himself to the language and capacity of a little child" (*Teachings*, p. 162). Dr. Wiltse, the nineteenth-century physician and near-death experiencer introduced previously, observed that phenomenon. "Thoughts not my own entered into my brain. These, I said, are his thoughts and not mine; they might be in Greek or Hebrew for all power I have over them, But how kindly I am addressed in my mother tongue that so I may understand all his will." (*The Return from Silence*, pp. 60–61.)

From any information we can gain, it seems that the most desirable method of communication may vary with circumstances, so that while thought and feeling sometimes serves best, verbal communication in one's own tongue (or perhaps even both) will often be the method used. For instance, one African man who found himself on the other side heard many languages which he could not understand, but finally he found someone who spoke in his own tongue, who was able to tell him he must return to mortal life. This would account for some experiences Latter-day Saints have had which, while they are not to be treated as doctrine, imply that some people are specifically called into the spirit world because their language skills are needed to further the Lord's work there (see, for example, Millet and McConkie, *The Life Beyond*, pp. 55–57).

Ultimately, however, the current languages of earth will be done away, being replaced by the Adamic language, the "pure and undefiled" language spoken by the first mortals (see *Mormon Doctrine*, p. 19). Brigham Young observed that the human language is "a good medium at ordinary times, yet it comes very far short of being such a medium, as man needs to convey thoughts, when he is inspired by the power of God, through the gift of the Holy Ghost, and is full of the revelations of Jesus." He then quoted Zephaniah 3:8–9: "Therefore wait ye upon me, saith the Lord, until the day that I rise up to the prey: for my determination is to gather the nations, that I may assemble the kingdoms, to pour upon them mine indignation, even all my fierce anger: for all the earth shall be devoured with the fire of my jealousy. For then will I turn to the people a pure language, that they may all call upon the name of the Lord, to serve him with one consent." (In *Journal of Discourses*, 10:353.)

Looking to a future state for the righteous, Elder Orson Pratt also confirmed that earthly languages pertain to a lesser state and will give way to more glorious means of communication. "These imperfect things will be done away, and we shall be able by the power of the Holy Ghost to obtain a language by which the angels speak, and by which a higher order of beings speak, and by these means attain to a greater degree of knowledge, that will produce a greater amount of happiness" (in *Journal of Discourses,* 3:103).

"The Same Sociality"

Both Joseph Smith and Brigham Young assured the Saints that our interaction with friends and loved ones after this life will merely be an eternal extension of our joyous associations with them here on earth. "Spirits will be familiar with spirits in the spirit world," President Brigham Young declared, "will converse, behold, and exercise every variety of communication with one another as familiarly and naturally as while here in tabernacles" (*Discourses of Brigham Young,* p. 380). Joseph Smith taught that we will continue to enjoy these blessings into the eternities. "And that same sociality which exists among us here will exist among us there, only it will be coupled with eternal glory, which glory we do not now enjoy" (D&C 130:2). Perhaps Swedenborg was also alluding to this state of sociality when he suggested that life goes on after the pattern we have grown accustomed to on earth, yet on a much higher and nobler plane. "Angels talk with each other just the way people in the world do, and they talk of various things—household matters, political matters, issues of moral life and issues of spiritual life, for example. There is no noticeable difference, except that they talk with each other more intelligently than men do, since they talk more profoundly, from thought." (*Heaven and Hell,* p. 170.)

Inexpressible Language

Not only do angels, and no doubt righteous, knowledgeable spirits, converse on a more enlightened level than humans, but it also seems that they communicate in words and ways which are far above those of the narrow mortal mind of man. We have record of this phenomenon in Latter-day Saint scripture. For instance, Oliver Cowdery made the following attempt to convey the indescribable nature of the language employed by John the Baptist when he appeared to Oliver and Joseph on the banks of the Susquehanna River to confer upon them the Aaronic Priesthood. "I shall not attempt to paint to you the feelings of this heart, nor the majestic beauty and glory which surrounded us on this occasion; but you will believe me when I say, that earth, nor men, with the eloquence of time, cannot begin to clothe language in as interesting and sublime a manner as this holy personage. No; nor has this earth power to give the joy, to bestow the peace, or comprehend the wisdom which was contained in each sentence as they were delivered by the power of the Holy Spirit!" (Joseph Smith—History 1:71, footnote.)

We find in 3 Nephi a moving description of the ineffability of the language of the higher realms. Referring to the prayer which Jesus offered to the Father in behalf of the people at the temple in the land Bountiful, we read this wondrous account. "And after this manner do they bear record: The eye hath never seen, neither hath the ear heard, before, so great and marvelous things as we saw and heard Jesus speak unto the Father; and no tongue can speak, neither can there be written by any man, neither can the hearts of men conceive so great and marvelous things as we both saw and heard Jesus speak; and no one can conceive of the joy which filled our souls at the time we heard him pray for us unto the Father" (3 Nephi 17:16–17).

In Elder Pratt's previously mentioned sermon, he contemplated some of the faculties of immortal beings which might facilitate the kind of miraculous communication described here.

> For instance, how do you suppose that spirits after they leave these bodies, communicate one with another? Do they communicate their ideas by the actual vibrations of the atmosphere the same as we do? I think not. I think if we could be made acquainted with the kind of language by which spirits converse with spirits, we would find that . . . they have . . . a more refined system among them of communicating their ideas. This system will be so constructed that they can not only communicate at the same moment upon one subject, as we have to do by making sounds in the atmosphere, but communicate vast numbers of ideas, all

at the same time, on a great variety of subjects; and the mind will be capable of perceiving them. . . . If the mind has such faculty as this, then there must necessarily be a language adapted to such a capacity of the mind. . . .

Well, inquires one, "can you imagine up any such system, or language in this world?" I can imagine up one, but it cannot be made practicable here, from the fact that the mind of man is unable to use it. For instance, the Book of Mormon tells us, that the angels speak by the power of the Holy Ghost, and man when under the influence of it, speaks the language of angels. Why does he speak in this language? Because the Holy Ghost suggests the ideas which he speaks; and it gives him utterance to convey them to the people. . . . Suppose, instead of having arbitrary sounds, such as we have here, to communicate these ideas, that the Holy Ghost itself, through a certain process and power, should enable him to unfold that knowledge to another spirit, all in an instant. (In *Journal of Discourses,* 3:100–101.)

Many NDErs have also borne witness of this inexpressible language. "Yet, although the language was English," noted Dr. Wiltse, the physician who was so "kindly addressed" in his native language, "it was so eminently above my power to reproduce that my rendition of it is far short of the original" (*The Return from Silence,* p. 61). Dr. Moody reports that the NDEr "cannot even translate the thoughts and exchanges which took place while he was near death into the human language which he must speak now, after his resuscitation" (*Life After Life,* p. 60). He quotes a woman who attempted to explain this ineffability. "Now, there is a real problem for me as I'm trying to tell you this, because all the words I know are three-dimensional. As I was going through this, I kept thinking, 'Well, when I was taking geometry, they always told me there were only three dimensions, and I always just accepted that. But they were wrong. There are more.' And, of course, our world—the one we're living in now—*is* three-dimensional, but the next one definitely isn't. And that's why it's so hard to tell you this. I have to describe it to you in words that are three-dimensional. That's as close as I can get to it, but it's not really adequate. I can't really give you a complete picture." (P. 26.)

Once again, Emanuel Swedenborg seems to have received substantial insight into this condition, also. He taught that "the sermons [in heaven] are characterized by such wisdom that none on earth can be cited in comparison: they are in the heavens, in a more inward light" (*Heaven and Hell*, p. 163). His explanation sounds very compatible with Oliver Cowdery's description. He explained further,

> . . . Their speech is so full of wisdom that they with a single word can express things that men could not compass in a thousand words. Then, too, their thought-concepts embrace things such as men cannot grasp, let alone verbalize. Consequently, the sounds and sights of heaven are called inexpressible, and such as ear simply has not yet heard, nor eye seen.
>
> I have been granted knowledge of this on the basis of experience. On occasion, I have been assigned to the state in which angels were, and in that state have talked with them. At such times I understood everything. But when I was sent back into my earlier state—hence to the natural thinking proper to man—and wanted to recall what I had heard, I could not. For there were thousands of things that had no equivalent in concepts of natural thought. (*Heaven and Hell*, pp. 172–73.)

Swedenborg also logically asserts that the more inwardly righteous a person in the spirit world (his "heaven") is, the more perfected his or her ability to communicate and to discern the thoughts of others. He claims that the angels of the "highest realm" speak a purer and more beautiful language, and that "more inward angels can know a person's whole life from the tone, from a few spoken words. From the tone, patterned by means of the concepts involved in the words, they perceive his dominant love [what or who is most important to him], which has recorded in it, so to speak, all the details of his life." (*Heaven and Hell*, p. 195.) This would, again, seem to coincide with Joseph Smith's description of celestial beings who would "see as they are seen, and know as they are known" (D&C 76:94; see also 1 Corinthians 13:12). Thus it seems that on the other side of the veil we will have the opportunity to progress toward perfection in our ability to communicate, as well as in all other areas.

Movement and Travel

In addition to their superior capacities for communication, there are spirit world beings who can travel at greatly accelerated speeds, as compared with mortal travel. Elder Parley P. Pratt, in a discourse on spiritual communication, taught that the nature and makeup of the spirit body are a factor in its proficiency in supernatural movement. "It is true that this subtle fluid or spiritual element is endowed with the powers of locomotion in a far greater degree than the more gross or solid elements of nature; that its refined particles penetrate amid the other elements with greater ease, and meet with less resistance from the air or other substances, than would the more gross elements. Hence its speed, or superior powers of motion." (In *Journal of Discourses*, 1:8.)

Elder Orson Pratt, in a discourse on communication in the next life, implied that because our spirits are composed of light we should be able to travel at the speed of light.

> What does the Lord say in one of the new revelations? "Ye shall live by every word that cometh out of the mouth of God; whatsoever is truth is light, and whatsoever is light is spirit," consequently the light that comes from the sun is spirit. How fast does that spirit travel? It can be demonstrated that it can travel [at the speed of light]; if then one portion of spirit can travel with that velocity, it is natural for us to suppose that any other portions of spirit can travel with the same velocity, and thus we shall be able to accomplish, and perform a greater amount of righteousness among other worlds and beings, than if we were compelled to lose three fourths, or nine tenths of our time on the journey. (In *Journal of Discourses*, 3:104.)

Brigham Young also taught that such a faculty would be a feature of the next life. He explained that in the spirit world we would not be "encumbered . . . so that when we advance in years we have to be stubbing along and to be careful lest we fall down. We see our youth, even, frequently stubbing their toes and falling down. But yonder, how different."

> They move with ease and like lightning. If we want to visit Jerusalem, or this, that, or the other place—and I presume we will be permitted if we desire—there we are, looking at its streets. If we want to behold Jerusalem as it was in the days of the Savior; or if we want to see the Garden of Eden as it was when created, there we are, and we see it as it existed spiritually, for it was created first spiritually and then temporally, and spiritually it still remains. And when there we may behold the earth as at the dawn of creation, or we may visit any city we please that exists upon its surface. If we wish to understand how they are living here on these western islands, or in China, we are there; in fact, we are like the light of the morning, or, I will not say the electric fluid, but its operations on the wires. God has revealed some little things with regard to His movements and power, and the operation and motion of the lightning furnish a fine illustration of the ability and power of the Almighty. If you could stretch a wire from this room around the world until the two ends nearly met here again and were to apply a battery to one end, if the electrical conditions were perfect, the effect of the touch would pass with such inconceivable velocity that it would be felt at the other end of the wire at the same moment. . . .
>
> When we pass into the spirit world we shall possess a measure of this power. (In *Journal of Discourses*, 14:231.)

In other words, President Young indicated that we will not only be able to travel to any place we desire as fast as the speed of electricity but that we may also be time-travellers. "As quickly as the spirit is unlocked from this house of clay," he said on another occasion, "it is free to travel with lightning speed to any planet, or fixed star, or to the uttermost part of the earth, or to the depths of the sea, according to the will of Him who dictates" (in *Journal of Discourses*, 13:77). From these statements we learn that our travelling abilities and possibilities will be limited only by two things—our own desires and the will of the Lord. Assuming that the Lord is in agreement, we will apparently be able to arrive at a destination almost instantaneously just by thinking about it or wishing ourselves there.

While such a notion may boggle the mortal mind, it is unquestionably the consensus of those who have had near-death experiences. Dr. George Ritchie reported that he travelled great distances across the United States in this manner during his NDE. "I had made two other discoveries about this strange out-of-body realm. First, one goes wherever his/her soul's sincere desire leads him/her. Secondly, time in this realm, if it exists at all, is much shorter than our normal human realm, or the capacity to cover great distances in a regular period of time is vastly increased, for the distance I knew I had traveled could not be covered in our fastest airplanes." (*My Life After Dying*, p. 14.)

Summarizing the accounts of many NDErs, Dr. Raymond Moody wrote: "Travel, once one gets the hang of it, is apparently exceptionally easy in this state. Physical objects present no barrier, and movement from one place to another can be extremely rapid, almost instantaneous." (*Life After Life*, p. 46.) "I felt as if I was being propelled forward at the speed of light or faster," claimed one man (*Return from Death*, p. 43). A Vietnam veteran whose body was lying wounded on an operating table in a medevac unit told that his spirit returned to the battlefield where he had been wounded. When he could not get his comrades to stop gathering up the dead bodies, he suddenly found himself back in the operating room. He described the swiftness of his transition by saying: "It was almost like you materialize there and all of a sudden the next instant you were over here. It was just like you blinked your eyes." (*Recollections of Death*, p. 33.)

A cardiac arrest victim described the elation of this new-found freedom. He said, "I could have moved away from my body anytime I wanted to. . . . There wasn't a thing that was mechanical about it, like an automobile or anything. It was just a thought process. I felt like I could have thought myself anywhere I wanted to be instantly. . . . I just felt exhilarated with a sense of power. I could do what I wanted to. . . . It's realer than here, really." (*Recollections of Death*, p. 34.)

Experiencers seem to be able to effect slower travel or

movement as well. Some speak of walking or strolling, others of gliding or floating. It usually seems to be a function of the desires of the individual spirit. In fact, when Emanuel Swedenborg commented on transportation within the spirit world, he alluded to another very interesting and perhaps understandable effect that the mind may have in relation to travel there. "When anyone travels from one place to another—be it within his community, within his own grounds, in his gardens, or to others outside his community—he gets there more quickly if he is willing and more slowly if he is unwilling. The route itself becomes longer or shorter in keeping with his willingness, even while it remains the same route." (*Heaven and Hell*, p. 146.)

Ability to Absorb, Comprehend, and Remember Information

Apparently the highly advanced capacities of the spirit body for communication and travel are also an integral part of its remarkable ability to gather, understand, and retain knowledge of all kinds. Brigham Young looked forward to these enhanced faculties for learning which we will enjoy in the next life. "I shall not cease learning while I live, nor when I arrive in the spirit-world; but shall there learn with greater facility; and when I again receive my body, I shall learn a thousand times more in a thousand times less time; and then I do not mean to cease learning, but shall still continue my researches" (in *Journal of Discourses*, 8:10). The highly refined and energized composition of the spirit body apparently can imbue it not only with perfect communication and instantaneous movement but also with enormously heightened senses.

Elder Orson Pratt contemplated the possibilities of spiritual senses. "We shall learn many more things there; we need not suppose our five senses connect us with all the things of heaven, and earth, and eternity, and space; we need not think that we are conversant with all the elements of nature, through the medium of the senses God has given us here. Suppose He should give us a sixth sense, a seventh, an eighth, a ninth, or a fiftieth. All these different senses would convey to us new ideas, as much so as the senses of tasting, smelling, or seeing communicate different ideas from that of hearing." (In *Journal of Discourses*, 2:247.) Elder Pratt also suggested how some of these senses might function in the next world in comparison to their operation on earth. He believed that the entire spirit body may be capable of sensing and absorbing knowledge and light.

> If we, by looking through these little eyes of ours, can see objects some thousands of millions of miles distant; if we can see objects that are existing at that immense distance through the medium of these little inlets; suppose that the whole spirit were uncovered and exposed to all the rays of light, can it be supposed that light would not affect the spirit if it were thus unshielded, uncovered, and unclothed? Do you suppose that it would not be susceptible of any impressions made by the elements of light? The spirit is inherently capable of experiencing the sensations of light; if it were not so, we could not see. You might form as fine an eye as ever was made, but if the spirit, in and of itself, were not capable of being acted upon by the rays of light, an eye would be of no benefit. Then unclothe the spirit, and instead of exposing a small portion of it about the size of a pea to the action of the rays of light, the whole of it would be exposed. I think we could then see in different directions at once, instead of looking in one particular direction; we could then look all around us at the same instant. (In *Journal of Discourses*, 2:243.)

Many spirit world experiences seem to bear witness to just such a rarified state of awareness. "My vision seemed to at once focus in front of me and at the same time cover a three hundred and sixty degree radius," related one individual who underwent an out-of-body experience (OBE). "All of my 'senses' were perceiving in similar intense fashion. I could 'hear' a wonderful harmony which seemed to accompany every movement of every particle." (As quoted in *The Return from Silence*, p. 207.) A man who was the victim of an attempted murder returned with a similar report. "As my senses expanded I became aware of colors that were far beyond the spectrum of the rainbow known to the human eye. My awareness stretched out in all three hundred sixty degrees." (As quoted in *Heading Toward Omega*, p. 65.) Dr. Kenneth Ring observed that "sometimes this heightened sensory awareness [is] not attributed to any particular sense organ per se." He then cited this account of a NDEr: "It was as if my whole body had eyes and ears. I was just so aware of everything." (*Life at Death*, p. 93.) Almost all NDErs report that they felt more alive, vibrant, and aware than they did during their physical life. They felt unlimited and unhindered by mortality in that new realm.

Emanuel Swedenborg also commented on the enhanced senses of spirits and angels. "People who are in heaven have far more delicate senses (that is, they see and hear far more precisely) and they think more wisely than when they were in the world. For they see by heaven's light, which surpasses earth's light by many degrees; they hear, too, through a spiritual atmosphere, which also surpasses the earthly one by many degrees." (*Heaven and Hell*, p. 359.)

Great Increase of Spirit Comprehension

Because of the immeasurably improved senses we will enjoy in the next life, we will not only be able to absorb masses of information at once but will also be able to comprehend it. We have several examples from latter-day revelation wherein great prophets—Enoch, the brother of Jared, and Moses—were quickened and privileged to view the existence of the world from beginning to end, comprehending every particle of it and every being who would ever occupy it. Moses' account of his experience provides us with the details. "And it came to pass, as the voice [of God] was still speaking, Moses cast his eyes and beheld the earth, yea, even all of it; and there was not a particle of it which he did not behold, discerning it by the spirit of God. And he beheld also the inhabitants thereof, and there was not a soul which he beheld not; and he discerned them by the Spirit of God; and their numbers were great, even numberless as the sand upon the sea shore." (Moses 1:27–28.)

It seems that the righteous will somehow possess this type of power in the spirit world. In a discourse entitled "The Increased

Powers and Faculties of the Mind in the Future State," Elder Orson Pratt propounded that they would enjoy just such a power. "When the Lord imparts to us a principle by which we can look upon the past and future, as well as the present—by which we can look upon many intricate objects of nature which are now hidden from our view—we shall find our capacity for obtaining and retaining knowledge to be greatly enlarged" (in *Journal of Discourses*, 2:247; see entire talk, pp. 235–48). In yet another oration, he further elaborated on these desirable abilities of the spirit.

> Here, then, is a new faculty of knowledge, very extended in its nature, that is calculated to throw a vast amount of information upon the mind of man, almost in the twinkling of an eye. How long a time would it take a man in the next world, if he had to gain knowledge as we do here, to find out the simplest things in nature? He might reason, and reason for thousands of years, and then hardly have got started. But when this Spirit of God, this great telescope that is used in the celestial heavens, is given to man, and he, through the aid of it, gazes upon eternal things, what does he behold? Not one object at a time, but a vast multitude of objects rush before his vision, and are present before his mind, filling him in a moment with the knowledge of worlds more numerous than the sands of the sea shore. Will he be able to bear it? Yes, his mind is strengthened in proportion to the amount of information imparted. It is this tabernacle, in its present condition, that prevents us from a more enlarged understanding.
>
> There is a faculty mentioned in the word of God, which we are not in possession of here, but we shall possess it hereafter; that is not only to see a vast number of things in the same moment, looking in all directions by the aid of the Spirit, but also to obtain a vast number of ideas at the same instant. . . .
>
> I believe we shall be freed in the next world, in a great measure, from these narrow, contracted methods of thinking. Instead of thinking in one channel, and following up one certain course of reasoning to find a certain truth,

knowledge will rush in from all quarters; it will come in
like the light which flows from the sun, penetrating every
part, informing the spirit, and giving understanding concerning ten thousand things at the same time; and the mind
will be capable of receiving and retaining all. (In *Journal of
Discourses*, 2:246.)

A passage from Emanuel Swedenborg's book hints that he
comprehended this same principle. "For the human mind is
just as discerning as the angelic mind," he asserted. "The reason it is not so discerning in the world is that it is within an
earthly body, within which a spiritual mind thinks in natural
fashion. But it is quite different when it is released from its tie
with the body. Then it no longer thinks in a natural way, but in
a spiritual way; and when it does, it thinks about matters unin-
telligible and inexpressible to the natural person—so it discerns
like an angel." (*Heaven and Hell*, p. 237.)

Other near-death experiencers have consistently and with
great detail reported this remarkable improvement in their understanding and comprehension. Dr. Raymond Moody characterized this enhanced intellectual and spiritual capacity as a
"vision of knowledge." In his second book, *Reflections on Life
After Life*, Moody summarized the findings concerning this significant element of the NDE which had come to his attention
subsequent to the publication of his first book, *Life After Life*.
Noting that NDErs state that a complete expression of the experience was impossible in mortality, he observed that they "got
brief glimpses of an entire separate realm of existence in which
all knowledge—whether of past, present, or future—seemed to
co-exist in a sort of timeless state. Alternately, this has been described as a moment of enlightenment in which the subject
seemed to have complete knowledge."

In his book Dr. Moody provided several specific examples.
One woman explained: "It seemed that all of a sudden, all
knowledge—of all that had started from the very beginning,
that would go on without end—that for a second I knew all the
secrets of all ages, all the meaning of the universe, the stars, the
moon—of everything." When questioned by Dr. Moody as to
how this knowledge was presented to her, she replied: "It was

in all forms of communication, sights, sounds, thoughts. It was any- and everything. It was as if there was nothing that wasn't known. All knowledge was there, not just of one field, but everything."

A young man who struggled to describe his experience put it this way. "Because this is a place where the *place* is knowledge. . . . Knowledge and information are readily available—all knowledge. . . . You absorb knowledge. . . . You all of a sudden know the answers." (*Reflections on Life After Life,* pp. 9–14.)

In *The Light Beyond*, Moody related further descriptions of this experience which correlate remarkably well with Brigham Young's statement on the ease of traveling wherever one desires in the next world. "Another man described this realm as a state of consciousness where whatever you want is available to you. If you think of something you want to learn about, it appears to you and is there for you to learn. He said it was almost as though information was available in bundles of thought. This includes information of any kind. For instance, if I wanted to know what it was like to be the president of the United States, I would need only to wish for the experience and it would be so. Or if I wanted to know what it was like to be an insect, I would merely have to 'request' the experience by wishing for it, and the experience would be mine." (P. 43.)

Finally, another experiencer related an occurrence which sounds somewhat similar to the vision of Moses. "Then I was told to shift my attention, and immediately I found that I could see the entire world as clearly as I had observed the details of my room" (*The Return from Silence,* p. 163).

While Moses and the other prophets may have been allowed to retain all that they learned in their visions, they have imparted to us only a fraction of their knowledge. It is interesting that all of the NDErs report that the knowledge gained in the eternal realm was erased from their memories when they returned to earth. Once again, this is in harmony with the understanding Latter-day Saints enjoy that a veil of forgetfulness as to the premortal life is drawn over our minds here in order to make the mortal testing valid. While the NDErs do not forget *everything* they experienced in the spirit world, it appears from the scriptures and the words of the prophets and is confirmed by the insights of experiencers that too much knowledge would indeed confound and destroy our schooling here on earth. "We are cocooned, as it were," Elder Neal A. Maxwell has taught, "in order that we might truly choose" (as quoted in, *The Life Before*, p. 173).

Perfect Spirit Memory

By contrast, there seems to be no memory loss as regards our mortal life once we pass out of this earthly "cocoon"; for in addition to and in concert with the superior abilities we have discussed, the spirit body enjoys perfect recall. In the next life we will remember everything we have learned and done in this life (except perhaps our forgiven sins) as well as being able to retain the magnificent knowledge that will be available to us in the next estate. We will no longer have to deal with the frustration of forgetting that plagues us in mortality. Elder Orson Pratt observed:

> We read or learn a thing by observation yesterday, and to-day, or tomorrow it is gone. . . . Some of the knowledge we receive here at one time becomes so completely obliterated, through the weakness of the animal system, that we cannot call it to mind, no association of ideas will again suggest it to our minds; it is gone, erased, eradicated from the tablet of our memories. This is not owing to the want of capacity in the spirit; no, but the spirit has a full capacity to remember. . . . It is not the want of capacity in the spirit of man that causes him to forget the knowledge he may have learned yesterday; but it is because of the imperfection of the tabernacle in which the spirit dwells; because there is imperfection in the organization of the flesh and bones, and in things pertaining to the tabernacle; it is this that erases from our memory many things that would be useful; we cannot retain them in our minds, they are gone into oblivion. It is not so with the spirit when it is released from this tabernacle. . . . Wait until these mortal bodies are laid in the tomb; when we return home to God who gave us life; then is the time we shall have the most vivid knowledge of all

the past acts of our lives during our probationary state. (In *Journal of Discourses*, 2:239.)

Elder George Q. Cannon also added his witness of this perfect memory of the eternal spirit.

> Memory will be quickened to a wonderful extent. Every deed that we have done will be brought to our recollection. Every acquaintance made will be remembered. There will be no scenes or incidents in our lives that will be forgotten by us in the world to come. You have heard of men who have been drowning or have fallen from a great height describe that in about a second or two every event of their lives passed before them like a panorama with the rapidity of lightning. This shows what power there is latent in the human mind, which, when quickened by the power of God, will make men and women recall not only that which pertains to this life, but our memories will stretch back to the life we had before we came here, with the associations we had with our Father and God and with those bright spirits that stand around His throne and with the righteous and holy ones. (*Gospel Truth*, pp. 60–61.)

The subject of perfect memory and perfect recollection will be treated more thoroughly in chapter 11. Experiences detailing the manifestation of this phenomenon will be extensively quoted there. We quote here, however, an interesting witness Swedenborg provided to the flawless performance of memory in the spirit world which goes beyond the life review. "I saw some books with writing in them, like the books in the world, and I was informed that these had come out of the memory of the people who had written them, without a word missing that had been in the book any one of them had written in the world. In the same way, the most minute details of everything can be drawn from someone's memory, even things he himself has forgotten in the world." (*Heaven and Hell*, p. 364.)

It is thrilling, uplifting, and almost overwhelming to contemplate the faculties we look forward to enjoying when released from our mortal tabernacles. Understanding that the more righteous we are, the more enhanced and perfected our capacity will be for using and enjoying these proficiencies, should inspire us to strive to live worthy lives and endure in faith to the end. In addition, such understanding also comforts us as we endure the deficiencies and limitations of mortal existence. Perhaps this explains why Elder Orson Pratt spoke so frequently and fervently upon this important subject. He admonished:

> And do not forget to look forward to those joys ahead, if we do [forget], we will become careless, dormant, and sluggish, and we will think we do not see much ahead to be anticipated, but if we keep our minds upon the prize that lays ahead—upon the vast fields of knowledge to be poured out upon the righteous, and the glories that are to be revealed, and the heavenly things in the future state, we shall be continually upon the alert. . . . Let these things sink down in our minds continually, and they will make us joyful, and careful to do unto our neighbors as we would they should do unto us. Lest we should come short of some of these things is the reason I have touched upon the future state of man the two Sabbaths past, to stir up the pure minds of the Saints that we may prepare for the things that are not far ahead, and let all the actions of our lives have a bearing in relation to the future. (In *Journal of Discourses*, 3:105.)

PART III

Conditions in the Spirit World

CHAPTER 5

_____

The Light

A nother capacity of the spirit body is its ability to behold
the brilliant light of the spirit realms which would blind the
human eye. NDErs seem to be introduced into this light in various ways. Many enter and are effortlessly transported at high
speed through what they describe as a tunnel with the light at
the end of it. Some seem to "float" in a calm, restful, and peaceful blackness for a time, or among the stars and planets, and
then are drawn overpoweringly toward a pinpoint of light
which grows until it engulfs them. Others may perceive the
light surrounding them as soon as they leave their mortal body
and immediately find themselves in the realms of the spirit.
(Those who have very limited NDEs may not encounter the
light at all.) Because the manner of entering into the light is so
divergent among experiencers, there may be no doctrinal significance to the tunnel or the blackness unless it somehow represents a transition through the veil into the spirit world. Perhaps the veil is literally some sort of shield or covering of
darkness between the mortal and immortal worlds which
keeps us from the knowledge-giving light of God that would

thwart our purpose here. "Without the veil, our brief mortal walk in a darkening world would lose its meaning—for one would scarcely carry the flashlight of faith at noonday and in the presence of the Light of the World," Elder Neal A. Maxwell has taught (as quoted in *The Life Before,* p. 173).

In any event, virtually all of those who encounter this singular light struggle to characterize its wondrous qualities, and many remark that though it is dazzling beyond the brightness of the sun, it is also easy on the eyes of the spirit. "I floated right straight . . . up into this pure crystal clear light, an illuminating white light," explained one experiencer. "It was beautiful and so bright, so radiant, but it didn't hurt my eyes. It's not any kind of light you can describe on earth." (As quoted in *The Return from Silence,* p. 228.) Dr. George Ritchie offered a similar observation: "[The light] continued to increase in intensity until it seemed to be equal to a million welders' lights. I knew if I had been seeing through my human eyes instead of those of my spiritual body I would have been blinded." (*My Life After Dying,* p. 16.) A woman who had a near-death experience at the age of four recalled, "It was yellow-white and brilliant, but not painful to look at even directly" (*Closer to the Light,* p. 119). "The best way to describe the light," wrote experiencer Dr. Raymond C. Babb, "is that it is exceedingly bright but does not hurt the eyes, or the beholder" (as quoted in *Vital Signs,* August–September, 1992, vol. 1, no. 3, p. 11).

The Prophet Joseph Smith used similar descriptive language in the narration of his vision of the Father and the Son. "I saw a pillar of light exactly over my head, above the brightness of the sun. . . . When the light rested upon me I saw two Personages, whose brightness and glory defy all description." (Joseph Smith—History 1:16–17.) Moses also spoke of beholding the glory of God with his spiritual rather than his natural eyes. "But now mine own eyes have beheld God; but not my natural, but my spiritual eyes, for my natural eyes could not have beheld; for I should have withered and died in his presence; but his glory was upon me; and I beheld his face, for I was transfigured before him" (Moses 1:11).

While the glory of God may be far more radiant than the refulgent light encountered in the spirit world, the same principle seems to apply. Joseph taught that there are also glorified beings in the spirit world. "The spirits of the just are exalted to a greater and more glorious work: hence they are blessed in their departure to the world of spirits. Enveloped in flaming fire, they are not far from us. . . . Flesh and blood cannot go there; but flesh and bones, quickened by the Spirit of God, can." (*Teachings*, p. 326.) Many of those who have experienced "death" reported that they were not only able to see an indescribable light but met a "being of light" as well, whose radiance was far, far greater than that of other spirit beings. Thus it appears that the spirit body is of such composition as to be able to behold the brilliance of the spirit world and of glorified spirit beings, which mortal bodies cannot withstand unless they are quickened.

This is a very simple and common doctrine to members of The Church of Jesus Christ of Latter-day Saints. However, there are other descriptions of this light which can enhance our understanding. Brilliance is only one of its unequalled qualities. In seeking to make this light understandable to those who have never enjoyed it, every NDEr gropes for words that don't seem to exist on earth. While the light is brilliant and dazzling, it is also soft and welcoming. "The whole thing was permeated with the most gorgeous light," explained one who had experienced it, "a living, golden yellow glow, a pale color, not like the harsh color we know on earth" (as quoted in *The Return from Silence*, p. 74). "Soft, silky, very brilliant gold," was another description (*Life at Death*, p. 61). "Living," "glowing," "all-pervading," "warm," "blue-white," "blue-gold," and "containing all colors" are other characterizations used. Furthermore, this light not only enlightens the senses but also penetrates the mind and the heart with unsurpassed joy, peace, love, and knowledge.

The aforementioned Dr. Babb went on to characterize this light as follows: "The closest thing I've been able to find that resembles it is in a candle flame . . . about halfway between the wick and the top of the flame [is] the top of an arc that is a little darker than the main flame. . . . If you look about halfway between [there] and the very top of the flame you will see a light orangish-white portion which does not offend the eye. That segment of the candle flame is the closest resemblance of the "light" that I'm aware of. Now then, if you can imagine going into that light, with the light merging with you, engulfing you, becoming one with you, you will begin to understand what happened. The light can perhaps best be described as personified love. Pure, unadulterated, magnificent, incredibly wonderful love." (In *Vital Signs*, August–September 1992, vol. 1, no. 3, p. 11.)

Another experiencer gave this interesting report. "I didn't actually see a person in this light, and yet it has a special identity, it definitely does. It is a light of perfect understanding and perfect love." (As quoted in *The Return from Silence*, p. 228.) "It wasn't God," explained one woman in an NDE study, "but it wasn't *not* God" (as quoted in *Transformed by the Light*, p. 189.)

The NDEr previously quoted who was the victim of attempted murder provided this captivating description of the light he encountered:

> I became aware of the most powerful, radiant, brilliant white light. It totally absorbed my consciousness. It shone through this glorious scene like the sun rising on the horizon through a veil which had suddenly opened. This magnificent light seemed to be pouring through a brilliant crystal. It seemed to radiate from the very center of the consciousness I was in and to shine out in every direction through the infinite expanses of the universe. I became aware that it was part of all living things and that at the same time all living things were part of it. I knew it was omnipotent, that it represented infinite divine love. It was as if my heart wanted to leap out of my body towards it. It was almost as though I had met my Maker. Even though the light seemed thousands and thousands of times stronger than the brightest sunlight, it did not bother my eyes. My only desire was to have more and more of it and to bathe in it forever. (As quoted in *Heading Toward Omega*, p. 66.)

Dr. Carol Zaleski writes that "the light radiates wisdom and compassion; it floods the mind, expanding awareness until one seems to comprehend everything in a single gaze." She then offers this exhilarating account from a woman who "nearly died" in childbirth and then returned to life. "It was a dynamic light, not like a spotlight. It was an incredible energy—a light you wouldn't believe. I almost floated in it. It was feeding my consciousness feelings of unconditional love, complete safety, and complete, total perfection. . . . It just *powed* into you. My consciousness was going out and getting larger and taking in more; I expanded and more and more came in. It was such rapture, such bliss. And then, and then, a piece of knowledge came in: it was that I was immortal, indestructible. I cannot be hurt, cannot be lost. We don't have anything to worry about. And that the world is perfect; everything that happens is part of a perfect plan. I don't understand this part now, but I still know it's true." (As quoted in *Otherworld Journeys,* pp. 124–25.)

Charles P. Flynn, who wrote a book chronicling the remarkable transformations in near-death experiencers, summarized that "NDErs refer to the Light as total love *and* total knowledge, . . ." He then offered this typical assessment of the light by one who had "died" and experienced this encounter with "the light." "Feeling myself enveloped in that love, feeling myself surrounded with the knowledge that came off of it, I felt like I knew the secrets of everything from the very beginning of time to infinity, and I realized that there was no end. I realized that we are but a very small part of something that's gigantic, but as people we interlock into each other's lives like puzzle pieces, and that we are just an infinitely small part of the universe. But we're also very special." (As quoted in *After the Beyond,* p. 12.)

These magnificent characterizations of the light are probably the most dominant and memorable element found in near-death experiences. Even those who only catch a glimpse of or have a momentary encounter with this effulgence are forever changed by it. It seems to pervade the entire experience and thereafter permeate the soul, mind, and heart of the individual. Not only does it feel and appear wonderful but also it has within it the power to enlighten the understanding and change a life for the better.

Light: Intelligence, Truth, and Love

Once again these descriptions of the light strike a familiar chord in Latter-day Saint theology. Modern revelation contains many references to light, its properties, and its effect upon man and his environment. In one of the most often-quoted of these passages, "The glory of God is intelligence, or, in other words, light and truth" (D&C 93:36), light is equated with glory, intelligence, and truth—and by inference with knowledge, wisdom, and righteousness. Perhaps we tend to think of this statement as telling us that God gained his glory by acquiring intelligence, or light and truth, through his righteousness, which is surely true. However, perhaps this declaration is also informing us that his glory is *literally* made up of light and truth in some material way that we cannot fully comprehend on earth. Indeed, the Lord has taught us that "whosoever is truth is light" (D&C 84:45). This seems to be not just a figure of speech but to signify a real light that somehow encompasses and transmits all truth. "And if your eye be single to my glory, your whole bodies shall be filled with light, and there shall be no darkness in you; and that body which is filled with light comprehendeth all things" (D&C 88:67). And again, "He that keepeth [God's] commandments receiveth truth and light, until he is glorified in truth and knoweth all things" (D&C 93:28).

In the eighteenth century, even before the restoration of the gospel in this dispensation, Emanuel Swedenborg was blessed with spiritual experiences that attested to the illuminating power of this light. His testimony is an interesting companion to the ideas and concepts the Lord would later reveal to the Prophet Joseph Smith. "The existence of a true light that enlightens the mind (quite distinct from the light called natural illumination) has been presented to my perception and sight many times. I have gradually been inwardly raised into that light; and as I was raised, my intellect was enlightened to the point that I could perceive what I had not perceived before—ultimately things totally incomprehensible to thought from natural illumination." (*Heaven and Hell*, p. 108.)

It appears that this property of heavenly light accounts for those near-death occurrences in which the experiencers suddenly feel filled with knowledge and understanding when they merge with or are bathed in the light yet lose all but a portion of such comprehension when they return to mortality. They seem to have been given a glimpse of their eternal possibilities and thereafter apparently act as witnesses that the Lord's promises to his children are quite literal—righteousness entitles us to be filled with light; this light contains truth; light and truth together constitute intelligence; the more intelligence a person possesses, the more glory [light] he or she radiates. Swedenborg also seems to have comprehended to some degree the connection between light and truth—intelligence. "People who are moved and delighted by the truth itself are moved and delighted by heaven's light," he wrote. "People who are engaged in this affection . . . are engaged in heavenly intelligence, and do shine in heaven like the radiance of the firmament." (*Heaven and Hell*, pp. 262–63.)

The love and peace and acceptance embodied in the light are not directly equated with it in scriptural passages. However, John the Apostle declared that "God is light, and in him is no darkness at all" (1 John 1:5) and later also stated, "God is love" (1 John 4:16), and "He that loveth his brother abideth in the light" (1 John 2:10). Perhaps this too is literal, and thus the light emanating from God transfuses its recipients with this perfect love and peace because "perfect love casteth out fear" (1 John 4:18). We also know that everything our Heavenly Father does, he does out of love for his children. Love is his motivation. Such divine love is likewise reflected in the ministry and atoning sacrifice of the Savior. "He doeth not anything save it be for the benefit of the world; for he loveth the world, even that he layeth down his own life that he may draw all men unto him" (2 Nephi 26:24).

In virtually all recorded near-death occurrences the love transmitted by the light is the most extraordinary and unforgettable aspect of the experience. The following expression is typical: "A dazzling brightness infiltrated the mist and, ultimately, cradled me in a way that I cannot describe. The awareness of my physical body left me. . . . My thoughts? I had none. But feelings my cup did, indeed, run over. Bliss . . . rapture . . . joy . . . ecstasy, all of the above, and in such measure that it cannot be compared or understood. As the light continued to surround me and engulf me, my consciousness expanded and admitted more and more of what the light embraces: peace and unconditional love." (As quoted in *The Return from Silence*, p. 122.)

In addition, Swedenborg continually equated God's love and this heavenly light with each other. "Heaven's light is not a natural light, like the world's light, but a spiritual one. It actually comes from the Lord as the sun, this sun being Divine love." (*Heaven and Hell*, p. 105.)

We also have some very moving accounts from Apostles of this dispensation who saw the Savior in dream or vision. The love they had for him and felt from him is the dominant element in these narratives too. Elder Orson F. Whitney was blessed with a vision in which he witnessed the Lord's agony in the Garden of Gethsemane. As he watched his Redeemer suffer, his "whole heart went out to Him," and he was overcome with love. "I loved Him with all my soul, and longed to be with Him as I longed for nothing else." (As quoted in *Exceptional Stories from the Lives of Our Apostles*, p. 267.) Elder George F. Richards saw the Savior in vision. "He spoke no word to me, but my love for him was such that I have not words to explain. I know that no mortal man can love the Lord as I experienced that love for the Savior unless God reveals it to him. . . . If only I can be with my Savior and have that same sense of love that I had in that dream, it will be the goal of my existence, the desire of my life." (As quoted by President Spencer W. Kimball in Conference Report, April 1974, pp. 173–74.) Elder Melvin J. Ballard also enjoyed a dream or manifestation of the Lord's love in which he was embraced and kissed by Him. He recounted: "The feeling that came to my heart then was: Oh! If I could live worthy, though it would require four-score years, so that in the end when I have finished I could go into His presence and receive the feeling that I *then* had in His presence, I would give everything that I am and ever hope to be!" (*Melvin J. Ballard: Crusader for Righteousness*, p. 66.)

Thus, in some inexplicable way, this light is also love; the light being the source of everything good in the world and in the eternities. The Doctrine and Covenants reveals to us that "intelligence, or the light of truth, was not created or made, neither indeed can be" (D&C 93:29), and therefore we understand that this light has always existed. Yet it is embodied, personified, and controlled by God, presumably because of his perfect righteousness.

The Light of Christ

Through the restored gospel we are led to understand that the light encountered by NDErs is yet infinitely more than all love and all knowledge. It is the Light of Christ. It embodies all of the spiritual and temporal power of the universe, which emanates from God. It gives life and light to all things. The Doctrine and Covenants clearly and unmistakably teaches this principle.

He that ascended up on high, as also he descended below all things, in that he comprehended all things, that he might be in all and through all things, the light of truth;

Which truth shineth. This is the light of Christ. As also he is in the sun, and the light of the sun, and the power thereof by which it was made.

As also he is in the moon, and is the light of the moon, and power thereof by which it was made;

As also the light of the stars, and the power thereof by which they were made;

And the earth also, and the power thereof, even the earth upon which you stand.

And the light which shineth, which giveth you light, is through him who enlighteneth your eyes, which is the same light that quickeneth your understandings;

Which light proceedeth forth from the presence of God to fill the immensity of space—

The light which is in all things, which giveth life to all things, which is the law by which all things are governed, even the power of God who sitteth upon his throne, who is in the bosom of eternity, who is in the midst of all things. (D&C 88:6–13.)

Elder Charles W. Penrose further expounded this principle and explained how the "Light of Truth" operates.

There is a spirit, an influence, that proceeds from God, that fills the immensity of space, the Holy Spirit, the Light of Truth. As the sun itself, a planet or heavenly body, is not

present in any other place except that which it actually occupies, so the individual Father occupies a certain locality;
and as the light that proceeds from the sun spreads abroad
upon all the face of the earth and lights up other planets as
well as this earth, penetrating to the circumference of an extended circle in the midst of God's great universe, so the
light of God, the Spirit of God, proceeding forth from the
presence of God, "fills the immensity of space." It is the
light and the life of all things. It is the light and the life of
man. It is the life of the animal creation. It is the life of the
vegetable creation. It is in the earth on which we stand; it is
in the stars that shine in the firmament; it is in the moon
that reflects the light of the sun: it is in the sun, and is the
light of the sun, and the power by which it was made; and
these grosser particles of light that illuminate the heavens
and enable us to behold the works of nature, are from that
same Spirit which enlightens our minds and unfolds the
things of God. As that light comes forth from the sun, so the
light of God comes to us. That natural light is the grosser
substance or particles of the same Spirit. (In *Journal of Discourses*, 26:21–22.)

Some of those who have near-death experiences, usually
Christians, seem cognizant that Jesus is light and is the source
of light. Dr. George Ritchie believed that he met the Christ in
his after-death journey. He described him in terms of light.

I stared in astonishment as the brightness increased,
coming from nowhere, seeming to shine everywhere at
once. All the light bulbs in the [hospital] ward couldn't give
off that much light. All the bulbs in the world couldn't! It
was impossibly bright: it was like a million welders' lamps
all blazing at once. And right in the middle of my amaze-
ment came a prosaic thought probably born of some biol-
ogy lecture back at the university: "I'm glad I don't have
physical eyes at this moment," I thought. "This light would
destroy the retina in a tenth of a second."
No, I corrected myself, not the light.
He.
He would be too bright to look at. For now I saw that it

was not light but a Man who had entered the room, or rather, a Man made out of light, though this seemed no more possible to my mind than the incredible intensity of the brightness that made up His form. (*Return from Tomorrow*, pp. 48–49.)

A man whose death certificate had already been signed also believed he met the Savior during his experience. He stated: "As for Jesus, in that place of light, Jesus was the light itself. This does not mean he was an abstraction, he was as much a 'person' as all the others. He was prophet, priest and king." (As quoted in *Return from Death*, p. 53.) A woman who had undergone open-heart surgery wrote: "The Light was yellow. It was in, around, and through everything. . . . It is God made visible. In, around, and through everything. One who has not experienced it cannot know its feelings. One who has experienced it can never forget it, yearns for its perfection, and longs for the embodiment of It." (As quoted in *Heading Toward Omega*, pp. 55–56.) Margot Grey, a British near-death researcher, author of *Return from Death* and a near-death experiencer herself, summarized the encounter with the light by saying: "From this point on, the light no longer served as a guide nor enveloped the experiencer in a warm and glowing radiance. It now illuminated the 'world within,' as perceived through the gates of death, and was understood to be the source from which all life and love springs." (P. 48.)

And once again, Emanuel Swedenborg also taught that the power and light emanating from the Lord is the source of all life and creation. "But the Divine-True [light] has intrinsic power, such power that through it heaven was created and earth was created, with all the things they contain" (*Heaven and Hell*, p. 113).

Thus we learn, though we may not fully comprehend, that everything, including man himself, is a product of and completely dependent on the Light of Christ. Our Savior is in reality—*literally* and not just figuratively, as we often tend to think—the *truth*, the *light*, and the *life* of this world.

All People Are Given the Light of Christ

Because the light of Christ is in and through all things, and is the source and the support of all life, each person born into this world possesses a portion of that light. The Doctrine and

Covenants is very clear on this point. "And . . . I am the true light that lighteth every man that cometh into the world" (D&C 93:2). Further: "For the word of the Lord is truth, and whatsoever is truth is light, and whatsoever is light is Spirit, even the Spirit of Jesus Christ. And the Spirit giveth light to every man that cometh into the world; and the Spirit enlighteneth every man through the world, that hearkeneth to the voice of the Spirit." (D&C 84:45–46.) Thus we all come to earth with the Light of Christ within us. "It is that light," President Harold B. Lee taught, "which our Father gives to every one of His children, no matter what color they are, or on what continent they live; every one of our Father's children has it at birth. No matter what might have been that spirit's condition before it came here, by the atonement and the blessing of the atonement, the Lord tells us that every spirit is innocent in the beginning. Each spirit comes into mortality lighted with that light." (*Ye Are the Light of the World*, p. 94.)

As we become accountable here in this mortal existence, we decided whether that light will grow and increase within us as we hearken to the Spirit or whether it will darken and dim as we shun the Spirit. President Joseph Fielding Smith explained how the Light of Christ works in our lives and how it may lead us on to the light of the gospel. "The light of truth . . . is the light or Spirit which emanates from God and fills the immensity of space. It is by this power that men are guided to right from wrong, for it quickens their understanding. If they will heed this Spirit it will lead them to the Gospel and then they may receive the greater light, even the Holy Ghost." (*Church History and Modern Revelation*, 1:339.)

It appears that in some way, not yet revealed nor understood, fundamental to the very composition of the individual's immortal spirit is this eternal, life-giving, truth-filled light. The more we accept truth and righteousness, the more light we receive and the more light our spirit body radiates, especially in the spirit world, where it is not hidden within the coarser mortal body. On the other hand, the wicked have darkened spirits because they have rejected truth and light. (This concept will be discussed further in a subsequent chapter.) This intrinsic connection between the Light of Christ and spirit substance is taught in the Doctrine and Covenants. While this intelligence, or light of truth, that makes up our being cannot be created nor destroyed (see D&C 93:29), it seems to be activated or controlled by the Light of Christ. Otherwise it would have no life. Brigham Young confirmed this principle. "God is the source, the fountain of all intelligence, no matter who possesses it, whether man upon the earth, the spirits in the spirit-world, the angels that dwell in the eternities of the Gods, or the most inferior intelligence among the devils in hell. All have derived what intelligence, light, power, and existence they have from God—from the same source from which we have received ours." (In *Journal of Discourses*, 8:205.)

It seems that Swedenborg also understood this concept to some degree in his day. He wrote: "For unless the Divine Human [Spirit of God] did flow into all the elements of heaven—and . . . into all the elements of earth—neither angel nor man would exist" (*Heaven and Hell*, p. 86). This fundamental connection may account for the reports of some NDErs who say that they feel they are one with the light, not separate from it.

Some Reject His Light

Although *all* are born into this world with a portion of the Light of Christ, some repudiate this inward light by their own evil thoughts and actions. Such wickedness diminishes that light. "And he that repents not, from him shall be taken even the light which he has received; for my Spirit shall not always strive with man, saith the Lord of Hosts" (D&C 1:33). Not only do the evil and rebellious darken the light they are born with but they also refuse to be receptive to the further light and understanding which is inherent in the Light of Christ, which permeates our existence and is always available for those who are willing and ready to enjoy it. "And every man whose spirit receiveth not the light is under condemnation" (D&C 93:32). Perhaps at least part of that condemnation is of their own doing; not a direct punishment from God but the natural and logical consequences of wilfully shutting out his light from their lives.

There have been observations by some who have visited or otherwise glimpsed the spirit world that would seem to add

credence to this concept. While it is important that such observations and descriptions not be viewed as doctrinal or definitive, they nonetheless provide some interesting insights that
may enhance our understanding of this doctrine. Dr. George
Ritchie stated that he was led through several different realms
by a being he understood to be Jesus Christ. He was shown disembodied beings on a crowded plain who were "the most frustrated, the angriest, the most completely miserable beings" he
had ever seen. It apparently looked like a great battle wherein
every individual sought to destroy every other individual. He
was sure that this was hell. He has offered the following assessment: "No condemnation came from the Presence at my side,
only a compassion for these unhappy creatures that was breaking His heart. Clearly it was not His will that any one of them
should be in this place. . . . Perhaps this was the explanation for
this hideous plain. Perhaps in the course of eons or of seconds,
each creature here had sought out the company of others as
pride and hate-filled as himself, until together they formed this
society of the damned. Perhaps it was not Jesus who had abandoned them, but they who had fled from the Light that showed
up their darkness." (*Return from Tomorrow*, pp. 63–66.)

Reflecting later on the spirit beings he had seen "tied" to
the earth by their own physical appetites and cravings, which
stayed with them after death, and upon these beings in hell
who did not even notice they were being hovered over and
watched over by other beings "seemingly made of light," Dr.
Ritchie again wondered why these beings could not see the
light of the angels and more especially the brilliant, magnificent, radiant light of Christ. He came to a similar conclusion.
"And suddenly I realized that there was a common denominator to all these scenes so far. It was the failure to see Jesus.
Whether it was a physical appetite, an earthly concern, an ab-
sorption with self—whatever got in the way of His Light created the separation into which we stepped at death." (*Return
from Tomorrow*, pp. 66–67.)

Swedenborg alluded to this same principle. It may be that it
is not so much that the Lord withdraws or withholds his light,
as it is that we block it out or hide from it by our wickedness.
"The reason why the Lord, out of His Divine Essence which is

the Good, Love, and Mercy, cannot deal in the same way with every individual, is that evil things and consequent false things are in the way, not only dulling but even rejecting His Divine inflow. The evil and consequent false elements are like black clouds that come between the sun and a person's eyes and cut off all its sunny and benign light, though all the while the sun keeps trying to break up the obstructing clouds. For the sun is behind them, working away, occasionally getting some shadowy light to the person's eye by various round-about routes." (*Heaven and Hell,* p. 455.)

Perhaps this is a literal manifestation of the idea, repeated many times in ancient and modern scripture, about the light—usually referring to Christ specifically—which "shineth in darkness; and the darkness comprehended it not" (John 1:5; see also D&C 6:21). Swedenborg also maintained that when evil persons are exposed to this light from heaven, they cannot bear it. "When heaven's light flows into true elements from what is good, it grants intelligence and wisdom. But when it flows into false elements from what is evil, it is turned into forms of madness and various kinds of hallucination. In all cases, then, it depends on how it is received." (*Heaven and Hell,* p. 473.) While we do not know for sure that this is literally the case, the scriptures do tell us that there are those who love "darkness rather than light, because their deeds [are] evil. For every one that doeth evil hateth the light, neither cometh to the light, lest his deeds should be reproved." (John 3:19–20; see also D&C 10:21.)

Who Is the "Being of Light"?

The unforgettable "being of light" encountered by some near-death experiencers often seems to be the source or at least an embodiment of this singular light of the spirit world. This entity may appear to NDErs as a human form made of light or as a presence or concentration of light. Whatever their perception, they feel it has an identity; a personality. Dr. Carol Zaleski summarizes: "Some might say that the light was more than a person, because it was a surrounding presence; others might say that it was more than a surrounding presence, because it was also a person. They agree, at any rate, in making an effort to communicate what was for them the supreme manifestation of existence." (*Otherworld Journeys*, p. 126.) Dr. Moody noted that the "description of the being of light is utterly invariable" but then added that "the identification of the being varies from individual to individual and seems to be largely a function of the religious background, training, or beliefs of the person involved." He states, for example, that a Christian might identify it as Christ, that a Jewish man called the light an "angel," and that a non-religious person called it "a being of light." (*Life After Life*, p. 59.)

It is interesting, however, to observe that many Christians are reluctant to identify the "being of light" as Jesus, and in fact some others make a point of noting that the being is *not* Christ but perhaps one of his messengers. A teenager who had "died" from kidney problems described meeting a person who was "about seven feet tall and wore a long white gown with a simple belt tied at the waist. His hair was golden, and although he didn't say anything, I wasn't afraid because I could feel him radiating peace and love." Yet he made this distinction, "No, he wasn't Christ, but I knew that he was sent from Christ. It was probably one of his angels sent to transport me to heaven." (*Closer to the Light*, p. 29.)

It is worthwhile to mention that Dr. Kenneth Ring (along with virtually all other researchers) makes this important distinction: "In my six years of research into NDEs, I cannot recall even one instance in which a being of light was said to have identified *himself* as Jesus" (*Heading Toward Omega*, p. 87). One NDEr actually asked the radiant being, for whom he felt great reverence, "Are you Jesus?" The being replied, "No, you will find Jesus and your loved ones beyond that door." After checking a book in front of him, the being in a dazzling white robe told the man he could enter the other room. While the man did meet his mother and father on the other side of the door, he was brought back to life before seeing Jesus. (As quoted in Maurice Rawlings, *Beyond Death's Door*, p. 80.) Nevertheless, no matter how they label it, all NDErs agree that this being of light is holy and loves them with a perfect and unconditional love that penetrates to their very souls.

Angel? Spirit of a Just Man Made Perfect?

There is no authoritative statement in LDS theology concerning a "being of light" who greets and welcomes those entering the spirit world and helps them pass judgment on their earthly accomplishments. (This latter aspect of the being of light will be discussed in a later chapter.) On the other hand, there are numerous scriptural passages and prophetic statements that give evidence of angelic messengers, escorts, and ministering agents who do the work of God through the power and authority of his priesthood. President George Q. Cannon alluded to those assigned to help mortals make the transition into immortality. "How delightful it is to contemplate the departure of those who have been faithful, as far as their knowledge permitted, to the truth which God has revealed! There is no sting nor gloom nor inconsolable sorrow about the departure of such persons. Holy angels are around their bedside to administer unto them. The Spirit of God rests down upon them, and His messengers are near them to introduce them to those who are on the other side of the veil." (*Gospel Truth*, p. 61.)

Near-death accounts of people of other faiths help us to understand that those decent and good-hearted people who have not received the gospel ordinances also experience a joyous welcome on the other side of the veil. It is a witness that the Lord is merciful and loving to all of his children. Once again, the principle of increased righteousness may apply—the more faithful the individual, the more glorious his or her reception in the spirit world.

From descriptions recorded in NDE accounts, both LDS and others, we learn that the being of light seems to be much more magnificent than the "guardian angels," friends and family, or other "normal" spirit beings encountered in the next life. This being possesses an infinitely greater portion of the light than does other spirits. He seems to function in some sort of official capacity. He is empowered to aid the NDEr in reviewing and judging his or her earth life, to answer "cosmic" questions about the universe and the meaning of life, and to assist the person in making a decision about returning to earth. Most notably, the being radiates the kind of complete love and compassion which originates only with God. In short, he must be either the Lord or some being commissioned to act just as the Lord would have him act in welcoming God's children home.

As set forth in the earlier section pertaining to the appearance of spirit beings (chapter 3), it is possible to become so united with Christ and so like him as even to appear as he does. The prophet Mormon exhorted us to seek and develop the gift of charity above all else and taught that disciples of Christ would one day become like Him—love as the Savior loves and be pure as he is pure: "Wherefore, my beloved brethren, pray unto the Father with all the energy of heart, that ye may be filled with this love, which he hath bestowed upon all who are true followers of his Son, Jesus Christ; that ye may become the sons of God; that when he shall appear we shall be like him, for we shall see him as he is; that we may have this hope; that we may be purified even as he is pure" (Moroni 7:46–48).

Given this understanding, it is reasonable to suppose that the "being of light" could well be a righteous spirit who has achieved a high spiritual level and serves in that official capacity. The Prophet Joseph Smith confirmed that "spirits [of the just] can only be revealed in flaming fire and glory." This characterization seems to correspond with some descriptions of the being of light as a presence or entity of light. Others say that the light is a man or has a body. Recall that the Prophet also taught that "angels have advanced further [than spirits of the just], their light and glory being tabernacled; and hence they appear in bodily shape." (*Teachings*, p. 325.) Thus there must be angels or spirits of just men made perfect who would have the compassion, knowledge, power, and glory to act in behalf of Jesus Christ as the "being of light," if so authorized.

It could be that Emanuel Swedenborg was referring, at least in some sense, to this phenomenon—that those who are filled with the Spirit of Christ take on his likeness—when he remarked: "Love for the Lord is what rules in heaven, because there the Lord is loved more than everything. As a result, the Lord is there the all in all, flows into each and all things, arranges them, *clothes them with His own likeness*, and so works things out that it is heaven where He is." (*Heaven and Hell*, p. 60, italics added.) Moreover, it has previously been mentioned that Dr. George Ritchie recorded his seeing beings who seemed to emit light almost as bright as that of the being he took to be Christ himself. He conjectured, "Could these radiant beings, I wondered, amazed, be those who had indeed kept Jesus the focus of their lives? Was I seeing at last ones who had looked for Him in everything? Looked so well and so closely that they had been changed into His very likeness?" (*Return from Tomorrow*, pp. 72–73.) Perhaps the above are additional witnesses to the literal nature of scriptural passages which testify that the righteous will one day be so patterned after our Savior that they will "be like him."

Divine Investiture of Authority

In fact, such beings may have become so like Jesus that some Christian (including LDS) NDErs believe the being of light actually is Christ when in reality that may not be so. This is understandable when we comprehend that these servants would be fully authorized to represent him—his presence, his power, his love—as if God himself were there. Indeed, there is another principle that adds credence to the possibility that in the near-death experience the being of light is an angel or other messenger authorized to act and speak as if he were Jesus himself. That principle is the tenet of our faith referred to as "divine investiture of authority."

This term is applied primarily to the complete delegation of authority from God the Father to his Son Jesus Christ to speak and act exactly as if he were the Father; but it also refers to transmitting to one of his angels the authority to speak as God. One such authorized minister appeared to John the Beloved, speaking as if he were the Lord. John may have believed it was the Lord himself, since he fell down on his knees to worship the messenger. The angel stopped him, saying, "See thou do it not: for I am thy fellowservant, and of thy brethren the prophets." The angel then resumed delivering his message just as if he were the Lord. (See Revelation 22:7–16). Also, in our dispensation the Lord has taught regarding prophecy the eternal truth that "whether by mine own voice or by the voice of my servants [earthly prophets or heavenly angels], it is the same" (D&C 1:38). It therefore seems that this investiture of authority is more perfect and literal than we can easily comprehend.

It is interesting and enlightening to note that in one of his writings Swedenborg seemed to be referring to the principle of divine investiture. While we do not know if his perception of this process was completely correct, his description leads us to understand that he was at least trying to convey the totality of this investiture. "I have also been shown what it is like for spirits to be filled with what is Divine by the Lord by means of a look. A spirit filled by the Lord with what is Divine has no awareness that he is not the Lord, or that it is not the Divine which is speaking. This lasts until he has finished speaking. Afterwards he realizes that he is a spirit, and that he has not spoken on his own, but rather from the Lord. Since this was the state of the spirits who spoke with the prophets, the prophets say that Jehovah spoke. Even the spirits themselves called themselves 'Jehovah,' as can be illustrated not only by prophetic passages, but even by historical passages of the Word." (*Heaven and Hell*, p. 183.)

Thus it may be that the NDEr experience with the being of light is in every way the same as if Christ were there himself to minister to these spirits, and naturally they therefore believe they have met the Christ. We have a few near-death reports, however, wherein the experiencers felt certain that the being of light they encountered was, in fact, Jesus Christ. They claim they knew with the kind of inner knowledge with which all doubt is removed.

Whether these feelings could have been evoked by a holy presence who in all essential respects was like the Lord himself but in fact was not the Lord is something we may not be able to determine on this side of the veil. Understanding the witness of the Spirit through their own mortal experiences, Latter-day Saints can relate to the kind of knowing these NDErs describe, and hence we would not dismiss the claims out of hand. One might wonder, however, whether the Lord's presumably cosmic concerns would allow him the leisure to greet new entrants to the spirit world, a function that could easily and apparently properly be delegated to many righteous servants.

In truth, of course, it does not really matter who functions as the being of light. "It is the same." No NDEr has ever felt slighted. All describe their experience with this personage in the same ineffable terms. All the superlatives on earth do not convey the love, peace, acceptance, and joy which are felt in the presence of this being and of which, regardless of the messenger, God is always the source.

_____

CHAPTER 6

Divine Love

Numerous scriptural passages speak of God and heaven in terms of light and love. Those who have had near-death experiences and glimpsed beyond the veil also testify of the profound love and light that prevail there. They often use the terms *love* and *light* almost interchangeably, for it appears there cannot be one without the other. Even though the light and love of the next realm are inextricably interwoven, the love in that place is so profound that it bears further examination.

Love Reigns Supreme

Love is the supreme element of the light and therefore the supreme element of heaven. It is the quality to be desired and developed above all others. The ability to give and receive love is the dominant and determining factor of true happiness in the next life as well as in this life. We are blessed with several passages of scripture that endeavor to teach us this principle here on earth. The prophet Nephi recorded the meaning of the tree of life in Lehi's dream, it being the ultimate goal of all of God's children. "And the angel said unto me: Behold the Lamb of God, yea, even the Son of the Eternal Father! Knowest thou the meaning of the tree which thy father saw? And I answered him, saying: Yea, it is the love of God, which sheddeth itself abroad in the hearts of the children of men; wherefore, it is the most desirable above all things. And he spake unto me, saying: Yea, and the most joyous to the soul." (1 Nephi 11:21–23.)

The Book of Mormon prophet Mormon and the New Testament Apostle Paul both preached of the preeminence of charity or love:

> Though I speak with the tongues of men and of angels, and have not charity, I am become as sounding brass, or a tinkling cymbal.
>
> And though I have the gift of prophecy, and understand all mysteries, and all knowledge; and though I have all faith, so that I could remove mountains, and have not charity, I am nothing.
>
> And though I bestow all my goods to feed the poor, and though I give my body to be burned, and have not charity, it profiteth me nothing. (1 Corinthians 13:1–3.)

> Wherefore, my beloved brethren, if ye have not charity, ye are nothing, for charity never faileth. Wherefore, cleave unto charity, which is the greatest of all, for all things must fail—
>
> But charity is the pure love of Christ, and it endureth forever; and whoso is found possessed of it at the last day, it shall be well with him. (Moroni 7:46–47.)

Jesus himself taught that the two most important commandments involve love, and that all other commandments are based on and founded in these two.

> Jesus said unto him, Thou shalt love the Lord thy God with all thy heart, and with all thy soul, and with all thy mind.
>
> This is the first and great commandment.
>
> And the second is like unto it, Thou shalt love thy neighbour as thyself.

On these two commandments hang all the law and the prophets. (Matthew 22:37–40.)

The underlying message of these passages is that "a love of God and of all men" (see 2 Nephi 31:20) must be the source of all of our works of righteousness or those efforts are of little avail. On the other hand, if we find ourselves falling short in our strivings for perfection, as we are always wont to do in this life, if we have a love of the Lord and of others rooted deep in our hearts some of our inadequacies will be overlooked. "And above all things," wrote Peter, "have fervent charity among yourselves: for charity shall cover the multitude of sins" (1 Peter 4:8). For these reasons, love will separate the righteous from the wicked, for we will seek after, serve, and eventually obtain that which we love.

Those who have had positive near-death experiences invariably testify to the ascendancy of love in the realm of righteous spirits. Here are some of their comments:

Love is the major impression I still retain. In heaven there is light, peace, music, beauty and joyful activity, but above all there is love and within this love I felt more truly alive than I have ever done before. (*Return from Death*, p. 53.)

I also felt and saw of course that everyone was in a state of absolute compassion to everything else. . . . It seemed, too, that love was the major axiom that everyone automatically followed. . . . There was nothing *but* love . . . it just seemed like the real thing, just to feel this sense of total love in every direction. (*Heading Toward Omega*, p. 40.)

There was the warmest, most wonderful love. Love all around me . . . I felt light-good-happy-joy-at ease. Forever— eternal love. Time meant nothing. Just being. Love. Pure love. Love. (*Heading Toward Omega*, p. 55.)

These are only a small sampling of the remarkable descriptions of the all-pervading love experienced in the spirit world.

Repeatedly in his writings, Emanuel Swedenborg also

made the point that love is the central theme of "heaven." His observations are insightful.

> The reason the formative Divine in heaven is love is that love is a spiritual bond. It joins angels to the Lord, and joins them to each other. It actually joins them in a way that makes them a "one" in the Lord's sight.
>
> Further, Love is the very Being of everyone's life. It is therefore the source of life for angel and man alike. Anybody can know that man's central vitality comes from love if he weighs the facts that love's presence warms him, love's absence chills him, and love's total removal means his death. . . .
>
> All the evidence in heaven bears witness to the fact that the Divine which emanates from the Lord, influences angels, and makes heaven, is love. All the people who are there are actual models of love and charity. They look bewilderingly beautiful; love radiates from their faces, their speech, and every detail of their lives. (*Heaven and Hell*, pp. 35–37.)

Perfect Love

The predominance of this love is not the only indelible impression reported by those who have been to that spiritual existence. Without exception, the perfect nature of that love is denoted, either explicitly or implicitly. The NDEr feels totally loved and accepted. This, however, does not imply that a person's sins are completely overlooked and will make no difference in the next life; and many of the NDErs who basked in this unparalleled love were also given to understand this principle. This dilemma will be discussed in a later chapter dealing with the life review, but the important thing to note here is that perfect love means that love which the Father possesses and feels toward all of his children, because they are literally his offspring. It is the perfect love that Jesus has for all mankind, as demonstrated by his supreme act of love—his atoning sacrifice, which redeems all from death and makes eternal life possible for all who will love and follow him. It is given freely to all of God's creations because they are a part of him and he "is love" (see 1 John 4:7–12). This love is as natural and integral to him as his very existence. To be in his presence is to experience this love—it is to be totally enveloped by his divine love and light. Again, we offer a few reports which attempt to capture the essence of this consummate love.

> What the light communicates to you is a feeling of true, pure love. You experience this for the first time ever. You can't compare it to the love of your wife, or the love of your children. . . . Even if all those things were combined, you cannot compare it to the feeling you get from this light. (*Return from Death*, p. 54.)

> The vast majority of near-death survivors have positive, uplifting experiences. Theirs is both the opportunity and the thrill of being totally engulfed by overwhelming love, a kind of love beyond precedent, beyond description. There is nothing else quite like it—a feeling, a knowing of oneness and worth, of total freedom and total acceptance. No demands. No stipulations. No conditions. No criteria. Just love—boundless, infinite, all-encompassing love—a love so forgiving, so total, so immense, nothing can contain it. Love encountered on "The Other Side" makes any kind of earthly love dim by comparison.
>   It is God's love. You just know. (*Coming Back to Life*, p. 65.)

> Above all, with that same mysterious inner certainty, I knew that this Man loved me. Far more even than power, what emanated from this Presence was unconditional love. An astonishing love. A love beyond my wildest imagining. This love knew every unlovable thing about me—the quarrels with my stepmother, my explosive temper, the sex thoughts I could never control, every mean, selfish thought and action since the day I was born—and accepted and loved me just the same. (*Return from Tomorrow*, p. 49.)

Some Reject God's Love

While God's love is available without cost to all of his children, his approbation, blessings, and ultimate rewards come at a price—the reciprocal love and its resultant obedience *from* his children. Thus it may be that while his love for all of his children never fails them—"charity *never* faileth"—they may fail him. Perhaps they bring their greatest misery upon themselves by rejecting this infinite, effulgent, exquisite, and supremely gratifying love. Scriptures inform us that God's presence is painful in the extreme to the wicked. They cannot bear his presence, his light and love, which exposes their darkness and malice. "In that day a man shall cast his idols of silver, and his idols of gold [symbolic of his love for himself and the things of the world], which they made each one for himself to worship, to the moles and to the bats; to go into the clefts of the rocks, and into the tops of the ragged rocks, for the fear of the Lord, and for the glory [intelligence—light, truth, and love] of his majesty, when he ariseth to shake terribly the earth" (Isaiah 2:20–21; see also Revelation 6:15).

The Book of Mormon teaches that the Lord desires that all people avail themselves of his redeeming love: "He doeth not anything save it be for the benefit of the world; for he loveth the world, even that he layeth down his own life that he may draw all men unto him. Wherefore, he commandeth none that they shall not partake of his salvation." (2 Nephi 26:24.) Dr. George Ritchie certainly had the understanding that such was the case in the hellish realm he was shown. He felt that angels were attempting to minister to the inhabitants there. He perceived that Jesus loved the wicked and depraved beings there with all his heart, but they would not receive him or his messengers. "No condemnation came from the Presence at my side, only a compassion for these unhappy creatures that was breaking His heart. Clearly it was not His will that any one of them should be in this place." (*Return from Tomorrow*, p. 65.)

From what he said were experiences with next-life conditions over a thirteen-year period, Emanuel Swedenborg also insisted that God's love is unconditionally extended to all and he desires to save everyone. Regrettably (especially to the Lord), some reject this love and salvation, just as they reject the light and enlightenment offered to them by Christ and his gospel. "This enables us to see that the Lord, through angels and through an inflow from heaven, leads every spirit toward Himself," asserted the eighteenth-century philosopher and theologian. "But spirits who are involved in what is evil resist strenuously and virtually tear themselves away from the Lord, with their evil—with hell, therefore—dragging them off like a rope. . . . The reason why the Lord, out of His Divine Essence which is the Good, Love, and Mercy, cannot deal in the same way with every individual, is that evil things and consequent false things are in the way, not only dulling but even rejecting His Divine inflow." (*Heaven and Hell*, pp. 454–55.)

Swedenborg also offered a fascinating observation which, while we have no specific doctrinal substantiation, seems possible and not at variance with the principles of the restored gospel. It is an interesting concept to contemplate.

> Hellish fire or love comes from the same source as heavenly fire or love—from heaven's sun, or the Lord. However, it is made hellish by the people who receive it. For all the inflow from the spiritual world varies depending on how it is received or depending on the forms into which it flows. There is no difference between this and the situation with the warmth and light that come from the world's sun. When warmth flows in from it into trees and flowering plants it brings about an enlivening and draws forth pleasing and sweet odors. But when the same warmth flows into fecal matter and dead flesh it brings about decay and draws forth rank and putrid stenches. In the same way, light from one and the same sun brings out beautiful and pleasing colors in one subject and ugly and unpleasant colors in another.
>
> This situation is similar with the warmth and light that come from heaven's sun, which is love. When the warmth or love flows into good things—as it does with good people and spirits and with angels—it makes their good qualities bear fruit. But with evil people it has an opposite effect. In fact, the evil qualities either stifle or corrupt it. (*Heaven and Hell*, p. 473.)

Are Spirit World Realms Divided According to Principle of Love?

Indeed, Swedenborg and George Ritchie seemed impressed with the idea that the spirit world is organized, at least to some degree, according to the kind and amount of love its inhabitants possess. "All the people who live in the celestial [highest] kingdom are involved in a love for the Lord," maintained the Swedish philosopher. He also believed that hell was similarly divided into realms. "And all the people in the opposite [lowest] kingdom in the hells are involved in self-love. All the people who are in the spiritual [next to the highest] kingdom are involved in a love toward the neighbor, while all the people in the opposite [next to the lowest] kingdom in the hells are involved in a love of the world." (*Heaven and Hell*, p. 500.)

In describing the realms he witnessed, Dr. George Ritchie seemed to concur with this idea. He commented on those vile, self-absorbed creatures whom the Savior loved, yet who would have nothing to do with him. "This was breaking the heart of the Son of God standing beside me. Even here were angels trying to get them to change their thoughts. Since they could not admit there were beings greater than themselves, they could not see or hear them. There was no fire and brimstone here; no boxed-in canyons, but something a thousand times worse from my point of view. Here was a place totally devoid of love. This was HELL." (*My Life After Dying*, p. 25.)

Dr. Ritchie also felt that he beheld a domain of beings who were still tied to the earth by the physical appetites and other desires for the things of the world which they had developed during earth life. More than forty years after his experience he summarized what he thought he was to learn from seeing these pitiful individuals: "We have to be careful of what we grow to love so much that we let it control us, for it can lead us into becoming bound on this Earth to the things that we made into false gods" (*My Life After Dying*, p. 22).

Furthermore, George Ritchie comprehended another realm where good and honorable people loved their fellowmen and sought the knowledge of the eternities in order to further the welfare of their fellow beings. They experienced their consummate joy in learning and thereby helping others. "Is this . . . heaven, Lord Jesus?" queried the young Ritchie. "The calm, the brightness, they were surely heaven-like! So was the absence of self, of clamoring ego. 'When these people were on earth did they grow beyond selfish desires?' *They grew, and they have kept on growing.* The answer shone like sunlight in that intent and eager atmosphere. But if growth could continue, then this was not all. Then . . . there must be something even these serene beings lacked. And suddenly I wondered if it was the same thing missing in the 'lower realm.' Were these selfless, seeking creatures also failing in some degree to see Jesus? Or perhaps, to see Him for Himself? Bits and hints of Him they surely had; obviously it was the truth they were so single-mindedly pursuing. But what if even a thirst for truth could distract from the Truth Himself, standing here in their midst while they searched for Him in books and test tubes." (*Return from Tomorrow*, p. 71.)

Finally, Ritchie was given a glimpse of a distant world he could not yet enter, a kingdom where the love of God and of all men reigned supreme. "Seeing these beings and feeling the joy, peace and happiness which swelled up from them made me feel that here was the place of all places, the top realm of all realms. The beings who inhabited it were full of love. This, I was and am convinced, is heaven. As marvelous as I thought the previous realm was, after glimpsing this new realm we were seeing, I began to understand for the first time what Paul was saying in the 13th Chapter of First Corinthians when he wrote: 'If I have the gift of prophecy and can fathom all mysteries and all knowledge, and if I have a faith that can remove mountains, but have not love, I am nothing.' I do not infer that the wonderful souls of the fourth realm did not have love because they did but not to the degree that the souls of this realm had reached." (*My Life After Dying*, p. 29.)

While Latter-day Saint scriptures do not always specifically use the criterion of love in delineating the requirements for different post-resurrection kingdoms (see D&C 76), there are those that clearly do so (e.g., see Matthew 25:31–46; Ether 12:34; Moroni 7:47–48; 10:21), and in any case the requirements the scriptures set forth surely imply such love. This correlates well with these NDE testimonies of spirit world realms when defined in terms of love. Interestingly, Orson Pratt did once define hell in such terms.

> If we should inquire what constitutes the misery of the fallen angels, the answer would be, they are destitute of love; they have ceased to love God; they have ceased to

have pure love one towards another; they have ceased to love that which is good. Hatred, malice, revenge, and every evil passion have usurped the place of love; and unhappiness, wretchedness, and misery are the results. Where there is no love, there will be no desire to promote the welfare of others. Instead of desiring that others may be happy, each desires to make all others miserable like himself; each seeks to gratify that hellish disposition against the Almighty which arises from his extreme hatred of that which is good. For the want of love the torment of each is complete. All the wicked who are entirely overcome by these malicious spirits will have the heavenly principle of love wholly eradicated from their minds, and they will become angels to these infernal fiends, being captivated by them, and compelled to act as they act. They cannot extricate themselves from their power, nor ward off the fiery darts of their malicious tormentors. Such will be the condition of all beings who entirely withdraw themselves from the love of God. (*The Seer*, vol. 1, no. 10, October 1853, pp. 156–57.)

Moreover, these NDE accounts add credence to the tenets Latter-day Saints have held that there are more divisions in the post-mortal life than the standard heaven and hell subscribed to by most of Christendom. Perhaps to those outside the understanding of the gospel, these divisions are best understood in terms of love. Conversely, such designations add understanding to our more specific and demanding doctrines. They especially enlighten us against the tendency to observe the outward commandments and ordinances of the restored gospel while lacking the essential inward motive and devotion. They confirm to us the verity of the Lord's identification of the two commandments about love as being, literally, the *greatest* commandments.

Peace, Joy, Rest

Also implicit in this divine love of which we have written are the blessings of peace, joy, and rest that spring from it. Swedenborg offered this insightful assertion. "The reason why the

Lord's Divine in heaven is love is that love is the vessel of everything heavenly—that is, of peace, intelligence, wisdom, and happiness. For love accepts any and all things suitable to it; it wants them, seeks them out, and soaks them in gladly, so to speak, from a desire constantly to be enriched and fulfilled with them. . . . We can see, then, that love emanating from the Lord is the vessel of heaven and of everything there." (*Heaven and Hell*, pp. 38–39.)

In other words, Swedenborg logically believed that divine love desires all goodness and therefore the complete happiness of its recipients. So good are these paradisiacal conditions in the spirit world that most NDErs dread coming back to earth life. This is the long-awaited respite for which the righteous strive. "And then shall it come to pass, that the spirits of those who are righteous are received into a state of happiness, which is called paradise, a state of rest, a state of peace, where they shall rest from all their troubles and from all care and sorrow" (Alma 40:12).

President Brigham Young spoke often of the joyous state of the "next apartment." "Here, we are continually troubled with ills and ailments of various kinds," taught that great prophet, "and our ears are saluted with the expressions, 'My head aches,' 'My shoulders ache,' 'My back aches,' 'I am hungry, dry, or tired;' but in the spirit world we are free from all this and enjoy life, glory, and intelligence; and we have the Father to speak to us, Jesus to speak to us, and angels to speak to us, and we shall enjoy the society of the just and the pure who are in the spirit world until the resurrection" (in *Journal of Discourses*, 14:231). On another occasion he remarked:

> If we could see things as they are, and as we shall see and understand them, this dark shadow and valley [of death] is so trifling that we shall turn round and look upon it and think, when we have crossed it, why this is the greatest advantage of my whole existence, for I have passed from a state of sorrow, grief, mourning, woe, misery, pain, anguish and disappointment into a state of existence, where I can enjoy life to the fullest extent as far as that can be done without a body. My spirit is set free, I thirst no more, I want to

sleep no more, I hunger no more, I tire no more, I run, I walk, I labor, I go, I come, I do this, I do that, whatever is required of me, nothing like pain or weariness, I am full of life, full of vigor, and I enjoy the presence of my heavenly Father, by the power of his Spirit. (In *Journal of Discourses*, 17:142.)

Those who have near-death experiences also bear testimony to this wonderful reality in the next life. Such depictions can be found in almost every recorded and every unrecorded report. "There was absolutely no pain whatsoever, just a great feeling of peace and joy," stated one man. "I saw no other being of any kind but felt a wonderful loving presence." (As quoted in *Revitalized Signs*, vol. 8, no. 4, November 1989, p. 6.) A woman reported: "I felt this great peace and the most exquisite joy, and felt I was floating up through the clouds and the sky. I had a new body, and it felt so good, and I was wearing something white." (As quoted in *Vital Signs*, vol. 10, no. 2, June 1991, p. 2.) Another woman described "the whole thing" as being "Just very *good*, very happy, very warm, very peaceful, very comforted, very—I've never known that feeling in my whole life" (as quoted in *Life at Death*, p. 63). One individual apparently struggled to find words that could approximate this remarkable feeling: "If you took the one thousand best things that ever happened to you in your life and multiplied by a million, maybe you could get close to this feeling" (as quoted in *Heading Toward Omega*, p. 62).

A woman who had an experience as a child portrayed the feelings in quainter, more familiar terms. "Everything was calm and peaceful and quiet. The feeling reminded me of when I was small, before my youngest sister and brother were born, and Daddy would hold me and my little sister and read bedtime stories to us; no matter what is happening anywhere else, right now I am safe and comfortable and loved. It's a sort of snuggly relaxed feeling, and very difficult to put into words. I liked the feeling. I liked being there. I wanted to stay." (As quoted in *Revitalized Signs*, vol. 9, no. 1, February 1990, p. 2.)

Many NDErs are surprised to find that they do feel so happy and peaceful, because they had expected death to be so painful and frightening. "I knew I was going to die at this point

and was willing to accept my life for what it was," philoso-
phized one person, adding, "Oddly enough it was the most
peaceful feeling I have ever had" (*Transformed by the Light*, p.
54). Some express feelings of sorrow at not being able to assure
their loved ones that they are "alive" and happy. "I felt bad because my wife was crying and she seemed so helpless and all,
you know. But it was nice. It didn't hurt." (As quoted in *Recollections of Death*, p. 19.) Others feel reassured about leaving children and other loved ones behind. They are amazed to discover
that the parting is not so terrible as they had thought. "I saw
the faces of my mother, husband, and baby boy who were all
living. They would be sad at my death but I didn't feel despon-
dent. In fact, it didn't seem to make much difference to me at
all! I wasn't unhappy and I couldn't understand why." (As
quoted in Maurice Rawlings, *Beyond Death's Door*, pp. 62–63.)

From these and other witnesses we are led to understand
that the spirit world into which we enter at death is the end of
all tribulation and sorrow for those who have lived lives of
goodness and love. It is also the source of every delight a righteous person could ever desire. Once again, Swedenborg offered a unique and thought-provoking viewpoint on this same
joy and happiness. "Heaven is intrinsically of such nature that
it is full of delights, even to the point that, seen in its own right,
it is nothing but blessed and delightful. This is because the
Divine-Good, emanating from the Lord's Divine Love, constitutes heaven in general and in detail for every individual there,
Divine Love being a will that everyone be saved and that
everyone be most profoundly and fully happy." (*Heaven and
Hell*, p. 307.)

He also submitted this fascinating and descriptive assertion: "I have perceived also that joy and delight seem to come
from the heart, spreading very gently through all the deepest
fibers and from there into gathered fibers, with such a profound feeling of pleasure that the fibers are virtually nothing
but joy and delight, with every derived perceptive and sensitive element alive with happiness. Next to these joys, the joys of
physical pleasures are like coarse and acrid dust relative to a
pure and very soft aura." (*Heaven and Hell*, p. 320.)

Phyllis Atwater, an NDEr and author, attested from her research that the ecstasy of the spirit world is beyond our comprehension, no matter what we already understand about it. "Even for those who profess a belief in life after death before their experience, it is still a jolt, for the enormity and diversity of what comes next stretches the imagination beyond what seems possible. You encounter more when you die. No matter what your previous beliefs, you encounter more." She went on to suggest: "And there is more beyond that. As near as I can tell there is no end to the 'mores' and the 'beyonds.' Death is a shift in consciousness, a doorway we pass through. What we encounter, no matter what it is, constitutes the mere tip of a bottomless iceberg, a wink in infinity!" (*Coming Back to Life*, pp. 13–14.)

Humor

An interesting and delightful side note to the joy and enjoyment of the next realm is the NDErs' frequent mention of the persistence of humor. Good humor brings us pleasure and happiness, even here on earth. It is comforting to know that we will still be able to let go and laugh in the life after death. Immortal life will not be all solemnity and seriousness. That delightful element of joy—humor—is also a part of the light and love of God which pervade that heavenly existence. Here are a few witnesses to that fact:

Dr. George Ritchie related: "If I'd suspected before that there was mirth in the Presence beside me, now I was sure of it: the brightness seemed to vibrate and shimmer with a kind of holy laughter—not at me and my silliness, not a mocking laughter, but a mirth that seemed to say that in spite of all error and tragedy, joy was more lasting still" (*Return from Tomorrow*, p. 54). One NDEr described the "being of light" as "a fun person to be with! And it had a sense of humor, too—definitely!" (*Life After Life*, p. 64.) Another described the two men who met him to show him the way into the spirit world. "These two men had a terrific sense of humor. They made jokes about different things as we were walking and made it very light." (*Recollections of Death*, p. 49.)

Several of those who have had near-death experiences

comment on the laughter and good humor they encountered as a reaction to their own spunky determination either to stay in that realm or to return to an unfinished life on earth, as the case may be. One nine-year-old girl was just climbing a lovely white fence in the spirit world to get to some beautiful horses when she was told it was not her time and she must go back. She said: "I pitched a royal fit. I grabbed onto the rail of the fence and wrapped my arms and legs around it and I wouldn't let go. The voice just laughed. 'Look, you can have it later, but this is not the time. And throwing a tantrum is not going to do you any good.'" (*Transformed by the Light*, p. 53.)

It is not hard to imagine that laughter and humor would persist in the afterlife. We can attest to its uplifting power here on earth. Life is so much richer when we can laugh. Almost every prophet in this dispensation has delighted and endeared the Latter-day Saints to himself through his quick refreshing wit and edifying sense of humor. Knowing that these men are representatives and role models of the Savior, we can pretty well rest assured that they and we will be rejoicing in the irreplaceable quality of humor in the world beyond. Such good-natured, loving, edifying heavenly humor is another interesting evidence of the divine love that prevails on the "other side of the veil"—where all is intended to uplift, encourage, and strengthen man's love for God and for his fellowmen.

CHAPTER 7

Descriptions of the Spirit World

As "unearthly" as the conditions of the spirit world may seem to us, President Brigham Young and others of the latter-day prophets and Apostles have instructed us that the spirit world is here on this earth. "Where is the spirit world? It is right here. Do the good and evil spirits go together? Yes, they do. . . . Do they go to the sun? No. Do they go beyond the boundaries of this organized earth? No, they do not. They are brought forth upon this earth, for the express purpose of inhabiting it to all eternity. Where else are you going? No where else, only as you may be permitted." (Brigham Young, in *Journal of Discourses*, 3:369.)

Elder Parley P. Pratt wrote that the spirit world "is here on the very planet where we were born, or, in other words, the earth and other planets of a like sphere have their inward or spiritual spheres as well as their outward, or temporal. The one is peopled by temporal tabernacles and the other by spirits. A veil is drawn between the one sphere and the other whereby all the objects in the spiritual sphere are rendered invisible to those in the temporal." (*Key to the Science of Theology*, p. 80.)

Though one woman was informed by her deceased relatives that she was in the "spirit world," like most of those who have experiences in that other realm she did not seem to comprehend that it was still on earth or, at least, she did not report any comprehension of it (see *Return from Death*, p. 80). Dr. George Ritchie, however, seems to be one of the very few experiencers who actually understood that the realms he was being shown were still connected in some manner to this earthly sphere. He reported this observation several times. "As fast as thought we travelled from city to city, seemingly on the familiar earth, even the part of the earth—the United States and possibly Canada—that I'd always known, except for the thousands of non-physical beings that I now observed also inhabiting this 'normal' space" (*Return from Tomorrow*, p. 58). Ritchie saw not only spirits but also cities in this spirit realm. He recorded: "What made me feel as though my vision was out of focus was seeing another city superimposed on our physical city. I came to realize this belonged to these astral beings. In the deepest sense most of the beings of one realm weren't aware of the existence of the other." (*My Life After Dying*, p. 23.)

Even the noble realm of learning and study appeared to him to be in the earthly sphere. "Up until this point I had had the impression that we were traveling—though in what manner I could not imagine—upon the earth itself. Even what I had come to think of as a 'higher plane' of deep thoughts and learning, was obviously not far distant from the 'physical plane' where bodiless beings were still bound to a solid world." The only exception to this perception of earthbound realms was the city of glorious, Christ-like beings which he was not allowed to reach. (Could these have been resurrected and exalted beings?) "Now however, we seemed to have left the earth behind. I could no longer see it." (*Return from Tomorrow*, p. 72.) Perhaps this is a reflection of the Prophet Joseph's pronouncement that "the angels do not reside on a planet like this earth; but they reside in the presence of God" (D&C 130:6–7).

The Rev. Norman Vincent Peale told of an experience he had at the death of his mother that taught him the nearness of the spirit world. Upon receiving word that his mother had died, he went into the church sanctuary to be alone to think, pray, and grieve the loss of his dear mother. His mother had often told him that whenever he went to the pulpit she would be there with him and he hoped that she would be now. He records:

> I sat for quite a while. Then, leaving the pulpit, I went into my office, stood in front of my desk, and put my hand on a Bible my mother had given me when I became minister of the Marble Collegiate Church, some 17 years earlier. At that moment, I felt two strong hands, cupped together, as light as a feather, on the back of my head. And I had the distinct impression of her person indicating to me that it was all right, and that she was happy, and to grieve no more.
>
> As a product of a scientific theological education, I had some trouble with this, even though I was a son longing for his departed mother. But then I began to read all the literature in this field, and discovered that something of a similar nature has happened to thousands of people.
>
> That leads me to the conclusion that this other world is not way off in the sky someplace, but that it is superimposed upon the world in which we live. That other world is simply on a higher, or, at least, a different frequency than we on earth occupy. And the line of demarcation becomes, under certain circumstances, so thin that there can be a vibration, or the sense of a presence, so that we know those whom we have loved and lost are not far from us. ("There is No Real Death," in *Plus: The Magazine of Positive Thinking*, March 1991, pp. 7–9.)

There are a couple of other veiled references to the idea, though not the fact, that the spirit world is very close at hand. Maurice Rawlings, a doctor and "born-again" Christian, admitted that "the 'departed' person can see and hear the people in the room but cannot be seen or heard in return. Apparently you and I are 'blinded' to this spiritual world in our present life." (Maurice Rawlings, *Beyond Death's Door*, p. 38.) A young girl who was dying, for whom the veil had been very thin, also made a comment about the nearness of the next life. "Two days before she died, . . . the superintendent of her Sunday school came to see her while she was enjoying a lucid period. As he was leaving, he turned to her and said, 'Well, Daisy; you will soon be over the dark river,' obviously referring to her imminent death. Daisy appeared puzzled by the reference. 'There is no river,' she replied, 'there is no curtain, there is not even a line that separates this life from the other life.'" (*The Return from Silence*, pp. 47–48.)

Incomparable Beauty and Desirability of Spirit World

While the two separate worlds inhabit the same earthly sphere, and the temporal is patterned after the spiritual (see D&C 77:2), the descriptions we have of positive near-death experiences in the spirit world show it as unquestionably the more desirable of the two. President Brigham Young mentioned the vast difference on more than one occasion. "I can say with regard to parting with our friends, and going ourselves, that I have been near enough to understand eternity so that I have had to exercise a great deal more faith to desire to live than I ever exercised in my whole life to live. The brightness and glory of the next apartment is inexpressible." (In *Journal of Discourses*, 14:231.) These desirable conditions may be a reason for the veil that hides this glorious reality from us, as suggested by Elder Benjamin F. Cummings:

> There is reason to believe that if too much knowledge concerning the world to come were given to us here in mortality, before we are better prepared than we now are to receive it, and conform our lives to it, it would interfere with the purposes for which our probation on earth was designed, and place us under condemnation that might be our utter ruin. . . . From certain sayings of President Brigham Young we are led to infer that one reason why the next world in so closely guarded from our eyes is that a knowledge of it, and of the joy, glory and happiness it holds in store for us, would so increase our discontent with this life

as to make us wretched and impatient for it to end. . . . (In "Editorial," *Liahona: The Elders' Journal,* vol. 6, November 14, 1908, p. 519.)

After having experienced the transcendent peace and beauty of the spirit world, a substantial number of those who had near-death episodes were indeed reluctant to return to the banality of earth life. Some report that they "threw a tantrum" or argued when informed that they would have to "go back" to mortality. A few were angry with those who resuscitated them. "Why did you bring me back? It was so beautiful there!" is a typical response. For those who have had positive experiences, there is no argument whatsoever about the superiority of the next realm.

Moreover, it is enchanting to read NDE descriptions of the scenery and circumstances of that mysterious existence. It is also remarkable to note how many of their reports coincide with and sound remarkably similar to the well-known Latter-day Saint account of Jedediah M. Grant as told to Heber C. Kimball. "[Brother Grant said] I have seen good gardens on this earth, but I never saw any to compare with those that were there. I saw flowers of numerous kinds, and some with from fifty to a hundred different colored flowers growing upon one stalk. He [Jedediah M. Grant] also spoke of the buildings he saw there, remarking that the Lord gave Solomon wisdom and poured gold and silver into his hands that he might display his skill and ability, and said that the temple erected by Solomon was much inferior to the most or-dinary buildings he saw in the spirit world." (Heber C. Kim-ball in *Journal of Discourses,* 4:136.)

Spirit World Scenery

The unequalled vegetation, landscape, and buildings of the spirit world are the most commonly described features. One frequently mentioned element of these is the striking color. This is color that surpasses all earthly imagination and mortal de-scription. "At first I became aware of beautiful colors which were all the colors of the rainbow," recounted the previously

mentioned murder victim. "They were magnified in crystal-
lized light and beamed with a brilliance in every direction. . . .
As my senses expanded I became aware of colors that were far
beyond the spectrum of the rainbow known to the human eye."
(As quoted in *Heading Toward Omega,* pp. 64–65.) Another re-
spondent to an empirical study of near-death experiences reported that "it seemed like, if there was any color, all the colors
were their brightest. . . . Like this is the way the colors are in
Utopia, perfect. Perfect to their natural color." (As quoted in
Life at Death, pp. 58–59.) "Not at all like the colors you see
here," and "the colors [on earth] are drab by comparison" are
typical comments. On the other hand, like the ineffable light of
the spirit world, the colors are brilliant but not offensive to the
eye. "I particularly noticed the colours," explained one British
experiencer; "the sky was a brilliant blue, but the colours were
so soft. The green of the trees, too, was brilliant but not harsh."
(As quoted in *Return from Death,* p. 49.)

A few witnesses of the afterlife either perceive a different
reality or perhaps contact a different portion of that realm.
More than colors, they seem to notice that a golden glow permeates everything there. A Florida housewife gave the following account after her cardiac arrest: "It was like a beautiful sun-
glow and sunset. It wasn't any blue sky or green water. The
water he [her deceased husband] was coming to me in was in a
yellow glow. . . . And everything was just beautiful. The trees
were there but they were all in the shadows of gold. There was
no green, no blue." (As quoted in *Recollections of Death,* p. 46.)

The early twentieth century "visit" to the spirit world of
Heber Q. Hale, the Mormon stake president from Boise, is well
known in the Church. Though it has never been officially en-
dorsed, it has been published in a variety of sources. President
Hale gave a description which seems to combine these two aspects of light and color. "The vegetation and landscape were
beautiful beyond description; not all green as here, but gold
with varying shades of pink, orange, and lavender—as the
rainbow." He also spoke of "spacious stretches of flowers,
grasses, and shrubbery, all of a golden hue, . . ." ("Everyone
Had Something to Do," in *Beyond the Veil,* 1:53–58.) While the
descriptions and perceptions may vary, the exhilarating theme

of unsurpassable beauty in rarified color and glorious light re-
sounds again and again from near-death accounts.

These reports of this magnificent beauty are as varied as, if
not more so than, descriptions of earthly landscapes would be,
but they are infinitely more remarkable and superior in every
detail, as noted in the previous reference of Jedediah M. Grant
by Heber C. Kimball. Accounts of NDErs of other faiths are
equally as compelling.

> I was in a field, . . . and it had high golden grass that was
> very soft, so bright. . . . The grass swayed. It was very
> peaceful, very quiet. The grass was so outstandingly beauti-
> ful that I will never forget it. (As quoted in *Life at Death*, p.
> 61.)

> Everything was very defined, on the one hand, but it also
> had a blending with everything else. The flowers and the
> flower buds . . . were all like precious stones, rubies and di-
> amonds and sapphires. One that I remember in particular
> had a yellow color to it and yet I would relate it to a dia-
> mond . . . all these things were just around flowers. [The
> flowers] looked like . . . tulips . . . and yet they had the fra-
> grance of roses. Strong fragrance of roses. (As quoted in
> *Heading Toward Omega*, p. 73.)

> The next thing I knew I'm standing at the end of a field and
> down the center of the field was a long path. Not wide but
> a well traveled path and over the fields were daisies. . . .
> They were beautiful. There was not a patch anywhere that
> wasn't covered with the daisy. The whole field on both
> sides covered. (Transcript of Experiencer's Panel Discus-
> sion, IANDS Conference, Washington D.C., August 1990, p.
> 2.)

> I was in a garden. All the colors were intense. The grass
> was a deep vibrant green, flowers were radiant reds, yel-
> lows, and blues, and birds of all beauty fluttered in the
> bushes. Everything was lit by a shadowless brilliance that
> was all-pervading.

This light did not cast a shadow, which I realized when I cupped my hands tightly together and the palm side was just as light as the back side. There were no sounds of motors or discord or commotions. No sound but the songs of birds and the sounds (yes, 'sounds') of flowers blooming. (As quoted in *Transformed by the Light*, p. 82.)

We were on an island, overlooking a wooded, rocky bay. The waters were bright with a living quality I had never seen in years of recreational boating. The trees were magnificent, each outlined in its own light. The mountains in the background were stately and calm, each with an indescribable aura. (As quoted in Kenneth Ring, "Amazing Grace: The Near-Death Experience as a Compensatory Gift," *Journal of Near-Death Studies*, vol. 10, no. 1, Fall 1991, p. 30.)

Just about every variety of scenery is mentioned in near-death accounts—mountains, hills, valleys, meadows, woodlands, lakes, rivers, streams, waterfalls—all described as "beautiful," "peaceful," and in glorious hues. Flowers there seem to be active rather than passive parts of the landscape. Cattle, horses, sheep, and lions are mentioned as well. Again, the differences in the accounts may be due to experiences in divergent areas of the spirit world and/or to individual perceptions and descriptive limitations. Over and over again, we see evidence that the Lord allows his children to perceive things in the way which is most understandable and comforting to them. Some researchers also posit that our outward perception of "heaven" may reflect our inner thoughts and character, or that we are brought into contact with that which we have desired in our hearts. This would seemingly be compatible with other such principles we have observed. Most likely, some combination of all of these is at work with every individual.

Cities of Light

A few NDErs saw buildings and cities as well as or instead of landscape. Like everything else in that realm, even the buildings were extraordinary. Emanuel Swedenborg advanced a simple and logical explanation for this. "Since angels are people, living together as people on earth do, they have clothes, houses, and many similar things. But there is this difference, that since angels are in a more perfect state, everything they have is more perfect." (*Heaven and Hell*, p. 137.) Here are some delightfully detailed explanations of those "more perfect" buildings.

> The building I went in was a cathedral. It was built like St. Mark's or the Sistine chapel, but the bricks or blocks appeared to be made of Plexiglas. They were square, they had dimension to 'em, except you could see through 'em and in the center of each one of these was this gold and silver light. And you could see the building—and yet could not for the radiance. . . . Now, this cathedral was literally *built* of knowledge. This was a place of learning I had come to. (As quoted in *Heading Toward Omega*, p. 72.)

> And then somehow she took me . . . somewhere [pause] and all I could see was marble all around me; it was marble. It *looked* like marble, but it was *very* beautiful. . . . The closest thing I could compare it to is possibly a mausoleum. . . . It was *immensely* filled with light, with light. . . . It was very beautiful and ornate. (As quoted in *Life at Death*, pp. 63, 65.)

> Then I was brought through a gate that was brighter than our light, into a dwelling-place where the entire floor shone like gold and silver (as quoted in *The Return from Silence*, p. 39).

> Here again, the colors and textures were outside my experience; and the road and the sidewalks appeared to be paved in some kind of precious metal. The buildings appeared to be constructed of a translucent material. (As quoted in "Amazing Grace: The Near-Death Experience as a Compensatory Gift," *Journal of Near-Death Studies*, vol. 10, no. 1, Fall 1991, p. 30.)

And from Swedenborg:

> Whenever I have talked face to face with angels I have been with them in their dwellings. Their dwellings are just like the dwellings on earth which we call homes, except

that they are more beautiful. They have rooms, suites, and bedrooms, all in abundance. They have courtyards, and are surrounded by gardens, flowerbeds, and lawns. . . .

I have seen palaces of heaven so noble as to defy description. The higher parts glowed as if they were made of pure gold, the lower as though made of precious gems; each palace was more splendid than the last. Inside, the same—the rooms were decorated with accessories such that words and arts fail to describe them.

Outside . . . there were parks where everything likewise glowed, with here and there leaves gleaming like silver and fruit like gold. The flowers in their plots formed virtual rainbows. (*Heaven and Hell*, pp. 141–42.)

Not only do the buildings themselves transcend earthly beauty but also they have been perceived by a few to be in some sort of perfect order or meaningful arrangement, which would be in keeping with the decree that God's house "is a house of order" (see D&C 132:8). George Ritchie reported such an impression from the experience he had in the realm of higher learning that he was shown. "Enormous buildings stood in a beautiful sunny park and there was a relationship between the various structures, a pattern to the way they were arranged, that reminded me somewhat of a well-planned university. Except that to compare what I was now seeing with anything on earth was ridiculous. It was more as if all the schools and colleges in the world were only piecemeal reproductions of this reality." (*Return from Tomorrow*, pp. 68–69. For more detail on these buildings, see George G. Ritchie, M.D., *My Life After Dying*, pp. 26–28.)

Indeed, some experiencers saw whole cities—glorious cities of light. As previously mentioned, Dr. Ritchie was allowed to see the "seemingly endless" city of light, whose "brightness seemed to shine from the very walls and streets," only from a distance (*Return from Tomorrow*, p. 72). Others report visiting that same type of city.

After soaring for a while, she (the angel) sat me down on a street in a fabulous city of buildings made of glittering gold and silver and beautiful trees. A beautiful light was everywhere. (As quoted in *Beyond Death's Door*, p. 78.)

And then I walked through the door, and saw on the other side this beautiful, brilliantly lit city, reflecting what seemed to be the sun's rays. It was all made of gold or some shiny metal with domes and steeples in beautiful array, and the streets were shining, not quite like marble but made of something I have never seen before. . . . The air smelled so fresh. I have never smelled anything like it. (As quoted in Maurice Rawlings, *Beyond Death's Door*, p. 80.)

Off in the distance . . . I could see a city. There were buildings—separate buildings. They were gleaming, bright. People were happy in there. There was sparkling water, fountains . . . a city of light I guess would be the way to say it. (As quoted in *Reflections on Life After Life*, p. 17.)

Though not included in each of the previous excerpts, the "happy people" were mentioned in each of these three narratives.

Another account echoes Ritchie's allusion to the vast size of the city. "I saw a city. . . . Even at tremendous distance, I realized that it was *immense!* It all seemed to have the same dimensions and there seemed to be nothing supporting it and no *need* for anything to support it. . . . The first thing that I saw was this street. And it had such a clarity. The only thing I can relate it to in this life was a look of gold, but it was clear, it was transparent. . . . Everything there had a purity and clarity. . . . The difference (between things here and there) was also—you think of gold as something hard and brittle; this had a smoothness and softness." (As quoted in *Heading Toward Omega*, pp. 72–73.)

Heavenly Music

Adding to these "perfectly heavenly" scenarios are pleasant fragrances and sounds—especially music. Like everything else in these realms, it far surpasses any earthly concept of music. Dr. Ritchie, even as a young soldier, realized the complexity of the music he heard. "There were complicated rhythms, tones not on any scale I knew. 'Why,' I found myself thinking, 'Bach is only the beginning!'" (*Return from Tomorrow*, p. 70.) Some NDErs hear singing, as did Alma the Younger when he was released from the pains of hell. "Yea, methought I saw, even as our father Lehi saw, God sitting upon his throne, surrounded with numberless concourses of angels, in the attitude of singing and praising their God; yea, and my soul did long to be there" (Alma 36:22). One individual believed, "I was seated by the tree of life . . . there I saw many thousand spirits clothed in white, and singing heavenly music—the sweetest song I have ever heard" (as quoted in *The Return from Silence*, p. 62). Here are some other captivating accounts of spirit world music.

> And I could hear beautiful music; I can't tell you what kind, because I never heard anything like it before. . . . It sounds—I could describe it as a combination of vibrations, many vibrations. [It made me feel] Oooh, so *good!* (As quoted in *Life at Death*, p. 63.)

> There were no sounds of any earthly thing. Only the sounds of serenity, of a strange music like I had never heard. A soothing symphony of indescribable beauty blended with the light I was approaching. (As quoted in *Heading Toward Omega*, p. 54.)

> My ears were filled with a music so beautiful no composer could ever duplicate it. . . . It was soothing, gentle, and warm and seemed to come from a source deep within me. (As quoted in *Heading Toward Omega*, p. 64.)

> There was tremendous sound, too. It was as if all the great orchestras in the world were playing at once; no special melody, and very loud, powerful but somehow soothing. It was a rushing, moving sound, unlike anything I could remember, but familiar, just on the edge of my memory. (As quoted in "Amazing Grace: The Near-Death Experience as a Compensatory Gift," *Journal of Near-Death Studies*, vol. 10, no. 1, Fall 1991, p. 29.)

This time we were audience to a choir of angels singing. . . . They sang the most lovely and extraordinary music I had ever heard. (As quoted in "Amazing Grace: The Near-Death Experience as a Compensatory Gift," *Journal of Near-Death Studies*, vol. 10, no. 1, Fall 1991, p. 30.)

In this dispensation the Lord declared, "For my soul delighteth in the song of the heart; yea, the song of the righteous is a prayer unto me, and it shall be answered with a blessing upon their heads" (D&C 25:12). Music is one of the most essential and truly expressive ways in which man can pour out his heart in praise to God for his goodness. Such anthems of worship and the peaceful strains of edifying music would surely play a central role in a world where a love of God reigns supreme.

No Time or Distance Intervenes

Another remarkable and apparently pleasant feature of the spiritual existence is the absence of the measure of time and space as we know it here on earth. "I found myself in a space, in a period of time, I would say, where all space and time was negated" (as quoted in *Life at Death*, p. 98). The reports of timelessness on the other side bear testimony to the statement of the prophet Alma that "all is as one day with God, and time only is measured unto men" (Alma 40:8). Elder Neal A. Maxwell confirmed that time as we understand it is a temporary fixture.

When the veil which now encloses us is no more, time will also be no more (see D&C 84:100). Even now, time is clearly not our natural dimension. Thus it is that we are never really at home in time. Alternately, we find ourselves impatiently wishing to hasten the passage of time or to hold back the dawn. We can do neither, of course. Whereas the bird is at home in the air, we are clearly not at home in time—because we belong to eternity! Time, as much as any one thing, whispers to us that we are strangers here. If time were natural to us, why is it that we have so many clocks and wear wristwatches? (Neal A. Maxwell, "Patience," *Ensign*, October 1980, p. 31.)

The mention of timelessness is prevalent in near-death reports. Almost without exception they remark or imply that they have no concept of whether their experience lasted seconds, minutes, hours, years, no time at all, or for an immeasurable duration. They report time as being changed, compounded, or absent altogether. Even Dr. Carl Jung, the famous psychoanalyst who himself had a near death-experience, recounted, "I can describe the experience as only ecstasy of a contemporal state in which present, past and future are one" (as quoted in Maurice Rawlings, *Beyond Death's Door*, p. 54).

On the concept of timelessness Emanuel Swedenborg presented a helpful discussion which seems compatible with Latter-day Saint teachings on time and eternity. He reasoned: "A natural person may believe that his thinking would cease if concepts of time, space, and matter were removed, since all man's thinking is based on them. It would help him to realize, though, that thoughts are limited and restricted to the extent that they draw upon time, space, and matter. They are not limited, and they expand, to the extent that they do not draw upon these, since the mind is proportionally raised above bodily and worldly matters." (*Heaven and Hell*, p. 132.)

Moreover, Swedenborg seemed to propound a principle pertaining to timelessness which Latter-day Saints have always taught. "Since angels have no idea of time," he wrote, "they have a different concept of eternity than people on earth do. Angels see in eternity an infinite *state*, not an infinite *time*." (*Heaven and Hell*, pp. 130–31, italics added.) The Lord revealed to Moses that his work and his glory were to "bring to pass the immortality *and* eternal life of man" (Moses 1:39, italics added). We have understood that eternal life does not refer exclusively to the unending duration of life. That is implied in the word *immortality*. Rather, eternal life refers to a state or quality of life which the Lord wants us to enjoy. Jesus gave us a hint of the meaning of this eternal type of life just before his crucifixion. "And this is life eternal, that they might know thee the only true God, and Jesus Christ, whom thou has sent" (John 17:3).

While we may not grasp the complete meaning of this statement, we believe that *knowing*—in the fullest sense of the word—our Heavenly Father and his Son encompasses living with them and becoming like them.

While we may have some inkling of what timelessness is like, it is even more difficult to conceive "this world where rules about space . . . were all suspended" (*Return from Tomorrow*, p. 45). Some of the comments of NDErs are quite enlightening in this regard, although, as one man explained, "Our normal spatio-temporal vocabulary is frustratingly inadequate to describe heaven" (as quoted in *Return from Death*, p. 52). Emanuel Swedenborg explained his understanding of how space and time are overcome or set aside there. Once again, it is similar to other faculties activated by thought. "Whenever an individual in the other life thinks about someone else, he sets the person's face before himself in his thought, together with many other things that belong to the person's life. When he does, the other person becomes present as though he were called and summoned. This kind of thing happens in the spiritual world because thoughts are communicated there and because distances do not have the same attributes as they have in the natural world." (*Heaven and Hell*, p. 400.)

While this may sound strange, modern-day visitors to the spirit world seem to be describing a process which sounds very similar. "It came then to my mind to see again those family members and loved ones who had passed on before, and no sooner had I thought the thought then [sic] they were there. . . . Next, I wanted to see Jesus, for I had always wished to thank him for the role he played in history and the example he set for others to follow. . . . He instantly appeared, without any effort on my part." (As quoted in *Coming Back to Life*, p. 35.)

Another individual described a process of relocation which echoes the prophecies of Brigham Young about travel in the next life. Recall that the prophet taught that "if we want to visit Jerusalem, or this, that, or the other place . . . there we are, looking at its streets. . . . If we wish to understand how they are living here on these western islands, or in China, we are there." (In *Journal of Discourses*, 14:231.) This experiencer reported instantaneous arrival at each destination: "About this time, while I was still marveling over what I had seen, my friend suggested we might be on our way; and becoming restless myself, I agreed. IMMEDIATELY we arrived at another location, on a beautiful street." After visiting this area, the NDEr remarked, "we relocated again, INSTANTLY." (As quoted in "Amazing Grace: The Near-Death Experience as a Compensatory Gift," *Journal of Near-Death Studies*, vol. 10, no. 1, Fall 1991, p. 30.) Dr. Ritchie related the same type of experience (see *My Life After Dying*, p. 25).

Another experiencer seems to bear witness of both aspects of this absence of intervening space in the spirit realm. Others have also mentioned the "telephoto lens effect" described here. "Whenever I would look at a person to wonder what they were thinking," marveled one woman who had left her body following an accident, "it was like a zoom-up, exactly like through a zoom lens, and I was there. But it seemed that part of me—I'll call it my mind—was still where I had been, several yards away from my body. When I wanted to see someone at a distance, it seemed like part of me, kind of like a tracer, would go to that person. And it seemed to me at the time that if something happened any place in the world that I could just be there." (As quoted in *Life After Life*, pp. 51–52.)

This may offer us a glimpse of the fulfillment of a promise which is basic to Mormon theology—that if we are faithful to all we have been taught, we will be with our loved ones forever, never to be separated again. In our earthly thinking it is almost impossible to comprehend how we might all be together without at least some intervening distances between us. Apparently we will have the power to overcome all obstacles—to visit and communicate with friends and loved ones, instantly, if we desire. Distance and separation will never again have the deterrent effect on relationships which they have here on earth.

As with accounts of the other unimaginable delights of the next life, the descriptions of this phenomenon could stretch on for pages, each as exhilarating as the one before. Those of us who have never experienced these views are at least blessed to have these wonderful reports to supplement our doctrinal understanding and can endeavor to imagine for ourselves the unimaginable joys that lie ahead.

CHAPTER 8

A House of Order

The perfect order of God's church and kingdom is a basic tenet of Latter-day Saint theology. "Behold, mine house is a house of order, saith the Lord, and not a house of confusion" (D&C 132:8). We believe that the divinely revealed priesthood organization of the Church is perfect even though, as fallible mortals, we may not follow or administer it perfectly here on earth. In the spirit world the Lord's influence is manifest more completely and his divine will followed more exactly, and therefore, the perfect order of heaven prevails. The prophets of this dispensation have instructed us that righteous spirits in that place are organized after the order of God as families. "These righteous spirits are close by us," taught President Ezra Taft Benson. "They are organized according to priesthood order in family organizations as we are here; only there they exist in a more perfect order. This was revealed to the Prophet Joseph." (In *The Teachings of Ezra Taft Benson*, pp. 35–36.)

President Jedediah M. Grant, a Counselor to President Brigham Young in the First Presidency, also marveled at this extensive organization of the spirit world as seen in his remarkable vision of the realm of departed spirits. President Grant shared his experience with President Heber C. Kimball, who later recounted: "'But O,' says he [Jedediah M. Grant], 'the order and government that were there! When in the spirit world, I saw the order of righteous men and women: beheld them organized in their several grades, and there appeared to be no obstruction to my vision; I could see every man and woman in their grade and order. I looked to see whether there was any disorder there, but there was none; . . .' He said that the people he there saw were organized in family capacities; and when he looked at them he saw grade after grade and all were organized and in perfect harmony." (In *Journal of Discourses*, 4:135.)

While those NDErs who are not of the LDS faith seem to have no specific perception as to the eternal significance of family organization, the majority of those who meet individuals in the next life most often say that those individuals are family members, often including many members of their immediate and extended families. Other than this we have from them no definite testimony to this principle. However, many comment on or allude to the organized and industrious nature of that domain. Swedenborg especially gave ample space in his writings to explaining the orderly nature of what he called "heaven." "Now heaven is a 'one' made up of different elements arranged in the most perfect form, for the heavenly form is of all forms the most perfect" (p. 58). "God is order" (p. 59). "There are necessarily governments there. For order must be kept, and matters of order cared for." (P. 157.)

Swedenborg further alluded to a condition which echoes President Grant's description of "grades" and "orders." He also believed that some order prevailed in hell (his reasons for this belief will be discussed in chapter 10). "All heaven's communities are very precisely arranged according to their good elements, their classes and sub-classes, while all the hells are similarly arranged according to their evil elements and their classes and sub-classes" (*Heaven and Hell*, p. 498).

Inherent in the concept of perfect organization is the necessity of the perfect usefulness and contribution of each individual. Again, Emanuel Swedenborg elaborated on this theme.

In similar fashion, uses exist in the heavens with all variety and diversity. The use of one person is in no case exactly like the use of another; so too the pleasure of one is in no case exactly like the pleasure of another. Beyond this, the pleasures of each particular use are countless, and these countless elements are likewise diverse. Still, they are closely connected in a pattern so designed that they depend on each other in the same way as do the uses of each member, organ, and inner part of the body. It is even more like the use of each tissue and fiber within each member, organ, and inner part, with all of them, every single one, so joined together that each sees its good within the other and therefore in all, and all see their good in each. On the basis of this all-encompassing and detailed view, they act as one. (*Heaven and Hell*, p. 314.)

This useful service and interdependence of spirit world inhabitants seems to be a major contributor to the happiness they enjoy. "Performing useful tasks is the delight of everyone's life," submits Swedenborg. "Clearly then, the Lord's kingdom is a kingdom of useful activities." (*Heaven and Hell*, p. 160.) It may also be responsible for the comments of some NDErs about the "busy" nature of the afterlife. Heber Q. Hale, mentioned previously, left this testimony. "The people I met there, did not think of [themselves] as spirit but as men and women, self-thinking, and self-acting individuals, going about important business in a most orderly manner. There was perfect order there, and everybody had something to do and seemed to be about their business." (As quoted in *Life Everlasting*, p. 79.) "I arrived at a place— it's very hard to put this into words, but I can only describe it as heaven," explained an experiencer. "It's a place of intense light, a place of intense activity, more like a bustling city than a lonely country scene, nothing like floating on clouds or harps or anything of that sort." (*The Return from Silence*, p. 232.) Another recalled: "I looked up and saw a beautiful, polished door, with no knob. Around the edges of the door I could see a really brilliant light, with rays just streaming like everybody was so happy in there, and reeling around, moving around. It seemed like it was awfully busy in there." (As quoted in *Life After Life*, p. 77.)

A woman who had lost her husband and two children was reassured from her own experience with death. Though others worried at her short-lived grief for her loved ones, she knew better. "They aren't dead. They are all alive, busy and waiting for me." (As quoted in *Heading Toward Omega*, p. 82.)

While some NDErs comment generally on the busy nature of the spirit world, a few comment on the specific activities or "uses" of the inhabitants there. "It seems that I saw one person carrying what looked like a *saw;* another was carrying a hammer, woodworking tools, but everyone was smiling," reported the victim of a cardiac arrest. "There was a great feeling of happiness around me." (*Life at Death*, p. 65.) Often those who have near-death episodes meet beings whom they describe as "guides," or "greeters," or "helpers." One man, a former alcoholic whose experience was quite extensive, visited several different areas of activity with his guide. His account seems to underscore the reality of the principle that joy is obtained through service and lives of usefulness in God's spiritual kingdom.

> IMMEDIATELY we arrived at another location, on a beautiful street. We appeared to be alone there, except for the street-sweeper, who was responsible for the spotless condition of the place. . . . I felt prompted to talk to the street-sweeper, and congratulated him on his efforts. He said work was a joy to him, and he derived his pleasure from doing the best job he could at all times. This statement nonplussed me somewhat, for I had never been enthusiastic about what I considered menial tasks. This man appeared absolutely sincere, however; and I was very impressed by his industry and the obvious love and care he brought to his work.

Next, this man was taken to visit an angelic choir and then an art gallery. "It contained the work of the great masters of all time and all places. . . . Some of the great works seemed familiar. Others were unlike anything I had ever seen, indescribable." Then he found himself in a computer room, where he perceived that he met a spirit being whom he recognized as Albert Einstein, a man whom he had always admired.

This great man took time away from his duties to encourage me. He asked me if I would care to operate the computer, which was very complex and beautiful. . . . I was flattered, but felt incompetent and unsure of myself in the presence of such greatness. I told him I would like to try, but I was afraid of making a mistake. He laughed gently, and reassured me, saying that error was not possible in this place. Encouraged, I seemed instinctively to know how to operate this unusual machine. . . . I knew instantly that the task had been performed perfectly, and it had somehow been of great benefit to someone. I was suffused with the joy of a job well done. I would gladly spend eternity here at this rewarding work if only for the tremendous feeling of well-being I had experienced as a result. (As quoted in "Amazing Grace: The Near-Death Experience as a Compensatory Gift," *Journal of Near-Death Studies*, vol. 10, no. 1, Fall 1991, pp. 30–31.)

Like Dr. George Ritchie, this man was also shown a vast library, seemingly containing all the wisdom of the ages. Dr. Ritchie further witnessed a building complex where serious study and research were ongoing. There he viewed beings using instruments which were totally foreign and incomprehensible to him during his near-death experience in 1943, but which he recognized years later in photographs in the December 1952 issue of *Life* magazine as some of the instruments in an atomic submarine engine. Looking back on that experience he surmised that these beings were assigned to provide help and inspiration for earthy inventions and progress that would benefit mankind. "Why is it that inventors in different parts of the earth come up with the same ideas about the same time, Ford in America, Bentley in England, Peugeot in France? I believe I was shown the place where those who have already gone before us are doing research and want to help us when we begin to seriously search and turn deep within for answers. I think this is true regardless of our fields of interest." (*My Life After Dying*, p. 27.)

It could be that the scenes viewed by Dr. Ritchie were perceived according to his own understanding. On the other hand, we have been informed through modern revelation that "I, the

Lord God, created all things, of which I have spoken, spiritually, before they were naturally upon the face of the earth" (Moses 3:5). It may well be that this, in fact, does apply to *all* things. At the very least, modern prophets have stated that the inspiration for the advancements of mankind come from the Lord. "Every good and perfect gift cometh from God," declared Brigham Young. "Every discovery in science and art, that is really true and useful to mankind, has been given by direct revelation from God, though but few acknowledge it." President Young went on to admonish the Saints to make use of these discoveries and prepare to do their part in the elevation of humanity through these means, as well. "It [the inspiration] has been given with a view to prepare the way for the ultimate triumph of truth, and the redemption of the earth from the power of sin and Satan. We should take advantage of all these great discoveries, the accumulated wisdom of ages, and give to our children the benefit of every branch of useful knowledge, to prepare them to step forward and efficiently do their part in the great work." (In *Journal of Discourses*, 9:369.)

Perhaps the studious beings observed in these spirit realms perform this work under the authority and direction of the Lord, thus enjoying the apparently exquisite happiness of doing what they love best, being useful in the Lord's kingdom, and serving their fellow beings on both sides of the veil.

As a final witness and source of insight, Swedenborg also provided some intriguing detail about spirit world occupations. He reiterated that "everyone there actively serves a use, for the Lord's kingdom is a kingdom of uses." He explained further: "Matters of the common good or use are cared for by wiser angels, while more limited matters are cared for by the less wise, and so on. They are ranked exactly as uses are in the Divine design." He illustrated this idea with the following specific examples.

> There are communities whose occupations involve taking care of infants. There are other communities whose occupations involve teaching and training them as they grow up. [See the section in chapter 12 on "Other Encounters," for more discussion of this concept.] There are others who similarly teach and train boys and girls who are well dis-

posed because of their training in the world and who therefore enter heaven. There are others who instruct good, simple folk from Christendom and lead them into the path to heaven. There are some which do the same for various non-Christian peoples. . . . There are some that help people who are in the lower earth, and some too who help people who are in the hells, . . .

Ecclesiastical concerns in heaven occupy people who in the world loved the Word and eagerly sought truths from it—not with an eye to prestige or profit, but the use both of their own lives and of the lives of others. . . . These people fill the function of preachers. . . .

Civic concerns occupy people who in the world loved their country and its common good more than their own, and who acted justly and rightly out of a love for the just and the right. . . . They have the capability of supervising areas of service in heaven. . . .

Beyond this, there are so many areas of service and supervision in heaven, so many tasks as well, that they cannot be listed for their abundance. There are few in the world by comparison. (*Heaven and Hell*, pp. 300–304.)

It seems, then, that at least some vocations in the world of spirits may be modeled to some extent after earthly ones, or vice versa. However, according to the flawless order which always exists in the Lord's house, in that world they are perfected and organized completely. Presumably other occupations are unique to the spirit world or to heaven. Among these are the many functions of angels referred to throughout holy writ. One such spirit world "assignment" that is also mentioned in near-death experiences merits examination because of its doctrinal significance. It is that of "guardian angel."

Guardian Angels

There is no specific scriptural passage or prophetic utterance that authoritatively states that one specific guardian angel is assigned to each and every mortal throughout his earthly sojourn, as has been the popular romantic notion, though this may be the case with certain individuals. However, Church leaders have in their sermons and writings occasionally referred to "guardian angels" and other "ministering angels" who are sent by the Lord to protect and help his children on earth as needed. We also have scriptural examples of this. Moreover, we have the assurance that God's angels are always watching over even the least among us. President George Q. Cannon taught: "There is not one of us that He has not given His angels charge concerning. We may be insignificant and contemptible in our own eyes and in the eyes of others, but the truth remains that we are the children of God and that He has actually given His angels—invisible beings of power and might—charge concerning us, and they watch over us and have us in their keeping. Those who otherwise might be thought to be contemptible and unworthy of notice, Jesus says, be careful about offending them, for 'their angels do always behold the face of my Father.'" (Matthew 18:10.) (*Gospel Truth,* p. 4.)

Swedenborg, claiming to have been well acquainted with the spirit world, also bore witness to this truth. "Since man has alienated himself from heaven, it has been arranged by the Lord that there be angels and spirits with each individual, and that the individual be led by the Lord by means of them" (*Heaven and Hell,* p. 178). George Ritchie reportedly observed that even the inhabitants of hell were not left completely alone. "Gradually I was becoming aware that there was something else on that plain of grappling forms. . . . The entire unhappy plain was hovered over by beings seemingly made of light. . . . All I clearly saw was that not one of these bickering beings on the plain had been abandoned. They were being attended, watched over, ministered to." (*Return from Tomorrow,* p. 66.) This is an interesting observation in light of the revealed knowledge we have that even resurrected telestial inhabitants will receive ministration from those of a terrestrial order (see D&C 76:86–88).

While we do not know exactly who these angels are, we occasionally get a glimpse of their functions. Such angels probably vary from time to time in number and identity according to the current needs of the one being ministered to. Consider the lone angel who was sent to protect the prophet Daniel in the den of lions (see Daniel 6:22) and the legions of angel warriors in horse-drawn chariots of fire who protected the prophet Elisha and his servant boy and smote the menacing Syrian encampment with blindness, "according to the word of Elisha" (see 2 Kings 6:16–18).

Moreover, we have record of members of the Church who have been watched over and helped by departed family members. Hyrum Smith the patriarch, brother of the Prophet Joseph, assured Bishop Edward Hunter, who had lost his young son, that the child would be sent to help him. "Your son will act as an angel to you; not your guardian angel, but an auxiliary angel, to assist you in extreme trials" (as quoted in *Life Everlasting*, p. 84). This indeed proved to be the case. Hyrum Smith's son, President Joseph F. Smith, believed that we are watched over here, especially by those who naturally cared for us as family, friends, and associates while they were on earth.

> I believe we move and have our being in the presence of heavenly messengers and of heavenly beings. We are not separate from them. We begin to realize more and more fully, as we become acquainted with the principles of the Gospel, as they have been revealed anew in this dispensation, that we are closely related to our kindred, to our ancestors, to our friends and associates and co-laborers who have preceded us into the spirit world. . . .
>
> . . . And therefore, I claim that we live in their presence, they see us, they are solicitous for our welfare, they love us now more than ever. For now they see the dangers that beset us; they can comprehend better than ever before, the weaknesses that are liable to mislead us into dark and forbidden paths. They see the temptations and the evils that beset us in life and the proneness of mortal beings to yield to temptation and to wrong doing; hence their solicitude for us and their love for us and their desire for our well being must be greater than that which we feel for ourselves. (As quoted in *The Life Beyond*, pp. 83–84.)

However, it is probably true that our loved ones who have passed on have other work to perform in the spirit world and aid us only as necessary. "As their family was their primary concern in this life, so it will continue to be their primary concern on the other side of the veil. We would demean the nature of their labors in the spirit world to suppose that they had nothing more to do than to conduct a daily watch over those they left behind; yet . . . on special occasions their presence will be felt." (*The Life Beyond*, p. 85.)

Few if any of those not of the LDS faith who had near-death or similar experiences identified as their guardian angel a deceased family member or any other person they knew on earth. However, some do speak of having met their guardian angel in terms which appear to agree with the principles we have set forth. "In a very few instances, people have come to believe that the beings they encountered were their 'guardian spirits,'" reported Dr. Raymond Moody. "One man was told by such a spirit that, 'I have helped you through this stage of your existence, but now I am going to turn you over to others.' A woman told me that as she was leaving her body she detected the presence of two other spiritual beings there, and that they identified themselves as her 'spiritual helpers.'" (*Life After Life*, p. 57.) Another eminent NDE researcher, Dr. Melvin Morse, remarked that he was "surprised to find that about 12 percent of the people in [his study] have regular contact with the guardian angels that they saw during their NDEs," and went on to cite some interesting examples of guidance, protection, and comfort rendered by these solicitous attendants (*Transformed by the Light*, p. 164). One NDEr, while not specifically calling the loving being who led him through the spirit world a guardian angel, described him in the following terms: "I knew he would be all the friends I never had, and all the guides and teachers I would ever need. I knew that he would be there if ever I needed him, but that there were others for him to look out for, so I needed to care for myself as much as I reasonably could." (As quoted in "Amazing Grace: The Near-Death Experience as a Compensatory Gift," *Journal of Near-Death Studies*, vol. 10, no. 1, Fall 1991, pp. 30–31.)

Thus, whether it be a "guardian angel" officially assigned to guide and protect us or a friend or family member allowed to be near and help us, it does not seem to matter. We can always rest assured that, seen or unseen, succor from the spirit world can come to us under the direction of our loving Father in Heaven through those who love us and have concern for our welfare. "I will go before your face," promised the Lord. "I will be on your right hand and on your left, and my Spirit shall be in your hearts, and mine angels round about you, to bear you up." (D&C 84:88.)

Ministers of the Gospel

There are other responsibilities in the spirit world which we believe are borne by spirits who in mortality were members of The Church of Jesus Christ of Latter-day Saints. As messengers of the restored gospel and as ordained administrators and officiators in the ordinances of salvation, we believe our work and service in the next life will be of a greater magnitude than it is here. President Wilford Woodruff explained:

> The same priesthood exists on the other side of the veil. Every man who is faithful is in his quorum there. When a man dies and his body is laid in the tomb, he does not lose his position. The prophet Joseph Smith held the keys of this dispensation on this side of the veil, and he will hold them throughout the countless ages of eternity. He went into the spirit world to unlock the prison doors and to preach the gospel to the millions of spirits who are in darkness, and every apostle, every seventy, every elder, etc., who has died in the faith, as soon as he passes to the other side of the veil, enters into the work of the ministry, and there is a thousand times more to preach there than there is here. (*Discourses of Wilford Woodruff*, p. 77.)

This belief stems from our understanding, unique in Christendom, that those who die without a full opportunity to accept and understand the gospel of Jesus Christ in this life will yet have the possibility of hearing, accepting, and obeying it and in turn receiving ordinances of salvation vicariously through the mortal ministrations of those who already enjoy the full blessings of the gospel.

But behold, from among the righteous, he organized his forces and appointed messengers, clothed with power and authority, and commissioned them to go forth and carry the light of the gospel to them that were in darkness, even to all the spirits of men; and thus was the gospel preached to the dead.

And the chosen messengers went forth to declare the acceptable day of the Lord and proclaim liberty to the captives who were bound, even unto all who would repent of their sins and receive the gospel.

Thus was the gospel preached to those who had died in their sins, without a knowledge of the truth, or in transgression, having rejected the prophets.

These were taught faith in God, repentance from sin, vicarious baptism for the remission of sins, the gift of the Holy Ghost by the laying on of hands,

And all other principles of the gospel that were necessary for them to know in order to qualify themselves that they might be judged according to men in the flesh, but live according to God in the spirit. (D&C 138:30–34.)

While broad hints of this doctrine appear in the Bible (see 1 Peter 3:18–19; 4:6; 1 Corinthians 15:29), most of Christianity has not yet come to understand its full meaning. This is perhaps one of the main reasons why many Christians—especially evangelical Christians who believe that a person must accept Christ before dying if he or she wants to avoid hell and enter "heaven"—have a great deal of trouble with near-death studies. (See Maurice Rawlings, *Beyond Death's Door,* p. 70.) They are quite perplexed as to how those who have not yet "accepted Christ as their Savior" can have such positive and heavenly experiences. Blessed with the understanding that death does not mark the final judgment and that even in the world of spirits opportunities to come unto Christ are afforded to mankind by a merciful, loving, and fair God, we as Latter–day Saints can learn from these positive experiences and be of even greater service to our fellowmen.

While no modern NDEr of another faith has reported observing anything that looked like genealogical or temple work or the teaching of the gospel, the eighteenth-century philosopher and theologian Emanuel Swedenborg did describe, in some detail, the spirit world preaching of the gospel to those who on earth lived good lives but did not there enjoy such knowledge. His teachings on this subject are quite remarkable and worth examining, since no earthly church in his day preached such doctrine. To many, it must have been considered heresy. Even today the notion of opportunities to exercise faith in Christ, repent of sins, and accept the fulness of the gospel after death—what we know as the doctrine of salvation for the dead—is foreign to virtually all Christian denominations. Consider the following excerpts from Swedenborg's book:

> For the Lord's church is universal, and exists in all people who recognize something Divine and live in charity. They are then taught by angels after death, and accept Divine truths. (P. 230.)

> It is known that Gentiles lead just as moral a life as Christians—some of them better than Christians. . . . Gentiles, consequently, although they are not involved in things genuinely true in the world, do ultimately accept them in the other life because of their love [for what is good]. (Pp. 241–42.)

> I have been taught in many ways about Gentiles who have led a moral life, living in obedience and good order and mutual charity according to their religious persuasion and who have thereby acquired some element of conscience. I have learned that they have been accepted in the other life and are taught there with painstaking care by angels about the good and true elements of faith. I have been told that when they are taught, they behave temperately, understandingly, and wisely, readily both accepting truths and absorbing them. (P. 242.)

In light of the great success of the Church and the restored gospel among African nations in modern times, the following statement by Swedenborg, which he makes more than once, is fascinating: "Among the Gentiles in heaven, the most beloved are the Africans. They accept the good and true elements of heaven more readily than others." (*Heaven and Hell*, p. 248.)

It stands to reason that the teaching of the gospel in the spirit world is also accomplished through perfect organization and order. As mentioned, it is carried out under priesthood authority there just as it is here. President Joseph F. Smith taught that sisters would teach sisters and that things here are typical of things there (see *Gospel Doctrine*, p. 461). David John, a member of the Church who was blessed with a spirit world experience, bore witness to the highly organized manner of teaching the gospel there. He saw people arranged according to age and gender.

> My guide led me to an apartment where I saw thousands of children between the ages of 4 to 8 years and [my guide] informed me that the first part of my mission should be to teach them to read and write. . . .
>
> He led me to the second department which appeared to be as numerous as the first which were from 8 to 16 years of age. He informed me that my mission to them should be to preach unto them the gospel and teach them the principles of life and salvation. . . .
>
> We then entered the third apartment and found them more numerous than in the first two. They consisted of persons from 16 to 40 years of age. . . . I was informed that my mission to them was to teach them the gospel and to superintend over them and to have the priesthood conferred upon them.
>
> I was led to the fourth apartment. They were as numerous as the third and were men from 40 to 100 years old. I was commanded to preach the gospel to them and see that they had the priesthood conferred upon them and that I should call all necessary help to accomplish this work. . . .
>
> Now in regard to this dream I wish to say that it was given by the inspiration of the Lord. I did not see any female person over 8 years of age which proves that I did not see all. I was led to understand that female administer to females. (As quoted in *Spirit World Manifestations*, pp. 103–4.)

It is interesting to note that nearly two centuries earlier

Swedenborg alluded to a similar pattern. "People who have died in early childhood [and] had been brought up to the age of early maturity in heaven are toward the front. People who are beyond their childhood state and the care of nurses are brought there by the Lord and taught. Behind them are areas where instruction is given to people who have died as adults, who were involved in an affection for what is true because of a goodness of life." (*Heaven and Hell*, p. 421.)

In addition, Swedenborg directly states that the people there are taught in the manner most suited to and most easily understood by them—a concept we find taught in the Book of Mormon—"according to their language, . . . unto their understanding" (2 Nephi 31:3). He testifies that ". . . each and every individual can be taught as befits his own intrinsic character and his ability to receive" (p. 420). He goes on to explain the heavenly organization further.

> Then behind these are people devoted to the Mohammedan religion who lived a moral life in the world, recognizing one Divine Being and recognizing the Lord as the Essential Prophet. Once they withdraw from Mohammed, because he cannot help them, they approach the Lord, worship Him, and recognize what is Divine about Him; then they are taught in the Christian religion.
>
> Behind these . . . are places for the teaching of various heathen who have in the world lived good lives in keeping with their own religions. . . . There are more of these than there are of the others; the best of them come from Africa.
>
> Not all people, however, are taught in the same way. . . . The ones who have been brought up in heaven from early childhood are taught by angels of more inward heavens because they have not absorbed false notions from false elements of religion or polluted their spiritual life with dregs drawn from prestige and profit in the world. . . .
>
> Mohammedans are taught by angels who were once involved in that religion and have turned to Christianity; the heathen too are taught by their own angels.
>
> . . . Christians are taught on the basis of a heavenly doctrine that is in full accord with the Word's inner meaning. Other people, such as Mohammedans and heathen, are

taught on the basis of doctrines suited to their level of comprehension, differing from the heavenly doctrine only in the fact that they teach spiritual life by means of a moral life consistent with the good tenets of their religion, the tenets on which they had based their life in the world. (*Heaven and Hell*, pp. 421–23.)

Finally, it appears that people who die without the gospel do not necessarily hear it preached as soon as they enter the spirit world, but only as they are ready. Swedenborg claimed that the angels "teach . . . [a new spirit] about the things that exist in the other life, but only as he can comprehend them" (*Heaven and Hell*, p. 347). A further consideration is the timing ordained by the Lord for that individual or group of individuals. Said Parley P. Pratt:

> The question naturally arises—Do all the people who die without the Gospel hear it as soon as they arrive in the world of spirits? To illustrate this, let us look at the dealings of God with the people of this world. "What can we reason but from what we know?" We know and understand the things of this world, in some degree, because they are visible, and we are daily conversant with them. Do all the people in this world hear the Gospel as soon as they are capable of understanding? No, indeed, but very few in comparison have heard it at all. . . .
>
> I have not the least doubt but there are spirits there who have dwelt there a thousand years, who, if we could converse with them face to face, would be found . . . ignorant of the truths, the ordinances, powers, keys, Priesthood, resurrection, and eternal life of the body. . . .

Interestingly, Elder Pratt noted that those in hell, being the least deserving because of their sinfulness, would be the last to hear the gospel preached to them.

> And why this ignorance in the spirit world? Because a portion of the inhabitants thereof are found unworthy of the consolations of the Gospel until the fulness of time,

until they have suffered in hell, in the dungeons of darkness, or the prisons of the condemned, amid the buffetings of fiends, and malicious and lying spirits.

As in earth, so in the spirit world. No person can enter into the privileges of the Gospel, until the keys are turned, and the Gospel opened by those in authority, for all which there is a time, according to the wise dispensations of justice and mercy. (In *Journal of Discourses*, 1:10–11.)

Thus, the Lord's house is a house of order in every aspect, down to every individual—from those who build and weave to those who do study and research for the advancement of mankind, to those who guard and guide mortals, to those who preach the gospel of Jesus Christ and administer the ordinances of salvation. It appears that this perfect organization makes each responsive spirit feel equally useful, needed, and important and is a source of infinite happiness and rejoicing in the eternal worlds.

CHAPTER 9

_____

Conditions, Companions, and Kingdoms

From President Joseph F. Smith's vision of the redemption of the dead (D&C 138) we learn not only of the Savior's organization of spirit world missionary work but also of many other truths pertaining to that realm. From this revelation we are led to understand that while the wicked and the righteous all go to the same world of spirits, as Brigham Young taught (see *Journal of Discourses,* 3:94), they do not mingle together but gather with those who are like themselves, in conditions suited to and dictated by their true inward, spiritual state (see Alma 41:5). "And there were gathered together in one place an innumerable company of the spirits of the just, who had been faithful in the testimony of Jesus while they lived in mortality. . . . The Son of God appeared, declaring liberty to the captives who had been faithful; and there he preached to them the everlasting gospel, . . . But unto the wicked he did not go, and among the ungodly and the unrepentant who had defiled themselves while in the flesh, his voice was not raised; neither did the rebellious who rejected the testimonies and the warnings of the ancient prophets behold his presence, nor look upon his face. Where these were, darkness reigned, but among the righteous there was peace." (D&C 138:20–22.)

"There were two grand divisions in the world of spirits," declared President Ezra Taft Benson. "Spirits of the righteous (the just) had gone to paradise, a state of happiness, peace, and restful work. The spirits of the wicked (the unjust) had gone to prison, a state of darkness and misery. (See Alma 40:12–15.)" (*The Teachings of Ezra Taft Benson*, p. 37.) Not only do we understand that there is a separation of the just and the unjust but we also comprehend that where the righteous are, the wicked are forbidden, unable, or unwilling to come—perhaps some combination of these three is in operation. Prophets of the Restoration have also advanced this idea. "Can those persons who pursue a course of carelessness, neglect of duty, and disobedience, when they depart from this life, expect that their spirits will associate with the spirits of the righteous in the spirit world?" asked Elder Heber C. Kimball. "I do not expect it, and when you depart from this state of existence, you will find it out for yourselves." (In *Journal of Discourses*, 2:150.) Brigham Young likewise confirmed, "Where the pure in heart are the wicked cannot come. This is the state of the spirit world." (In *Journal of Discourses*, 14:229.) Even the New Testament speaks of the uncrossable gulf that separated the sinful, greedy rich man and the devout, deserving Lazarus (see Luke 16:19–31). Only the atonement of Christ made it possible to bridge that gulf.

Through the missionary labors of the Saints who must minister to them in their confined and darkened state, the wicked may at some point learn the truth, repent, exercise faith in Christ, and escape their hellish prison if they are willing. Until then, they remain. "Knowledge saves a man," explained the Prophet Joseph Smith; "and in the world of spirits no man can be exalted but by knowledge. So long as a man will not give heed to the commandments, he must abide without salvation. . . . But when he consents to obey the gospel, whether here or in the world of spirits, he is saved." (*History of the Church*, 6:314.) President Heber Q. Hale, an LDS stake president who had an NDE-like vision of the spirit world and was asked by the First Presidency to recount his experience in a special genealogy conference of the Church, claimed also to have been witness to this condition. "Particularly was it observed that the wicked and unrepentant are confined to a certain district by themselves, the confines of which are as definitely determined and impassable as the line marking the division of the physical from the spiritual world, a mere film but impassable until the person himself has changed. . . . There was much activity within the different spheres and the appointed ministers of salvation were seen coming from the higher to the lower spheres in pursuit of their missionary appointments." (As quoted in *Life Everlasting*, p. 87.)

Not only are there two distinct and separate realms in the spirit world, but within these two greater divisions there seem to be all manner and degree of conditions, communities, and orders. "Well, says one, is there no more than one place in the spirit world?" queried Elder Parley P. Pratt. "Yes," he answered, "there are many places and degrees in that world, as in this." (In *Journal of Discourses*, 1:9.) This, of course, must be due to the endless variety of spirits and their levels of progression and goodness or digression and evil. "There will be just as much distinction between spirits there as you find between spirits here," taught President George Q. Cannon. "Those who have made good use of their opportunities here will have the benefit of their diligence and faithfulness there. Those who have been careless and indifferent and have not acquired knowledge and power through the exercise of faith will find themselves lacking there." (*Gospel Truth*, p. 60.)

Thus, to a large extent, the conditions and circumstances we experience in the spirit world will be of our own making. The prophet Alma's teachings on the doctrine of perfect restoration in the resurrection no doubt apply equally to our life in the spirit world: "The one raised to happiness according to his desires of happiness, or good according to his desires of good; and the other to evil according to his desires of evil; for as he has desired to do evil all the day long even so shall he have his reward of evil when the night cometh. And so it is on the other hand. If he hath repented of his sins, and desired righteousness until the end of his days, even so he shall be rewarded unto righteousness." (Alma 41:5–6.)

In our generation, Elder Hartman Rector, Jr., of the Seventy offered this helpful example: "The scriptures speak of the spirit world as being two different places—as paradise at one time, and as spirit prison at another time. But as a matter of fact, the spirit world is really just one place; it merely depends on the condition we are in when we go there as to what it will be for us. If we go there addicted to drugs, bad habits, or evil desires, it will be a prison." (In *Improvement Era*, December 1970, p. 76.)

Dr. George Ritchie stated that in his near-death experience he observed at least four different and separate realms in the world of spirits. He clearly saw that the beings in these realms had created and were creating their own circumstances through their own desires and choices. Emanuel Swedenborg offered even more detail and enlightenment to the people of his day on what he saw as the many varying conditions of heaven and hell. "Almost all the people who enter the other life think that hell is the same for everyone and that heaven is the same for everyone. Yet in each case there are infinite varieties and differences—nowhere is hell exactly the same, nowhere is heaven exactly the same for one person as for another. In the same way, no person, spirit, or angel exists anywhere who is exactly like another, even in his facial features." (*Heaven and Hell*, p. 313.)

Like Spirits Are Drawn Together

Besides the heavenly or hellish conditions we create for ourselves to enjoy in the next life, we further reinforce and enhance these circumstances because we are drawn to associate with those who are most like us. This is an eternal principle. "For intelligence cleaveth unto intelligence; wisdom receiveth wisdom; truth embraceth truth; virtue loveth virtue; light cleaveth unto light; mercy hath compassion on mercy and claimeth her own; justice continueth its course and claimeth its own" (D&C 88:40). This is true even in this life. In the next life too we will be most comfortable with those who think and act as we do, at least in matters of righteousness or wickedness. Speaking to the unrighteous and unbelieving, the Book of Mormon prophet Moroni declared:

Do ye suppose that ye shall dwell with [God] under a consciousness of your guilt? Do ye suppose that ye could be happy to dwell with that holy Being, when your souls are racked with a consciousness of guilt that ye have ever abused his laws?

Behold, I say unto you that ye would be more miserable to dwell with a holy and just God, under a consciousness of your filthiness before him, than ye would to dwell with the damned souls in hell.

For behold, when ye shall be brought to see your nakedness before God, and also the glory of God, and the holiness of Jesus Christ, it will kindle a flame of unquenchable fire upon you. (Mormon 9:3–5.)

George Ritchie observed that this precept indeed seemed to be in effect in the hellish realms he witnessed. "Since hypocrisy is impossible because others know your thoughts the minute you think them, they tend to group with the ones who think the same way they do. In our own plane of existence, earth, we have a saying, 'Birds of a feather flock together.'"(*My Life After Dying*, p. 23.) Seeing the miserable, hateful beings of that place who seemed unwilling to leave it, Ritchie wondered if "there was a kind of consolation in finding others as loathsome as [themselves], even if all [they] could do was hurl [their] venom at each other" (*Return from Tomorrow*, p. 65).

Swedenborg explained, "People are borne by their own natures, as it were, toward those who are like them. With people like themselves, they feel as though they were with their own family, as though they were at home; while with others they feel as though they were with foreigners, as though they were abroad." He described these groupings of spirits as "communities," saying: "The whole heaven is divided into communities on the basis of differences in the good [the various kinds of service] that comes from love. Every single spirit who is raised into heaven and becomes an angel is taken to the community where his love is [in this case, not only his righteousness, but also that which he loves to do], and once he is there he is where he belongs . . . as though he were at home, where he was born. An angel senses this, and makes close friends with others like himself." (*Heaven and Hell*, pp. 50–51, 380.) Likewise, he wrote, "Evil people are promptly attached to the hellish community where, as to their ruling love [the desires of their hearts], they were during their life in the world; . . ." Whether "assigned" or "drawn" (though these apparently work in combination) to these "communities" or groups of beings, the result is the same and the person is perfectly situated, ". . . because likeness forms bonds, and unlikeness severs" (*Heaven and Hell*, pp. 333–34).

In addition, George Ritchie attested to the discomfort of associating with those who hold values and ideas at odds with those we may hold dear. "Just as there are areas in our own cities which are divided by . . . moral standards so it is, in the astral realm. There were definite areas of this dimension that I would not want to be caught in, just as there are areas in our own towns and cities that we don't feel safe in." (*My Life After Dying*, p. 23.) Interestingly, Elder Orson Pratt, an Apostle and one of the Church's great theologians and thinkers, referred to this situation with reference to the preaching of the gospel to those in spiritual darkness.

> Suppose you were a righteous spirit, and you . . . were sent out, on a mission to the abodes of darkness, or to those who are not as righteous as yourselves; though you might have peace of conscience and happiness dwelling within your own bosoms in reflecting upon your past conduct, yet the society with which you are compelled to mingle for a short period, in order to impart knowledge and wisdom and such information as is calculated to benefit them, is, in a measure, disagreeable; you are compelled, for a season, to mingle with those who are inferior to yourself in their capacities. When you go and associate with them there is something disagreeable in the nature of this association; you feel to pity them in their ignorance, in their condition and circumstances; their conversation is not agreeable to you as that of your own associates in the presence of God. (In *Journal of Discourses*, 2:241.)

Even in this life, as Ritchie said, we often find ourselves in just such an uncomfortable situation, whether by choice or otherwise. However, in this earthly sphere, though the behavior may be abhorrent, we cannot see into the hearts of others. In the spirit world, though, the thoughts and intents of every being are discernible. The differences between righteousness and unrighteousness will be readily apparent to all. Though they must be filled with the pure love of Christ, it may be even more unpleasant for the pure in heart to associate with those of an evil disposition in the next life when such may no longer disguise their diabolical deeds and desires. The wicked may further shrink from the agonizing light of the righteous when their dark and sinister natures can no longer be hidden behind the "coarser organization" of the mortal flesh. Swedenborg claimed that such differences can even separate families. "I have seen a father talking with his six children and recognizing them, and many others talking with their relatives and friends. But since they were of different dispositions because of their lives in the world, it was not long before they were separated." (*Heaven and Hell*, p. 334.) Hopefully, the great work of the spirit realm will be to tie families and friends together again through the leavening and unifying influence of the eternal gospel and its ordinances.

Celestial, Terrestrial, and Telestial Spirit Beings

From modern scripture, we know that there are at least three main kingdoms in the post-final-judgment heaven (telestial, terrestrial, celestial—see D&C 76). If spirits in the next life tend to congregate with those like themselves, it would be reasonable to believe that, to some extent, these general distinctions manifest themselves in the spirit world as well. Even here in mortality we demonstrate our affinity for certain conditions and associations. "We shall enter into the other sphere of existence with the same spirit that we have here," warned President George Q. Cannon. "If we were animated by the spirit of the Telestial Kingdom we shall have that, if by the spirit of the Terrestrial Kingdom we shall have that, if by the spirit of the Celestial Kingdom we shall have that. We shall go from this condition of existence into the other sphere with the same feelings, to some extent at least, as we have here. If we have had knowledge, we shall have it there." (*Gospel Truth*, p. 60.)

If we can accept the testimonies of Ritchie and Swedenborg, we have a further witness that such general divisions exist. Ritchie attempted to name the two heavenly realms he visited. For the lower of the two, where spirits loved knowledge and their fellowmen, he tentatively suggested several names: "Realm of Knowledge, Paradise?, Terrestrial?" (*My Life After Dying*, p. 25.) The qualities Ritchie attributes to the beings of this realm could be reflective of one of the qualifications listed in Doctrine and Covenants section 76 for those of the terrestrial world—"honorable men of the earth" (v. 75). For the highest kingdom, where light-filled spirits radiated an intense love he thought of as that which Paul describes in 1 Corinthians 13 (which we would call charity, or the pure love of Christ), he suggested "The Celestial Realm, or Heaven" (*My Life After Dying*, p. 28). These beings, it seems, could be representative of the descriptions of the celestial beings revealed in section 76 as "the church of the Firstborn," and those "who have received of his fulness, and of his glory" (vv. 54, 56). On the other hand, Swedenborg confidently made these distinctions: "There are three heavens quite distinct from each other—an inmost or third heaven, an intermediate or second, and an outmost or first" (*Heaven and Hell*, p. 43).

Moreover, these men declare that (as with the celestial, terrestrial, and telestial kingdoms in Latter-day Saint doctrine) the righteous are in the highest realm. Ritchie's descriptions of the inhabitants of these heavenly kingdoms have been quoted and examined in previous chapters. However, the words of Emanuel Swedenborg are also fascinating to study and ponder. Noting that "the angels in the Lord's celestial kingdom are vastly superior in wisdom and glory to the angels in the spiritual [middle] kingdom" (*Heaven and Hell*, p. 41), he delineated the differences in these various kingdoms as he understood them. While his concept of the lowest heaven does not generally accord with ours, it is important to know that Swedenborg rarely even mentioned or described this realm. His distinctive depictions of the inhabitants of the two higher realms are interesting and insightful and may prompt helpful introspection.

It is worth realizing fully that the more inward elements of angels determine which heaven they will be in.
As more inward elements are more open to the Lord, they
are in a more inward heaven. There are three levels of the
more inward elements of everyone, angel, spirit, or man.
People whose third level has been opened are in the inmost heaven; people whose second, or just whose first has
been opened, are in the intermediate heaven or the outmost one.

These more inward elements get opened by the acceptance of what is Divinely good and Divinely true. People
who are moved by Divine truths and let them right into life
(that is, into intention and action) are in the inmost or third
heaven, located there according to their acceptance of the
good as a result of their affection for the true. Others, who
do not let these truths right into life, let them instead into
their memory and consequent understanding, and from
there intend and do them. They are in the intermediate or
second heaven. Then there are people who live upright
lives and believe in a Divine Being, but do not much care
about learning. They are in the outmost or first heaven. (In
Heaven and Hell, pp. 44–45.)

The Divine which flows in from the Lord and is accepted in the third or inmost heaven is called celestial, so
the angels there are called celestial angels. The Divine
which flows in from the Lord and is accepted in the second
or intermediate heaven is called spiritual, so the angels
there are called spiritual angels.

But the Divine which flows in from the Lord and is accepted in the outmost or first heaven is called natural. (Pp.
43–44.)

Angelic perfection lies in intelligence, wisdom, love—in
everything good and every resultant happiness. . . . For angels of the inmost heaven . . . their perfection vastly exceeds
the perfection of angels in the intermediate heaven, whose
more inward elements are opened on the second level. The
perfection of angels of the intermediate heaven exceeds the

perfection of angels in the outmost heaven to a similar degree. (P. 45.)

Since this distinction exists between angels of the celestial kingdom and angels of the spiritual kingdom, they do not live together or socialize with each other. . . . The Lord always furnishes intermediate angels . . . as agents of communication and connection. (P. 42.)

In addition, Swedenborg provided further credence for the principle of perfect order and associations based on righteousness. He declared that even within the "communities" in these segregated "kingdoms," people are divided by gradations of worthiness. "Within a given community, all the individuals are distinguished from each other in a similar way. The more perfect ones are in the central region—that is, those who are outstanding in goodness and thus in love, wisdom, and discernment. The less outstanding ones are around the outside, at distances proportional to lessening levels of perfection. It is arranged the way light decreases from a center toward the periphery. The people at the center are in the greatest light, those toward the fringes progressively in less." (Pp. 50–51.)

Remarkably in accord with Latter-day Saint revelations which teach that only those in the highest realm of the celestial kingdom will enjoy continued family life, Swedenborg also testified that only the "best of angels" live in families. While we cannot be sure that this represents the same familial state that one may enjoy in the celestial kingdom, it is an extraordinary parallel. "There are also some people who live apart, home by home, so to speak, and family by family. Spread out as they are, they are still arranged like the people in communities. That is, the wisest of them are in the center, and the simpler toward the borders. These people are more closely under the Lord's Divine guidance, and are the best of angels." (*Heaven and Hell*, p. 54.)

It is rare that we find among Christian faiths a belief in more than one level of reward in "heaven," and this makes Swedenborg's teachings all the more bold and unusual, even though in his epistles the Apostle Paul alludes to the "third heaven" (2 Corinthians 12:2) and "celestial bodies" and "bodies terrestrial" (1 Corinthians 15:40–41). While he may have been limited in what he was allowed to witness and understand, Swedenborg was undoubtedly sincere in what he reported and was unafraid to report conditions which ran counter to the popular beliefs of his day. While his accounts are not offered here (nor needed) to validate the doctrines of The Church of Jesus Christ of Latter-day Saints, they often provide supporting evidence from an unexpected and unbiased source.

"Clans and Societies"

As further evidence that there are many different realms and areas of association and affinity in the spirit world, President Brigham Young taught, "If they associate together [in the spirit world], and collect together in clans and in societies as they do here, it is their privilege" (in *Journal of Discourses* 2:137). There seems to be some evidence from near-death experiences that this may indeed be the case. We have already established the principle that spirits there are taught the gospel by those who are most like themselves and best able to understand and communicate with them. In addition, it seems that many newly arrived spirits are greeted and welcomed by former friends and family members. Finally, there are some fascinating studies of near-death experiences in several countries which may also add credence to the idea of differing cultural realms in the next life, though these reports are limited at present.

One of the great riddles for both Latter-day Saints and other Christians is the fact that NDErs of non-Christian religions almost invariably have experiences which coincide with and reinforce their own religious beliefs. The premier study on cross-cultural NDEs found that "on the whole, Christians tended to . . . [see what they believe to be] angels, Jesus, or the Virgin Mary, whereas Hindus would most usually see Yama (the god of death), one of his messengers, Krishna, or some other deity" (*At the Hour of Death*, p. 66). While such religious figures rarely do anything to correct or discourage these perceptions, it is vitally important to note that they also do not necessarily identify *themselves* as any of these beings. "Let us be aware that such apparitions do not wear name tags or speak their names. It is the patient who announces the apparition's name and title." (*At the Hour of Death*, p. 154.)

Many other aspects of these experiences also seem to vary, not only according to religion but also—seemingly an even stronger influence—according to culture and nationality. In his encounter with death, a man from Papua, New Guinea, followed a path to a village where he climbed a ladder up to a house which seemed to be on posts, but which he later recognized was suspended in the air and turning as if on an axle. He was not allowed to enter the house because, he was told, "It isn't time for you to come" (*The Return from Silence*, pp. 148–49). A college-educated woman from India who had suffered an allergic reaction to penicillin felt that she was brought to heaven on a cow and saw that the way there was beautifully decorated; a college-educated American woman, by contrast, experienced her journey to a world of "beautiful, endless gardens" as taking place in a taxi cab (see *At the Hour of Death*, pp. 155, 165).

A sixty-year-old African truck driver who was attacked and nearly killed by a lioness saw an endless, star-lined highway to the sky open up before him. An African grandmother felt she was put into a big calabash (hollow shell of a gourd). Notably, a couple of African subjects seemed to have contacted realms which did not immediately reflect their own culture. "I went to a place where I found a lot of people dressed in white robes— children and adults," explained a thirty-five-year-old clerk. "I couldn't make out their races." A sixty-year-old charcoal burner also couldn't find anyone familiar at first. "During this time of collapse, I had gone on a long journey. I heard people talking in different languages. I couldn't however make out what they were saying. Then someone spoke to me in my language—Bemba. He said, 'you have come a day earlier than we expected you. Please go back.' Later I recovered from my unconsciousness." (*Transformed by the Light*, pp. 121–23.) Additionally, according to studies, it seems that Japanese tend to see long dark rivers and beautiful flowers, and Micronesians see the next life as something "similar to a large, brightly lit American city with loud noisy cars and tall buildings" (*Transformed by the Light*, p. 127).

Many other interesting cultural differences are apparent in near-death experiences. While those of different religions identify "the being of light" and other religious figures according to their own beliefs, and those of different nationalities tend to experience the surroundings of the spirit world according to their cultural conditioning, there are yet other culturally inspired proclivities. In their previously noted cross-cultural study, Dr. Karlis Osis and Dr. Erlendur Haraldsson, noted psychologists and NDE researchers, compared the death-bed visions and NDEs of Americans, mostly Christian, and of Indians (people from India), both Christian and Hindu. They found that similarities ran more along lines of nationality than of religion. Indians, regardless of sect, tended to see religious figures serving as "guides" who had come to take them away more than they saw deceased friends or family members acting in that capacity. Americans were just the opposite. Osis and Haraldsson offer this explanation: "A positive bias in favor of religious figures might also be at work. Indians often seem to experience their deities in an intimate, personal way, and bring offerings of food and flower garlands to the statues of their gods. Americans, especially those of liberal Protestant denominations, often tend to interpret the divine as an abstract, spiritual force." (*At the Hour of Death*, p. 94.)

Another difference noted in the study was the gender and age of this "take away" figure. In India, where there are more inhibited sensitivities about the role of women in society, seeing a female messenger was infrequent. Only 23 percent reported such an experience, with 13 percent fewer Indian men than women seeing females. By contrast, in the American NDEs 61 percent of these guiding spirits were reportedly women. With respect to age, Osis and Haraldsson reached this conclusion.

When probing into another cultural force, we made a discovery. In India, there is a strong respect, even veneration, for elders to an extent that is unusual in the United States. Because of this, would more of the patients in India be received by these esteemed elders than in youth-loving America? Indeed, they would. In the United States, 41 percent of the peaceful take-away apparitions belonged to the previous generation, while this was true in India in 66 percent. Apparitions of members of the same generation as the patient comprised 44 percent of the cases in the United States and 29 percent in India, while the next-generation relatives appeared in 15 percent of the American cases and in only 5 percent of the Indian ones. Although in the United States 14 percent of the apparitions portrayed deceased sons or daughters, no such youngsters seemed to be entrusted with the take-away mission in India. (Pp. 94–95.)

There is one other very captivating aspect of these figures or messengers and the differences in how they perform their duties. The researchers observed that while "experiences of this sort [near-death experiences where the subject is sent back to earth] are remarkably similar in both cultures. . . . the manner in which the ostensible mission was performed showed cultural flavoring. The spirit guides of Americans were experienced as friendly and understanding of the patients' needs and unfinished tasks, as evidenced by one typical comment: 'You have work to do.' The manners of the Indian apparitions were sometimes more bureaucratic—the messenger of death (Yamdoot) might bring the patient before a desk where his record would be looked up by a man with a white beard (Karma?). It then turned out that the otherworldly messenger had brought up the wrong person." (P. 161.)

On the other hand, the study found this similarity. "Characteristically for India, an authoritarian manner is attributed only to the lower echelon of heavenly personnel, the messengers. The man with the 'book of accounts' is always pictured as a benign ruler. An aura of sacredness rests upon him regardless of whether he is called 'the man in a white robe' or 'God.' The same aura of sacredness appears in the visions of religious figures seen by patients in the United States." (P. 183.)

Undoubtedly, then, there could be as many different experiences as there are people and cultures, though the core elements remain the same. There are several possible reasons for this. Near-death researchers are virtually unanimous in believing that the experiences are definitely shaded by cultural interpretation. Scott Rogo reached this typical conclusion: "So it is beginning to look as if the NDE is some sort of archetypal experience which is perceived slightly differently from place to place, from culture to culture. . . . It also seems obvious that cultural factors influence the specific way the prototypical NDE is experienced." (*The Return from Silence*, p. 175.) He added this essential qualification: "Let me say, though, that I don't discount the possibility that some NDEs represent direct contacts with the Great Beyond. Cultural tradition may cloud the witness's perceptions, so that he or she 'sees' or interprets the observations in the form of familiar objects, settings, landscapes, and so forth." (P. 236.)

In other words, Rogo and other researchers believe that a person may actually *experience* an NDE in a way suited to his cultural and religious sensitivities or he may only *interpret* it that way. While perception is undoubtedly a major factor, it is not out of harmony with Latter-day Saint beliefs to accept that, to some extent, there actually is a continuation of cultures, customs, languages, and so forth in the spirit world. Therefore, an NDEr might actually be contacting the spirit realm where his predecessors have gathered together, possessing the same personalities and proclivities they enjoyed on earth, to perpetuate the positive aspects of their culture. "Almost everything that we see here is the same in the spirit world," advanced Elder Orson Pratt. "They are mixed up with every variety, and are as liable to be deluded [or ignorant of the gospel and therefore retaining previous belief systems] there as here." (In *Journal of Discourses*, 2:370.)

Moreover, we have already demonstrated the profound condescension of the Lord in teaching and leading his children along "according to their understanding" (2 Nephi 31:3). These glimpses of the spirit world which seem to reinforce cultural beliefs might suggest to Latter-day Saints that the Lord has respect for the cultural traditions of his children. Apparently he does not "shock" them with radical changes to their way of thinking, but starts with what they already understand—the truths that they have previously received through their cultural and religious traditions—and guides and persuades them "line upon line, precept upon precept, here a little and there a little" (2 Nephi 28:30). Swedenborg alluded to this when he explained the teaching process in "heaven." "Then behind these are people devoted to the Mohammedan religion who lived a moral life in the world, recognizing one Divine Being and recognizing the Lord as the Essential Prophet. Once they withdraw from Mohammed, because he cannot help them, they approach the Lord, worship Him, and recognize what is Divine about Him; then they are taught in the Christian religion. . . . Mohammedans and heathen, are taught on the basis of doctrines suited to their level of comprehension, . . . consistent with the good tenets of their religion, the tenets on which they had based their life in the world." (*Heaven and Hell*, pp. 421, 423.)

Despite the differences in perceptions and interpretations across cultures, the core elements of virtually all near-death experiences bespeak a universal, single spirit world. Osis and Haraldsson explain: "Allowing for cultural differences to exert some influence, we should expect Indians to see the beyond with somewhat different coloring from the way Americans see it. However, the basic characteristics of the world that they both see should be recognizable over and above the differences in the influences of the cultural milieu, just as we can recognize the same mountain whether it is painted by an American or an Indian artist." (*At the Hour of Death*, p. 61.)

This is, in fact, what virtually all near-death studies in recent years have found. Indeed, one of the reasons why NDE researchers have not been able to dismiss these experiences and similar spirit-world visions and visitations as hallucinations or some other psychological or paranormal phenomena is the consistency and similarity of thousands of these reports, even across cultural barriers. Summarizing the many common characteristics, Osis and Haraldsson wrote: "The only unity which transcends the bewildering variety of imagery is experiential rather than perceptual. Common to most is the experience of 'great beauty beyond reality,' joy, peace, and serenity. Most of the dying seem to experience something completely gratifying, a value fulfillment—they don't want to 'come back.' Sometimes these experiential qualities seem to irradiate the visitors with lightened brightness and intensified colors." (*At the Hour of Death*, p. 184; see also pp. 186–89.)

Thus, it seems to be much as it is with the spreading of the gospel here on earth: the eternal principles are the same for every person, but the practice and implementation of some Church programs and organizations may be adapted according to the needs, abilities, and cultures of those who receive it. The sacrament service is always the same, but the Sunday dress of those who administer it may vary widely. The baptismal prayer never varies, and complete immersion is always required, but the fonts and the Church buildings (or lack thereof) often differ. These principles are apparently still applicable in the spirit world to a great extent. The Lord mercifully allows for and perhaps even encourages the individuality and affinities of each of his children, while making the same eternal blessings available to all: despite the diversity in some aspects there is a common thread of unity and conformity in the ordinance. President Brigham Young spoke about this diversity, including cultural divergence.

> Let the people bring out their talents, and have the variety within them brought forth and made manifest so that we can behold it, like the variety in the works of nature. See the variety God has created—no two trees alike, no two leaves, no two spears of grass alike. The same variety that we see in all the works of God, that we see in the features, visages and forms, exists in the spirits of men. Now let us develop the variety within us, and show to the world that we have talent and taste, and prove to the heavens that our minds are set on beauty and true excellence, so that we can become worthy to enjoy the society of angels, and raise ourselves above the level of the wicked world and begin to increase in faith, and the power that God has given us, and so show to the world an example worthy of imitation. (In *Journal of Discourses*, 11:305.)

The most important distinctions and divisions, however, will be those established by our levels of righteousness or unrighteousness. These are the ones that will have the greatest impact upon our happiness, both in the intermediate spirit world and in the eternal realms of resurrected beings. Knowing that these conditions begin to take effect as soon as we enter the next life and that they will be a reflection and a perfect restoration of our desires and actions in mortality should encourage us to strive all the more diligently to be of a celestial nature while still on earth. As President Wilford Woodruff declared: "And that eternal variety of character which existed in the heavens among the spirits—from God upon his throne down to Lucifer the son of the morning—exists here upon the earth. That variety will remain upon the earth in the creations of God, and for what I know, throughout the endless ages of eternity. Men will occupy different glories and positions according to their lives—according to the law they keep in the flesh." (In *Journal of Discourses*, 25:9.)

CHAPTER 10

Hell

O ne cannot understand the spirit world and its relationship to the overall plan of salvation without also gaining an increased awareness and understanding of the doctrine of hell. "Latter-day scriptures describe at least three senses of hell: (1) that condition of misery which may attend a person in mortality due to disobedience to divine law; (2) the miserable, but temporary, state of disobedient spirits in the spirit world awaiting the resurrection; (3) the permanent habitation of the sons of perdition, who suffer the second spiritual death and remain in hell even after the resurrection" (M. Catherine Thomas, "Hell," in *Encyclopedia of Mormonism*, 2:585). Hell, therefore, can be both a place and a state of mind.

The focus of this chapter is on hell as a temporary abode of spirits in the spirit world. In the early stages of near-death studies, there were no reports of hellish or negative NDEs. Some researchers, and perhaps some experiencers, began to believe that hell was a myth—that the arms of death would extend the same forgiving welcome to all. Gradually, however, reports of frightening, dark, gruesome encounters began to come forth. Those involved in NDE studies posited that subjects who had negative experiences were probably less likely to report them because of the connotation of having such experiences. In his book *Beyond Death's Door*, Dr. Maurice Rawlings also advanced the theory that such terrifying encounters with hellish realms and beings might be more likely to be repressed or forgotten than positive experiences. He, himself, had resuscitated patients who described horrifying ordeals in the domains of evil, only to forget them completely when later questioned about them. Nonetheless, the most remarkable thing about negative NDEs is that they, too, tend to change for the better those who have them, even though the actual incident may be subsequently forgotten.

While these unpleasant accounts vary considerably in their details, like the positive episodes they have general traits in common. Scott Rogo summarized the "core" elements of negative or "hellish" NDEs.

Phase 1. The subject feels fear and feelings of panic instead of peace and joyfulness.

Phase 2. Just as with the more classic NDE, the subject experiences leaving the body.

Phase 3. Again similar to the classic NDE, the dying person enters into a dark region or void.

Phase 4. Instead of experiencing the presence of comforting religious figures, friendly deceased relatives, or a great white light, the subject is overwhelmed by a sense of foreboding and senses the presence of an evil force.

Phase 5. The subject finally enters a hellish environment, different from the beautiful and peaceful Elysium of the classic NDE. (*The Return from Silence*, pp. 140–41.)

As with heavenly near-death experiences, the subject may or may not go through all of these stages. Researcher Margot Grey differentiated between a negative NDE and a hell-like

NDE, which seems to be much more intense. She provides the following general description of these two different but related types of experiences.

> A negative experience is usually characterised by a feeling of extreme fear or panic. Other elements can include emotional and mental anguish, extending to states of the utmost desperation. People report being lost and helpless and there is often an intense feeling of loneliness during this period coupled with a great sense of desolation. The environment is described as being dark and gloomy, or it can be barren and hostile. People sometimes report finding themselves on the brink of a pit or at the edge of an abyss, and state that they needed to marshal all their inner resources to save themselves from plunging over the edge. Alternatively, some people felt that they were being tricked into death and needed to keep their wits about them to prevent this from happening.
>
> The hell-like experience is defined as being one which includes all the elements comprehended in the negative phase, only more so in that feelings are encountered with a far greater intensity. There is often a definite sense of being dragged down by some evil force, which is sometimes identified with the powers of darkness. At this stage, visions [of] wrathful [or] demonic creatures that threaten or taunt the individual are occasionally described, while others recount being attacked by unseen beings or figures which are often faceless or hooded. The atmosphere can either be intensely cold or unbearably hot. It is not uncommon during this phase of the experience to hear sounds that resemble the wailing of "souls" in torment, or alternatively to hear a fearsome noise like that of maddened wild beasts, snarling and crashing about. Occasionally, respondents will report a situation that resembles the archetypal hell in which the proverbial fire and an encounter with the devil himself are experienced. (*Return from Death*, p. 58.)

In describing his battle with the powers of hell as he endeavored to pray in the grove, the Prophet Joseph Smith employed some of the same terms and images alluded to in the earlier stages of the classic negative and/or hell-like near-death experiences. He recalled:

> I kneeled down and began to offer up the desires of my heart to God. I had scarcely done so, when immediately I was seized upon by some power which entirely overcame me, and had such an astonishing influence over me as to bind my tongue so that I could not speak. Thick darkness gathered around me, and it seemed to me for a time as if I were doomed to sudden destruction.
>
> But, exerting all my powers to call upon God to deliver me out of the power of this enemy which had seized upon me, and at the very moment when I was ready to sink into despair and abandon myself to destruction—not to an imaginary ruin, but to the power of some actual being from the unseen world, who had such marvelous power as I had never before felt in any being . . . I found myself delivered. (Joseph Smith—History 1:15–17.)

Other leaders from the early days of Church history have also chronicled their contests with the forces of Satan as they endeavored to spread the message of the new restoration. They likewise spoke in terms which echo Grey's references to attempted attacks by evil spirits and to the horrible and malicious appearance of such beings. Heber C. Kimball recalled an onslaught of demons which even caused him intense physical pain.

> While thus engaged, I was struck with great force by some invisible power, and fell senseless on the floor. The first thing I recollected was being supported by Elders Hyde and Richards, who were praying for me; . . . Elders Hyde and Richards then assisted me to get on the bed, but my agony was so great I could not endure it, and I arose, bowed my knees and prayed. I then arose and sat up on the bed, when a vision was opened to our minds, and we could distinctly see the evil spirits, who foamed and gnashed their teeth at us. We gazed at them about an hour and a half

(by Willard's watch). We were not looking towards the window, but towards the wall. Space appeared before us, and we saw the devils coming in legions, with their leaders, who came within a few feet of us. They came towards us like armies rushing to battle. They appeared to be men of full stature, possessing every form and feature of men in the flesh, who were angry and desperate; and I shall never forget the vindictive malignity depicted on their countenances as they looked me in the eye; and any attempt to paint the scene which then presented itself, or portray their malice and enmity, would be vain. . . . We distinctly heard those spirits talk and express their wrath and hellish designs against us. However, the Lord delivered us from them, and blessed us exceedingly that day. (Orson F. Whitney, *Life of Heber C. Kimball*, pp. 130–31.)

The scriptures, even in modern revelation, speak of the torment and bitterness of hell only in very general terms. Descriptive designations of hell from modern revelation are the most graphic in portraying what we do know of hell, and they definitely reflect some of the same conditions described by Margot Grey.

[Some] terms or phrases used in the Book of Mormon to refer to hell are "eternal gulf of misery and woe" (2 Nephi 1:13), "kingdom of the devil" (2 Nephi 2:29; 28:19; Alma 41:4), "spiritual death" (2 Nephi 9:12), "awful monster" (2 Nephi 9:10), "lake of fire and brimstone" (2 Nephi 9:19, 26; 28:23), "misery and endless torment" (Mosiah 3:25; Moroni 8:21), "awful chains" (2 Nephi 28:22), . . . "place of filthiness" (1 Nephi 15:34), "endless night of darkness" (Alma 41:7), "misery which never dies" (Mormon 8:38), and "dregs of a bitter cup" (Alma 40:26). ("The Concept of Hell," Larry E. Dahl, in *Doctrines of the Book of Mormon*, p. 44.)

With these descriptions in mind, to discover what constitutes hell we may examine the reports of near-death experiencers in light of scriptural teachings and the doctrines of the restored gospel.

A State of Mind

Despite the phrases "lake of fire and brimstone" and "everlasting fire," Latter-day Saint theology has never subscribed to the traditional Christian view of hell as a place where wicked people burn eternally in a fire which never actually consumes them. We tend to take such terminology as more figurative than literal, although we acknowledge there may indeed be some physical aspect of pain and suffering involved. "We might inquire, what is the cause of this intense suffering and misery?" queried Elder Orson Pratt. "Is it the action of the elements upon the spirit? Is it the materials of nature, operating from without upon it, that causes this distress, this weeping, wailing, mourning, and lamentation?" He postulated, "It may be in some measure; it may help to produce the misery and the wretchedness; but there is something connected with the spirit itself that no doubt produces this weeping, wailing, and mourning. What is this something? It is memory, and remorse of conscience." (In *Journal of Discourses*, 2:239.)

In addition, Joseph Smith taught that at least one aspect of the suffering in that realm would come from a tormented state of mind. "The great misery of departed spirits in the world of spirits, where they go after death, is to know that they come short of the glory that others enjoy and that they might have enjoyed themselves" (*Teachings*, pp. 310–11). In his classic doctrinal discourse known in the Church as the King Follett sermon, which was delivered in Nauvoo shortly before his martyrdom, the Prophet further revealed that "a man is his own tormentor and his own condemner. Hence the saying, They shall go into the lake that burns with fire and brimstone. The torment of disappointment in the mind of man is as exquisite as a lake burning with fire and brimstone." (*History of the Church*, 6:314.) Finally, the ancient Book of Mormon prophet Alma spoke of the spirit world hell in terms of the "state of the soul" being in "misery" (Alma 40:21) and "a state of awful, fearful looking for the fiery indignation of the wrath of God upon them" (Alma 40:14).

Emanuel Swedenborg also attempted to convey a picture of hell which was at variance with the traditions of his Christian contemporaries. "To date, hardly anyone knows what the eternal fire and gnashing of teeth are which the Word attributes to people in hell. This is because people have thought about the Word's contents in material terms, unaware of its spiritual meaning. . . . For every word, and every meaning of words in the Word has a spiritual meaning within it because the Word is spiritual at heart. What is spiritual can be conveyed to man only in natural terms because man is involved in a natural world and does his thinking in terms of the things that exist in it." (*Heaven and Hell*, p. 471.)

Swedenborg went on to give a rather complicated explanation of the meaning of these two terms, giving them a very specific spiritual meaning which we Latter-day Saints, while not necessarily disagreeing, would probably not attempt to define with such precision. Nevertheless, his definition reflects the concept that the torment of hell is partially a state of mind. "Because 'hellish fire' means every craving to do what is evil that wells up from self-love, this same fire also means the kind of torment that exists in the hells. For the craving that arises from that love is a craving to injure other people who do not respect or do homage or offer worship." (*Heaven and Hell*, p. 477.)

Conditions

It is worthwhile to note, then, as Dr. Grey reported, that relatively few people who have negative near-death experiences actually experience the traditional perception of hell. However, the depictions of the hellish conditions apprehended during NDEs are equally as horrifying, grim, and literal. It is logical, therefore, to believe that the same principle of individuation which operates in the paradisiacal realms is also in effect in the realms of hell. Just as there are infinite levels of righteousness, there are innumerable grades of wickedness. It may be that the descriptions of hell found in holy writ apply generally to the overall conditions of that world, with each of its condemned inhabitants perfectly restored (see Alma 41:5) to those personalized conditions which he or she fostered during mortality and which are most communicative, instructive, and/or punitive to the individual; in other words, they reap exactly what they have sown in terms of conditions, companions, and kingdoms, just as those in the higher regions have done. "And if their works are evil they shall be restored unto them for evil," declared the prophet Alma. Although he may have been speaking specifically of the resurrection, the concept of restoration surely must apply also to the different rewards and varying levels of happiness that one may experience in the world of spirits.

> Therefore, all things shall be restored to their proper order, everything to its natural frame—mortality raised to immortality, corruption to incorruption—raised to endless happiness to inherit the kingdom of God, or to endless misery to inherit the kingdom of the devil, the one on one hand, the other on the other—
>
> The one raised to happiness according to his desires of happiness, or good according to his desires of good; and the other to evil according to his desires of evil; for as he has desired to do evil all the day long even so shall he have his reward of evil when the night cometh (Alma 41:4–5; see also Alma 40:13–14).

As previously mentioned, Swedenborg declared that neither heaven nor hell is exactly alike for any two people. We also know from the vision of the glories of heaven given to the Prophet Joseph Smith that "as one star differs from another star in glory, even so differs one from another in glory in the telestial world" (D&C 76:98). Furthermore, the Prophet often refuted the sectarian belief that there is "one universal heaven and hell, where all go, and are all alike and equally miserable or equally happy" (*Teachings*, p. 311). There *is* variation in hell. President Spencer W. Kimball offered the following illustration of this principle: "They will not be put into two categories but in as many as there are individuals who have different degrees of accomplishment and performance, and this is just. Think for one moment how unjust it would be to put all law-breakers—the murderer, adulterer, thief, and car-parking violator—in the same penitentiary with the same punishments, deprivations, and the same period to serve." (*The Teachings of Spencer W. Kimball*, p. 47.)

Perhaps, as with positive NDEs, this would account for the many divergent descriptions of hellish encounters which nevertheless have the same underlying patterns. Logically, we could expect to hear reports of conditions which are exactly the opposite of those found in the heavenly areas of the spirit world. Indeed, Emanuel Swedenborg believed there were two areas of hell which are the precise counterparts of the two highest realms of heaven. "All the people who live in the celestial kingdom are involved in a love for the Lord," he wrote, "and all the people in the opposite kingdom in the hells are involved in self-love. All the people who are in the spiritual kingdom are involved in a love toward the neighbor, while all the people in the opposite kingdom in the hells are involved in a love of the world." (*Heaven and Hell*, p. 500.)

The warmth and light of the higher realms described in more pleasant NDEs would be replaced in hell with darkness and a discomfiting spiritual, emotional, and physical coldness. Instead of love, hatred rules; instead of peace, fear. We have already established that the absence of love is part of what constitutes the misery of those in hell (see chapter 6). Indeed, some researchers have also concluded that living without God's love would be a kind of hell. "Once you experience what I call the Awesome Presence, its absence becomes even more deadly. When I read [one researcher's] account, I thought immediately of a traditional Christian teaching about hell: that it is the total absence of God and of God's love. What could burn one up more than that, to get a glimpse of the Ultimate Goodness and Love of the Universe, and then, to know that you would be utterly separated from Him?" (John M. McDonagh, Ph.D., "Book Review," in *Journal of Near-Death Studies*, vol. 8, no. 1, Fall 1989.)

Further, while perfect love casts fear out (1 John 4:18), the total lack of the Lord's love makes hell the epitome of fear. Moses experienced a gripping fear and the accompanying bitterness of hell which almost overcame him (see Moses 1:20). The transcendent beauty, heavenly fragrances, and pleasing sounds of the more spiritual realms are replaced by filth, ugliness, unpleasant odors, and disconcerting noises in hellish realms devoid of the Spirit and love of God. Interestingly, Elder Parley P. Pratt explained that spirits from hell, when possessing a human body "will cause a disagreeable smell about the person thus possessed which will be plainly manifest to the senses of those about him, even though the person thus afflicted should be washed and change his clothes every few minutes" (*Key to the Science of Theology*, pp. 72–73). And President Brigham Young declared that "there is no music in hell, for all good music belongs to heaven" (*Discourses of Brigham Young*, p. 242). (Since Brother Brigham's day we have seen the emergence of the kind of evil, discordant music that may actually reflect the true spirit of hell.) As illustrated, these and other equally negative and unpleasant conditions are, in fact, the very types of things that are being reported to NDE researchers.

Companions

As with the higher spirit realms, the people in the hellish areas are drawn to others like themselves. Association with those who hate them as much as they hate others and who desire to perpetrate the same evils makes them feel "at home" and yet compounds their misery and creates some measure of their punishment. "There is something that is calculated to render their society disagreeable to themselves, which increases as the degradation of the society is increased," elucidated Elder Orson Pratt. "Then a wicked man entering into the company of such beings has not only a hell within himself—a conscience gnawing like a worm—but he sees misery and wretchedness; and they cleave one to another in their wickedness, and in their conversation, and acts, and doings, and intercourse with each other; all these things are calculated in their nature to produce misery and wretchedness, as well as their own consciences." (In *Journal of Discourses*, 2:241.)

Dr. George Ritchie's description of this wretchedness reflects this idea. "Perhaps this was the explanation for this hideous plain. Perhaps in the course of eons or of seconds, each creature here had sought out the company of others as pride-and-hate-filled as himself, until together they formed this society of the damned." (*Return from Tomorrow*, p. 66.) According to Emanuel Swedenborg, evil people are so drawn to hell and to others like themselves that the Lord does not have to force them there—they put themselves there. "They do enter of their own free will; and the ones who enter because of a burning love of what is evil look as though they were being thrown straight in, head first and feet up. It is because of this appearance that they seem to be cast down into hell by Divine power. So now we can see from this that the Lord does not cast anyone into hell; each individual casts himself in, not only while he is living in the world, but after death, when he arrives among the spirits." (*Heaven and Hell*, p. 455.)

While the Lord himself says that he has the power to cast the wicked down to hell (see D&C 63:4), it may be that he does not have to personally impose such punishment upon the wicked. It may instead take place as the result of his perfect utilization of eternal laws. Perhaps it is more the law and its natural consequences that effects the punishment of hell. "But there is a law given, and a punishment affixed, and a repentance granted; which repentance, mercy claimeth; otherwise, justice claimeth the creature and executeth the law, and *the law inflicteth the punishment*; if not so, the works of justice would be destroyed, and God would cease to be God" (Alma 42:22, italics added). Or, as Swedenborg declared, "For an evil thing and its punishment are so closely joined that they cannot be separated. . . ." He went on to elaborate. "We may conclude from these considerations that the Lord does not do evil to anyone. This is much the way it is in the world, since neither the ruler nor the law is responsible for the punishment of the criminal because they are not responsible for the evil element within the evildoer." (*Heaven and Hell*, p. 456.) President George Q. Cannon confirmed: "Therefore, when men lift up their eyes in torment, the misery of their torment will be increased by the knowledge that they themselves through their own action and through the exercise of their own agency have brought upon them this condemnation and not because any human being forced them there, for there is no such thing possible" (*Gospel Truth*, p. 110).

Furthermore, it seems that an assignment in hell with others like themselves may actually be an act of mercy toward the wicked. As we have previously noted, Moroni warned the rebellious that they would be miserable in the presence of a holy and just God. "For behold, when ye shall be brought to see your nakedness before God, and also the glory of God, and the holiness of Jesus Christ, it will kindle a flame of unquenchable fire upon you" (Mormon 9:5). The prophet Alma confirmed that as he endured the pains of hell which the memory of his sins induced, "The very thought of coming into the presence of my God did rack my soul with inexpressible horror!" (Alma 36:14. For a further discussion of the nature of suffering in hell, see *Life Everlasting*, pp. 170–74.)

Thus, as with the conditions in hell, so with the companions of that diabolical place—they are the inverse of the beautiful, helpful, solicitous spirits of the realms of light. Elder Heber C. Kimball stated that he could not begin to paint a picture of the heinous appearance of those evil spirits who confronted him and his companions. If the righteous are beautiful in accordance with their level of goodness and perfection, it stands to reason that those who are void of righteousness are also lacking in beauty and that the more they delight in evil the more hideous they would tend to be. Swedenborg propounded this principle. "Angels of the inner heavens . . . are in the loveliest and most perfect human form. Angels of lower heavens are less perfect and lovely in form. It is the other way around in hell. People there, in heaven's light, hardly look like people at all, but rather like monsters. . . . As a result, their life is not even called 'life,' but 'spiritual death.'" (*Heaven and Hell*, p. 76; see also 2 Nephi 9:12.) He further indicated that the beings in hell look and sound grotesque and inhuman to the spirits of the higher realms who see in "heaven's light."

When the spirits in the hells are examined in any of heaven's light, they appear in forms appropriate to their evil qualities. Each one is in fact a model of his evil quality because for each one the more inward and the more outward elements act in unison, with the more inward ones displaying themselves in the more outward ones, which are the face, the body, speech, and behavior. So it is possible to recognize the spirits' quality by looking them over carefully. . . .

In general, their faces are frightful, lifeless as corpses. Some are black, some like fiery little torches, some swollen by pimples, distorted veins, and sores. Many have no visible face, but only something hairy or bony instead; with some, only the teeth stand out. Their bodies are grotesque, and their speech apparently arises from anger or hatred or revenge because each one talks out of his own false nature and has a voice quality that stems from his evil nature. In short, all of them are reflections of their own hells. . . .

. . . For in heaven's light, everything looks the way it really is. (*Heaven and Hell*, pp. 459–61.)

Although such an idea is not to be viewed as official LDS doctrine, it is fascinating to consider that such manifestations may be the way in which Swedenborg and other NDErs who have described similar visages were allowed to perceive and understand the wicked, malicious, and bestial nature of the inhabitants of hell—those most rebellious and disobedient of the spirits of mankind. George Ritchie did not see hellish beings as being physically distorted or as "monsters." However, he did bring back a report of their sickening behavior.

Now, however, although we were apparently still somewhere on the surface of the earth, I could see no living man or woman. The plain was crowded, even jammed with hordes of ghostly discarnate beings; . . . they were the most frustrated, the angriest, the most completely miserable beings I had ever laid eyes on. . . .

At first I thought we were looking at some great battlefield: everywhere people were locked in what looked like fights to the death, writhing, punching, gouging. . . . No weapons of any sort, . . . only bare hands and feet and teeth. And then I noticed that no one was apparently being injured. . . .

They could not kill, though they clearly wanted to, because their intended victims were already dead, and so they hurled themselves at each other in a frenzy of impotent rage.

. . . These creatures seemed locked into habits of mind and emotion, into hatred, lust, destructive thought-patterns.

. . . Whatever anyone thought, however fleetingly or unwillingly, was instantly apparent to all around him, more completely than words could have expressed it, faster than sound waves could have carried it.

And the thoughts most frequently communicated had to do with the superior knowledge, or abilities, or background of the thinker. "I told you so!" "I always knew!" "Didn't I warn you!". . . (*Return from Tomorrow*, pp. 63–64.)

This is remarkably reflective of the "malignant" behavior described by Heber C. Kimball and others who have encountered the spirits from hell, who hate righteousness. One man who had an NDE called the countless people he saw "downstairs" in hell "miserable and hateful" and he was told he wasn't wanted there and had to leave because he wasn't "mean enough" (as quoted in *The Light Beyond*, pp. 26–27). Likewise, Swedenborg testified that "an absolutely incredible malice displays itself. There are thousands of things that erupt from this malice, among them some things such that they are beyond description in the vocabulary of any language. . . . I can bear solemn witness to the fact that they have so many forms of malice that scarcely one in a thousand can be described." (*Heaven and Hell*, p. 482.) Thus there are many witnesses of the horrific reality of hell and the evil designs of some of its inhabitants.

Kingdoms and Powers

While hell is a realm for unrepentant sinners, it is still a part of the spirit world and subject to the universal power and influence of the Lord. Though the inhabitants there may refuse to submit to his will, they cannot escape from his power or go beyond the bounds he has set. "If the wicked wish to escape from His presence," taught President Brigham Young, "they must go where He is not, where He does not live, where His influence does not preside. To find such a place is impossible, except they go beyond the bounds of time and space." (In *Journal of Discourses*, 2:94.) On the other hand, President Young explained that they will not enjoy any of the benefits of his presence. "Any person knowing and understanding the Scriptures as they are, and understanding the mind and will of God, can understand at once that when he is shut out from the presence of the Lord, when he does not hear His voice, sees not His face, receives not the ministering of His angels or ministering spirits, and has no messenger from the heavens to visit him, he must surely be in hell" (in *Journal of Discourses*, 2:137). George Ritchie said he saw angels hovering over those wicked creatures he observed. "All I clearly saw was that not one of these bickering beings on the plain had been abandoned. They were being attended, watched over, ministered to. And the equally observable fact was that not one of them knew it." (*Return from Tomorrow*, p. 66.)

Swedenborg declared that the Lord governs hell in order to keep all things in balance, ". . . the uprisings in the hells are mitigated as much as they can be, and the cruelties are confined so that they do not burst out against each other beyond the proper bounds. This is done by countless methods that belong to Divine power." (*Heaven and Hell*, p. 500.) Nonetheless, the inhabitants there cannot partake of the blessings of his presence because "evil things and consequent false things are in the way, not only dulling but even rejecting His Divine inflow" (*Heaven and Hell*, p. 455).

Moreover, the inhabitants of hell are not only restricted by the Lord in their bounds and their powers, but they are subject to the devil as well. One little boy, who reported to have met the devil during his NDE, was wise enough to discern the trickery of Satan in this matter.

> "On the way back, I saw the devil. He said if I did what he wanted, I could have anything I want."
>
> I [his mother] said, "You know God is good and the devil is evil."
>
> He said, "The devil said I could have anything I wanted, but I didn't want him bossing me around." (*The Return from Silence*, pp. 111–12.)

Thus the kingdom of Satan's followers is limited and confining, and their freedom from evil is forfeited. They are vassals of the devil until they repent or are released from their bondage at the end of the Millennium (except sons of perdition). He utilizes their hateful natures in an effort to accomplish his evil purposes in the world.

Furthermore, such are slaves to the evil passions, cravings, and desires they fostered in mortality. As mentioned, George Ritchie reports of witnessing a situation wherein spirit beings were desperately bound to the earth, futilely trying to regain the things they set their hearts on in life. For instance, some strove endlessly to obtain the mortal substances like alcohol and cigarettes which had mastered them in the flesh. Other experiencers have reported sensing the presence of other beings in the tunnel or dark void through which they passed on their way to the light. They somehow comprehended that these individuals are "stuck" there or that they had no desire to move toward the light. One woman attempted to explain:

> It's a dusky, dark, dreary area, and you realize that the area is filled with a lot of lost souls, or beings, that could go the same way I'm going [to the Light] if they would just look up. The feeling I got was that they were all looking downward, and they were kind of shuffling, and there was a kind of moaning. There were hundreds of them, looking very dejected. The amount of confusion I felt coming off of it was tremendous. When I went through this, I felt there was a lot of pain, a lot of confusion, a lot of fear, all meshed into one. It was a very heavy feeling. They weren't turning toward the Light. In fact, they didn't even know the Light existed. (As quoted in *After the Beyond*, pp. 82–83.)

Perhaps some of these spirits could account for hauntings and seances and what Brigham Young termed "spirit-rapping, spirit-knocking, and so forth." He taught that these things are "produced by the spirits that the Lord has suffered to communicate to people on the earth, and make them believe in revelation." He added, "There are many who do not believe this; but I believe it, and have from the beginning." (In *Journal of Discourses*, 7:239.) Heber Q. Hale, the stake president from Boise who had a near-death experience, returned with a report on the activities of evil spirits which appears very much in harmony with the scriptures and teachings of the prophets. "The wicked and unrepentant spirits having still like all the rest, their free agency, and applying themselves to no useful or wholesome undertaking, seek pleasure about their old haunts and exult to the sin and wretchedness of degenerate humanity. To this extent, they are still the tools of Satan. It is these idle mischievous and deceptive spirits who appear as miserable counterfeits at the spiritualistic scenes, table dancing and ouija board operations. The noble and great do not respond to the call of the mediums and to every curious group of meddlesome inquirers." (Quoted in *Life Everlasting*, pp. 117–18.)

Additionally, Dr. Ritchie observed that some of the disembodied beings he saw were greedily waiting for a chance to enter the bodies of the evil and weakened human beings on earth who would do their bidding. (See *Return from Tomorrow*, pp. 60–61.) Leaders of the Church have often warned of the reality and influence of evil spirits and their heinous obsession with destroying both bodies and souls. Whether they be the premortal followers of Satan, who have never had a physical body of their own, or spirits of the wicked deceased, they are all in hell together and seek to thwart any and all works of righteousness. "You can see the acts of these evil spirits in every place," observed Brigham Young; "the whole country is full of them, the whole earth is alive with them, and they are continually trying to get into the tabernacles of the human family, and are always on hand to prompt us to depart from the strict line of our duty."

Interestingly, President Young went on to explain that such opposition is necessary, "Could we do without the devils? No, we could not get along without them. They are here, and they suggest this, that, and the other." (In *Journal of Discourses*, 3:369.) We have already established the certainty of guardian-type angels (see chapter 9), but a couple of those who have had otherworld experiences have spoken of the existence of both good and evil spirits who seek to influence humans. One of Swedenborg's most important themes is related to this and will sound very familiar to Latter-day Saints. "There are spirits from hell and angels from heaven with every single person," he wrote. "The person is involved in his evil aspect by means of the spirits from hell, and in his good aspect from the Lord by means of the angels from heaven. In this way, he is in a spiritual balance—that is, in a freedom." (*Heaven and Hell*, p. 503.) In other words, this is the Swedish philosopher and theologian's way of perceiving and saying, "For it must needs be, that there is an opposition in all things" (2 Nephi 2:11) in order for us to make our own choices. His explanation for this freedom also has a familiar ring. "This freedom is granted to every individual by the Lord, and is not in any manner taken away. It is something that by virtue of its origin belongs to the Lord and not to the individual, because it comes from the Lord. Yet it is given to the individual as a possession, along with his life, the purpose being his reformation and salvation. For without freedom, there can be no reformation or salvation." (P. 501.)

Swedenborg advances two other principles about these spirits which are in harmony with teachings of the restored gospel. First, "The spirits connected to a person are of the same quality as the person himself. . . . But the good spirits are put in connection with him by the Lord, while the evil ones are invited by the person himself." (P. 217.) Also that "evil spirits . . . have no greater desire than to destroy someone—not only as to his soul . . . but even as to his body" (p. 216).

Elder Parley P. Pratt likewise alluded to these precepts in his doctrinal treatise *Key to the Science of Theology*. "Those who are habitually given to vice, immorality and abomination; . . . who would sacrifice every finer feeling at the shrine of lawless pleasure and brutal desires—those persons will not understand and appreciate these views, because their good angels, their kindred spirits, have long since departed and ceased to attend them, being grieved and disgusted with their conduct" (p. 76). And, speaking of evil spirits, he further explained, "If permitted, they will often cause death. Some of these spirits are adulterous, and suggest to the mind all manner of lasciviousness, all kinds of evil thoughts and temptations." (P. 72.) The witness of one female experiencer sums it up well. "There was a war going on between good and evil. The evil face came into view from time to time, but the Being of Light was stronger." (As quoted in *Transformed by the Light*, p. 160.)

Who Has Negative or Hellish
Near-Death Experiences?

Does all this mean that those who have negative near-death experiences are evil people and are bound for hell? The research would suggest that this is not necessarily so. Undoubtedly some are wicked, though there is certainly no way to judge this by outward appearances alone. For instance, some might have supposed the member of the motorcycle gang whose NDE was discussed in the first chapter to be a likely candidate for such an experience, whereas actually his was a very loving, warm experience. Some regular church attenders, on the other hand, have suffered through frightening, hellish encounters. Yet with the exception of the confrontation with the devil quoted previously (and this little boy was not frightened by it) there seem to be no dark or hellish episodes in reported childhood NDEs.

One possibility may be that these are good and honorable people who were allowed to be witnesses of the reality of hell. The idea of hell is a very unpleasant one, implying greater individual accountability; and many in the world dismiss it quite casually, while others go to great lengths to refute its reality. Dr. Bruce Greyson, a respected psychiatrist and near-death researcher, "admitted that people like himself had not been asking the right questions to identify those who might have undergone 'dark' or distressing episodes. He confessed, 'We didn't try to find them because we didn't want to know.'" (Phyllis Atwater, "Is There a Hell? Surprising Observations About the Near-Death Experience," in *Journal of Near-Death Studies*, vol. 10, no. 3, Spring 1992, p. 150.) Yet now the evidence of a hellish existence in the afterlife is just as plausible and compelling as that of the heavenly reward. Many of those who have had this type of experience insist on how "real" it was to them, just as with those who have the good experiences. A man declared to an NDE researcher: "You've got to tell people about hell. There is one. I know. I've been there. . . . There's a hell, and people go there." (Phyllis Atwater, "Is There a Hell? Surprising Observations About the Near-Death Experience," in *Journal of Near-Death Studies*, vol. 10, no. 3, Spring 1992, p. 159.) One woman confessed: "I have never believed in hell, I feel God would never create such a place. But it was very hot down there and the vapour or steam was very hot. At the time I did not think very much about it, but in the intervening years I have realised both good and evil exist. The experience has transformed my life." (As quoted in *Return From Death*, p. 63.)

Indeed, another reason why some people undergo these unpleasant confrontations with a hellish domain of the spirit world may be that they provide the experiences and understanding most needed by such individuals, whether righteous or wicked. Moreover, perhaps it does not matter, for some, whether they have a positive or a negative encounter with the spirit world, but only that they are able to comprehend that life goes on after death. At any rate, most NDErs tend to change their lives for the better, regardless of the type of NDE. Nancy Evans Bush, a prominent NDE researcher, struggled with the meaning of her own frightening near-death experience. She reached some important conclusions.

> For starters, it is untrue that "bad" people have "bad" experiences; the saints of all traditions have reported experiences of terror and despair. Secondly, a terrifying experience has every bit as much potential for being transformative as an encounter with the Light, although the process and the paths will be quite different. Third, both the radiant and the dark experience contain seeds of temptation as well as transformation: the temptation for the classic NDE experiencer is to grandiosity, ego-inflation, the sense of self-admiration for being worthy of an exalting experience; the temptation of a terrifying experience is to despair. The danger of yielding to the temptation is that it short-circuits both the message and the journey. (In *Vital Signs*, vol. 1, no. 2, April–June 1992, p. 8.)

It is important here to make a further examination of Bush's third point. While most NDEs are positively transformed by their experiences, some NDEs are not so enthusiastically welcomed, including positive experiences. Researcher Phyllis Atwater recounted the following occurrence:

A man in the audience related his near-death story, one so
positive and so inspiring it brought tears to the eyes of most
of those attending. Yet, to everyone's surprise, he went on to
reveal how cursed he felt to have had such an experience and
how difficult his life had been ever since it had happened.
Then a woman jumped up and excitedly recounted her story.
Even though her scenario centered on a life-or-death struggle
in semi-darkness at the edge of a whirlpool, while high winds
and the presence of evil threatened, she was overjoyed to
have experienced anything so inspiring and so revealing
about how life really worked and how salvation is guaranteed by our willingness to correct our own mistakes. Here
were two people: one traumatized by a heaven-like experience, the other uplifted and transformed by a hellish one.

Atwater went on to determine that "it is almost as if the phenomenon is a particular kind of growth event that allows for a
'course correction,' enabling the individual involved to focus on
whatever is weak or missing in character development . . ." and
that the "value and meaning [of the experience] depend entirely
on each person involved and his or her response to what happened during the near-death experience and its aftereffects." ("Is
There a Hell? Surprising Observations About the Near-Death Experience," in *Journal of Near-Death Studies*, vol. 10, no. 3, Spring
1992, pp. 155, 157.) For these and other reasons we can never judge
a person's eternal possibilities by the type of near-death experience he or she has. A wicked person who has a loving, positive,
and uplifting NDE is no more guaranteed salvation by that experience than a righteous person is doomed to damnation because
he/she may glimpse the evil side of the spirit world. As with any
of life's events, what is important is how those experiences are understood and are utilized by the individuals concerned to progress
or regress—to live lives of love, compassion, and worthiness or to
be self-centered, hedonistic, and estranged from God.

Saved from Hell

In addition to these negative experiences, there are accounts
of those who undergo both a hellish and a heavenly NDE in the

same episode. This is because they are rescued or saved from hell after exerting some effort to call upon or exercise faith in Jesus Christ. Their experiences are stunningly parallel to that of Alma the Younger as recorded in the Book of Mormon. Remember that Alma had been seeking to destroy the Church among the Nephites when, because of the faith and prayers of his father, an angel appeared to him and those who were with him and commanded him to cease the trouble-making or he would be destroyed. Alma was completely overcome and could not speak or move. He later told his son what he endured.

> And now, for three days and for three nights was I racked, even with the pains of a damned soul.
> And it came to pass that as I was thus racked with torment, while I was harrowed up by the memory of my many sins, behold, I remembered also to have heard my father prophesy unto the people concerning the coming of one Jesus Christ, a Son of God, to atone for the sins of the world.
> Now, as my mind caught hold upon this thought, I cried within my heart: O Jesus, thou Son of God, have mercy on me, who am in the gall of bitterness, and am encircled about by the everlasting chains of death.
> And now, behold, when I thought this, I could remember my pains no more: yea, I was harrowed up by the memory of my sins no more.
> And oh, what joy, and what marvelous light I did behold; yea, my soul was filled with joy as exceeding as was my pain! (Alma 36:16–20.)

Alma experienced hell in terms of suffering because of his sins. Although NDErs define more in visual terms the hell they confront, note the parallels in the following reports of near-death experiences.

> I was standing some distance from this burning, turbulent, rolling mass of blue fire. As far as my eyes could see it was just the same. A lake of fire and brimstone. . . .
> The scene was so awesome that words simply fail. . . .

There is no way to escape, no way out. You don't even try to look for one. This is the prison out of which no one can escape except by Divine intervention. I said to myself in an audible voice, "If I had known about this I would have done anything that was required of me to escape coming to a place like this." But I had not known.

As these thoughts were racing through my mind, I saw another man coming by in front of us. I knew immediately who He was. He had a strong, kind, compassionate face, composed and unafraid, Master of all He saw. It was Jesus Himself.

A great hope took hold of me and I knew the answer to my problem was this great and wonderful Person who was moving by me in this prison of the lost, confused judgment-bound souls. I did not do anything to attract His attention. I said again to myself, "If He would only look my way and see me, He could rescue me from this place because He would know what to do." He passed on by and it seemed as though He would not look my way, but just before He passed out of sight He turned His head and looked directly at me. That is all it took. His look was enough.

In seconds I was back entering into my body again. (As quoted in Maurice Rawlings, *Beyond Death's Door*, pp. 87–88.)

In another fascinating and detailed NDE account, Howard Storm recounted his own battling with evil spirits whom he perceived were in hell. He finally got them to leave him alone by shouting "God bless America" and anything else he could remember that had a religious connotation, though he had not been a "religious" man.

I lay there for a long time. I was in such a state of hope-lessness, and blackness, and despair, that I have no way of measuring the time. I was just lying there in an unknown place—all torn and ripped. And I had no strength; it was all gone. I felt as if I were sort of fading out, that any effort on my part would expend the last energy I had. My conscious sense was that I was perishing, or just sinking into the darkness.

Then a most unusual thing happened. I heard, very clearly, once again in my own voice, something that I had learned in nursery Sunday School. It was the little song: "Jesus loves me, yes I know, . . ." and it kept repeating. I don't know why, but all of a sudden I wanted to believe that. I didn't have anything left, and I wanted to cling to that thought. And . . . I, inside, screamed: "Jesus, please save me." I screamed that with every ounce of strength and feeling left in me.

When I did that, I saw, off in the darkness somewhere, the tiniest little star. . . . Then I realized it was coming toward me. It was getting very bright, rapidly.

As it came up to me, and its radiance was all over me, I just rose up—not with my effort—I just lifted up. Then I saw . . . and I saw this very plainly, I saw all my wounds, all my torn spots, all my brokenness just melt away. And I became whole in this radiance. (As quoted in Arvin S. Gibson, *Glimpses of Eternity*, pp. 255–56.)

And finally, another (unnamed) person testified of the spiritual power of Christ and His righteousness in overcoming the terrifying powers of the evil one.

I was going through this long tunnel and I was wondering why my feet weren't touching the sides. I seemed to be floating and going very fast. It seemed to be underground. It may have been a cave, but the awfullest, eery sounds were going on. There was an odor of decay like a cancer patient would have. Everything now seemed to be in slow motion. I can't recall all of the things I saw, but some of the workers were only half human, mocking and talking to each other in a language I didn't understand. . . . But there was a large person in radiant white clothes that appeared when I called, "Jesus, save me!" He looked at me and I felt the message "live differently!" I don't remember leaving there or how I got back. There are a lot of other things that may have happened that I don't remember. Maybe I'm afraid to remember! (As quoted in Maurice Rawlings, *Beyond Death's Door*, pp. 90–91.)

While it is important to keep in mind that these beings perceived to be Christ may instead have been symbolic or representative beings, the most important lesson to be learned from these experiences has to do with the perfect mercy of the Savior and the literal fulfillment of his promises to save us from death and hell (see 2 Nephi 9:15–18). If we will even desire or begin to have faith in him (see Alma 32:27) and follow him, his redemptive powers can conquer the effects of evil in this life and break the bands of death and the chains of hell in the life to come. Again, his love is extended to all and he desires to save everyone who will let him. And, though it may seem to fall on deaf ears, we must continue to teach and testify of Christ and his salvation. His is the message that can and does save—both physically and spiritually.

PART IV

Experiences in the Spirit World

CHAPTER 11

The Life Review

Many of the abilities of the spirit body and conditions in the spirit world combine to precipitate or make possible the experiences one has there. For example, the presumably perfect memory of the spirit body and the timelessness of the spirit realm facilitate a singular experience which some NDErs enjoy—that of a life review. In this review the person sees, senses, and experiences all or parts of his or her mortal life again, sometimes down to the most minute detail, reliving it once again as if it were happening at that very moment. This life review experience may take place at various times in the near-death episode. Some aspects of it may even take place before a person dies, as he or she first approaches the "doors of death." The expression, "my life passed before me," may be quite literal in these cases.

This examination of the mortal existence may also seem to take place in different ways. Most describe it in terms of a "panoramic, wrap-around, full-color, three-dimensional vision" (Raymond Moody, *Reflections on Life After Life*, p. 31). By contrast, one woman perceived that scenes of her life were floating past her in bubbles, and another person saw everything about his life written in a book. A Vietnam veteran likened it to someone showing slides of his life, and still another individual perceived a life review only in thought form. The difference may be partly due to the manner in which it is perceived by the person experiencing it. Moreover, it may also be that these experiencers are describing a phenomenon of immortality in mortal terms, sometimes comparing it to movies or other modern technological inventions which may only be a metaphor or an approximation. In any case, it seems that those who have more extensive NDEs tend to experience the fuller and more formal review of their mortal lives, usually in the authoritative presence of a "being of light."

Out of Our Own Memories

In chapter 4 we discussed the capacity of the spirit body to remember absolutely every thought, word, and deed, and every detail, circumstance and occurrence of the individual's mortal life. Perhaps this is why the ancient American prophet Jacob could, with certainty, declare that in the next life "we shall have a perfect knowledge of all our guilt, and our uncleanness, and our nakedness; and the righteous shall have a perfect knowledge of their enjoyment, and their righteousness, being clothed with purity, yea, even with the robe of righteousness" (2 Nephi 9:14). Another Book of Mormon prophet, Alma, also testified that the wicked would have a "perfect remembrance" (Alma 5:18) and a "bright recollection" (Alma 11:43) of their iniquities. He further proclaimed that every aspect of our being—thoughts, words, and deeds—would be weighed in the balance of judgment (see Alma 12:14). While these passages may be referring to the final judgment, which will take place at the end of the resurrection, the principle of perfect recall is apparently also in effect to some degree in the world of spirits. President John Taylor declared:

The spirit lives where the record of his deeds is kept—that does not die—man cannot kill it; there is no decay associated with it, and it still retains in all its vividness the re-membrance of that which transpired before the separation by death of the body and the ever-living spirit. . . . It would be in vain for a man to say then, I did not do so-and-so; the command would be, Unravel and read the record which he has made of himself, and let it testify in relation to these things, and all could gaze upon it. . . . That record will stare him in the face, he tells the story himself, and bears witness against himself. . . . When we get into the eternal world, into the presence of God our Heavenly Father, his eye can penetrate every one of us, and our own record of our lives here shall develop all. (In *Journal of Discourses*, 11:78–79.)

There is a striking similarity between this doctrine ex-pounded by President Taylor and the Book of Mormon prophets and the following observation of Emanuel Sweden-borg. His vision of the spirit world provides us with an inter-esting glimpse of the judgment of deceased souls that confirms the doctrine taught by the prophets and helps illuminate the life review experiences of NDErs.

There were people who denied crimes and disgraceful things they had committed in the world. So lest people be-lieve them innocent, all things were uncovered and re-viewed out of their memory, in sequence, from their earliest age to the end. Foremost were matters of adultery and whoredom.

There were some people who had taken others in by evil devices and who had stolen. Their wiles and thefts were recounted one after another—many of them things hardly anyone in the world had known other than the thieves themselves. They admitted them, too (since they were made clear as daylight), together with every thought, intent, pleasure, and fear which had then combined to agi-tate their spirits.

There were people who took bribes and made a profit out of judicial decisions. These people were examined from their memory in similar fashion, and from this source everything they had done from the beginning to the end of their tenure of office was reviewed. There were details about how much and what kind, about the time, about the state of their mind and intent, all cast together in their remembrance, now brought out into sight, running past several hundred [people]. . . .

There was one person who thought nothing of disparaging others. I heard his disparaging remarks repeated in their sequence, his defamations as well, in the actual words—whom they were about, whom they were addressed to. All these elements were set forth and presented together in wholly life-like fashion; yet the details had been studiously covered up by him while he had lived in the world. . . .

In short, each evil spirit is shown clearly all his evil deeds, his crimes, thefts, deceits, and devices. These are brought out of his own memory and proven; there is no room left for denial, since all the attendant circumstances are visible at once. . . .

Let no one then believe that there is anything a person has thought within himself or done in secret that remains hidden after death. Let him rather believe that each and everything will then be visible as in broad daylight. (*Heaven and Hell*, pp. 361–64.)

These descriptions seem to correlate well with scriptural teachings prophesying that the Lord will "reveal the secret acts of men, and the thoughts and intents of their hearts" (D&C 88:109), and that "there is nothing which is secret save it shall be revealed; there is no work of darkness save it shall be made manifest in the light" (2 Nephi 30:17). Indeed, some experiencers have verified that their memories seemed to be replayed in "living color" before themselves and others, almost like a movie, perhaps more like a holograph, except that it seems to take place all at once or in a timeless state. For the most part, NDErs report that scenes from their lives appear chronologically, or simultaneously, or in some other meaningful order. At any rate, this all seems to happen almost instantaneously or in a very short time. "Yet, it was slow enough that I could take it all in," recalled one experiencer (as quoted in *Life After Life*, p. 68).

Observe Swedenborg's declaration that these "instant replays" were seen by "several hundred." He also added that these scenes were viewed as if they were presently happening. "I have even heard the things which a person thought during a month seen and reviewed by angels out of his memory, a day at a time without error—things recalled as though the person were engaged in them at the time they happened." (*Heaven and Hell*, pp. 362–63.) The latter-day Apostle, Elder Orson Pratt, confirmed that the recollections of past actions would be lifelike. "Things that may have been erased from your memory for years will be presented before you with all the vividness as if they had just taken place" (in *Journal of Discourses*, 2:239). Perhaps King Benjamin was by revelation made familiar with this spiritual process when he declared that the doers of evil would be "consigned to an awful *view* of their own guilt and abominations" (Mosiah 3:25, italics added). On the other hand, we may suppose that the righteous will be rewarded with a wonderful view of their faithfulness, obedience, and personal righteousness and that their secret prayers in behalf of others and their unheralded acts of goodness and compassion will be made known, to their credit and joy.

Like others, Dr. George Ritchie has provided a further witness of these elements of the life review process. "When I say He knew everything about me, this was simply an observable fact. For into that room along with His radiant presence—simultaneously, though in telling about it I have to describe them one by one—had also entered every single episode of my entire life. Everything that had ever happened to me was simply there, in full view, contemporary and current, all seemingly taking place at that moment." (*Return from Tomorrow*, pp. 49–50.)

And from another person: "It was like I knew everything that was stored in my brain. Everything I'd ever known from the beginning of my life I immediately knew about. And also what was kind of scary was that I knew everybody else in the room knew and there was no hiding anything—the good times, the bad times, everything. . . . I had total complete clear knowledge of everything that had ever happened in my life—even little minute things that I had forgotten. . . . Everything was so clear." (As quoted in *Heading Toward Omega*, pp. 68–69.)

Also consider this insightful observation by near-death researcher Raymond Moody about this process of having secret deeds and thoughts "exposed."

> In thinking about all this, it has occurred to me that a very common theme of near-death experiences is the feeling of being *exposed* in one way or another. From one point of view we human beings can be characterized as creatures who spend a great deal of our time hiding behind various masks. We seek inner security through money or power; we try to make ourselves feel that we are better than others by priding ourselves on our social class, the degree of our education, the color of our skin, our money, our power, the beauty of our bodies, . . . etc. We adorn our bodies with clothes; we hide our innermost thoughts and certain of our deeds from the knowledge or sight of others.
>
> However, in the moments around the time of death all such masks are necessarily dropped. Suddenly the person finds his every thought and deed portrayed in a three-dimensional, full-color panorama. If he meets other beings he reports that they know his every thought and vice versa. . . .
>
> This situation can be regarded as being most unpleasant indeed, and it is no wonder that quite frequently people may come back from this feeling that they need to make a change in their lives. (*Reflections on Life After Life*, pp. 33–35.)

Judged by Appearance

Besides having their lives displayed in these lifelike replays, spirits may be exposed in other ways. We have quoted many witnesses of the literal nature of the inspired saying, "For as he thinketh in his heart, so is he" (Proverbs 23:7). A person's spirit will be a continual and inescapable "exposé" of his or her inward life. Unlike the situation in mortality, we will be able to judge by appearances. Prophets of the restored gospel have taught that in the final judgment we will indeed be judged out of the "book of life" which comprises every cell of our being. Elder Bruce R. McConkie wrote:

The book of life is the record of the acts of men as such record is written in their own bodies. It is the record engraven on the very bones, sinews, and flesh of the mortal body, That is, every thought, word, and deed has an effect on the human body; all these leave their marks, marks which can be read by Him who is Eternal as easily as the words in a book can be read.

By obedience to telestial law men obtain telestial bodies; terrestrial law leads to terrestrial bodies; and conformity to celestial law—because this law includes the sanctifying power of the Holy Ghost—results in the creation of a body which is clean, pure, and spotless, a celestial body. . . . Men's bodies will show what law they have lived. (*Mormon Doctrine*, p. 97.)

How else would these impressions be made on the human body, but by the spirit, which is the living, acting, controlling agent. "The spirit that we have here," observed President George Q. Cannon, "will be the spirit that will animate us in the resurrection" (*Gospel Truth*, p. 13). Therefore, it is reasonable to believe, as we have already established, that the quality of a person's life is as visible in his or her spirit as it will be in the resurrected body. Emanuel Swedenborg described a judgment process which supposedly takes place as soon as a spirit enters the spirit world. It sounds very much like the final judgment described previously by Elder McConkie.

When a person's deeds are being laid bare to him after death, the angels who are given responsibility for examining him look carefully at his face. The examination then spreads through his whole body, beginning with the fingers of one hand, then the other, and continuing in this fashion through the whole.

Because I was puzzled as to the reason for this, it was unveiled, as follows. Just as the details of thought and intention are written on the brain because their origins are there, so they are written on the entire body as well, because all elements of thought and intention move out from their origins into the entire body, where they are bounded as being in their final forms. . . .

It is indeed the fact that everything—both deeds and thoughts—is written on the whole person, seeming to be read in a book when called from the memory, and to be seen in visual likeness when the spirit is examined in heaven's light. (*Heaven and Hell*, pp. 363–64.)

Perhaps this process and what NDErs have called the "life review" are part of what Latter-day Saints have always referred to as a partial or preliminary judgment which takes place at death. Elder McConkie taught that at the time of death, "the spirit undergoes a partial judgment and is assigned an inheritance in paradise or in hell to await the day of the first or second resurrection" (*Mormon Doctrine*, p. 402). It seems this is exactly what Swedenborg claimed to have witnessed, except that he thought these assignments to "heaven" or hell were final and that there would be no resurrection and subsequent judgment.

Not the Final Judgment

From revealed doctrine, we know that there is indeed a final judgment which will come after all people have been resurrected. "Every living soul shall then stand before God," writes Elder McConkie, "the books will be opened, and the dead will be judged out of those things written in the books, according to their works. (Revelation 20:11–15). 'And it shall come to pass,' Jacob said, 'that when all men shall have passed from this first death unto life, insomuch as they have become immortal, they must appear before the judgment-seat of the Holy One of Israel; and then cometh the judgment, and then must they be judged according to the holy judgment of God.' (2 Nephi 9:15–16.)" (*Mormon Doctrine*, p. 403.) Comparing the circumstances related by NDErs about this life review to the conditions set forth in this passage of scripture—resurrection and appearing before Christ to be judged of him—we can ascertain that it is in no way a "final" judgment. Dr. Raymond Moody similarly believes it neither represents the final reckoning, which is slated for the "end" of the world, nor implies that such will not come about. (See *Reflections on Life After Life*, pp. 36–37.)

The fact that this is not the final judgment may account for reports from NDErs that the "being of light" who seems to officiate at their life review does not pass judgment on them, even though some *perceive* this being to be Christ or some other holy person clothed with power and authority. The scriptures teach us that the final right to condemn or reward at the end of the resurrection lies only with Jesus Christ. "For the Father . . . hath committed all judgment unto the Son" (John 5:22). The Nephite prophet Mormon sent his people and us a message reminding them of this sobering truth. "And for this cause I write unto you, that ye may know that ye must all stand before the judg-ment-seat of Christ, yea, every soul who belongs to the whole human family of Adam; and ye must stand to be judged of your works, whether they be good or evil. . . . And I would that I could persuade all ye ends of the earth to repent and prepare to stand before the judgment-seat of Christ." (Mormon 3:20, 22.)

From these and other authoritative and inspired pronounce-ments from the scriptures we can be certain that this judgment is literal and not a mere figure of speech. Yet how merciful the Lord is in withholding judgment until we have had every rea-sonable chance to prepare ourselves. This is certainly a pattern for us to follow in dealing with our fellowmen.

Therefore it seems reasonable that, as reported, this helpful being would pass no judgment on the actions revealed in the life review. In negative NDEs, on the other hand, a person may encounter beings who are trying to pass judgment on and con-demn him, but such does not seem to be the role of the being of light. Rather, he seems to be a source of complete love and sup-port for the spirit who is reviewing his or her own life. This must never be construed to mean, however, that the "being of light" approves of or excuses any behavior, whether right or wrong; rather, he aids the person in fairly evaluating himself or herself. Most often this is done with some sort of question. "What have you done with your life?" or "What is in your heart?" or "What have you done to benefit mankind?" Latter-day Saints are well acquainted with the dream or near-death encounter of President George Albert Smith with his grand-father, George A. Smith the Apostle. Acting much like the

"being of light" as recounted in NDE experiences, his grand-
father inquired, "I would like to know what have you done
with my name." At that point, President Smith experienced a
simultaneous and panoramic life review and was able to report
to his honored progenitor that he had never done anything to
bring dishonor to his name.

A Perfect Restoration

At this point, the person experiencing the life evaluation
process is aided in making judgments on his or her own actions
because of the way in which this review is usually experienced.
As mentioned previously, most NDErs reexperience their lives
as if they were taking place at the moment. This vividness is
often so complete that they feel exactly the same feelings and
perceive the same sensations they enjoyed or suffered at the
time those first occurred. One account revealed that "it was not
my life that passed before me nor was it a three-dimensional
caricature of the events in my life. What occurred was every
emotion I have ever felt in my life, I felt. And my eyes were
showing me the basis of how that emotion affected my life."
(*Heading Toward Omega*, p. 71.) Barbara Harris, who recorded
her NDE in a book entitled *Full Circle*, offers this detailed delineation of her life review. It offers an unforgettable illustration of
perfect sensory recall.

> Barbara saw herself at the age of six, sitting in Miss Ham-
> den's second-grade class at MacDowell Elementary School.
> Miss Hamden was standing on a small chair, putting things
> on a bulletin board. Suddenly, and without warning, she fell,
> just as Barbara remembered her doing. Barbara had disliked
> Miss Hamden intensely, and hated being in her class. When
> Miss Hamden fell that day, Barbara had had to stifle her
> laughter, and that is what she saw herself doing now.
>   . . . Miss Hamden was on the floor writhing in pain. She
> screamed for someone to get help. Barbara looked around
> and saw that no one was moving. She raced out of the
> room, heading toward the principal's office, while her class-
> mates stood in the room looking on, horrified.

. . . Barbara could smell the pungent odor of that classroom. Miss Hamden never used deodorant, and her body odor filled the room with a musky smell. Floating high above this scene now, that same awful smell returned to her as strong as if she were again sitting in Miss Hamden's classroom.

As she watched herself run out into the hall, she immediately picked up the strong smell of the heavily waxed floors at the school. As she watched herself race down the metal-tipped stairs, she could clearly hear the pinging noise they always made when anyone went down them. Her senses were sharper than mere imagination, more distinct than memory. She was reliving these experiences. (*Full Circle*, p. 25.)

As can be seen from the foregoing, the life review seems to encompass much more than the mere repetition of past events. It is an opportunity to view one's life from a new and much clearer perspective. Barbara Harris apparently saw the particular episode recounted above because it helped her realize some important things about herself as a child. She had felt terrible guilt for laughing when Miss Hamden fell, and "internalized a feeling of being bad. . . . She could see clearly now that she had always believed that she was an unworthy child who felt undeserving and bad. As these scenes of her life were paraded before her now, she could see herself acting out this role. In this review, it became clear to her that this feeling of low self-worth had affected every relationship in her life. This realization had a profound and immediate healing effect on her. It was like years of psychotherapy in an instant." (*Full Circle*, p. 26.)

Dr. George Ritchie reported a similarly instructive understanding that came to him. "I felt my stepmother was growing to love me until she had her first child, Henry, my half-brother. Then I saw something different from the way I had recalled it. I had been certain Mother was the one who had changed the most, particularly after the birth of my half-sister, . . . The picture of my life showed I had grown jealous of my younger siblings and had become sullen. Then Mother had begun to change in her attitude." (*My Life After Dying*, p. 20.)

Added to these instructive components of the life review is one more—probably the most enlightening and educating of all. Those who are assessing their own lives are often blessed with the miraculous ability to perceive and experience how their lives affected other people and other things. Phyllis Atwater witnessed this effect down to the last ripple of her actions. "Mine was not a review, it was a reliving. For me, it was a total reliving of *every* thought I had ever thought, *every* word I had ever spoken, and *every* deed I had ever done; *plus* the effect of each thought, word, and deed on everyone and anyone who had ever come within my environment or sphere of influence whether I knew them or not (including unknown passersby on the street); *plus* the effect of each thought, word, and deed on weather, plants, animals, soil, trees, water, and air." (*Coming Back to Life*, p. 36.)

"When I would see something," recounted one man concerning his life review, "when I would experience a past event, it was like I was seeing it through eyes with (I guess you would say) omnipotent knowledge, guiding me, and helping me to see. That's the part that has stuck with me, because it showed me not only what I had done but *even how what I had done had affected other people.*" (*Reflections on Life After Life*, p. 35.) This process may be yet another aspect of the eternal "law of restoration" of which the prophet Alma spoke.

> And it is requisite with the justice of God that men should be judged according to their works; and if their works were good in this life, and the desires of their hearts were good, that they should also, at the last day, be restored unto that which is good.
>
> And if their works are evil they shall be restored unto them for evil. . . .
>
> The one raised to happiness according to his desires of happiness, or good according to his desires of good; and the other to evil according to his desires of evil; for as he has desired to do evil all the day long even so shall he have his reward of evil when the night cometh. (Alma 41:3–5.)

According to those who claim to have experienced this life review, this facet of the law of restoration is an absolutely perfect and just return for our actions. We get what we gave. We reap what we sowed. We experience all of the effects of our own choices. This restoration of good for good and evil for evil is also found in the New Testament in the teachings of Jesus and the Apostle Paul. In the Sermon on the Mount, the Savior gave several examples of restoration or reciprocity that may be reflected in these life-review descriptions. "Blessed are the merciful: for they shall obtain mercy" (Matthew 5:7). Later he admonished his disciples to teach: "Judge not unrighteously, that ye be not judged: but judge righteous judgment. For with what judgment ye shall judge, ye shall be judged: and with what measure ye mete, it shall be measured unto you again." (JST Matthew 7:1–2.) The Apostle Paul described this restoration that is part of our judgment as a "harvest." "Be not deceived; God is not mocked: for whatsoever a man soweth, that shall he also reap. For he that soweth to his flesh shall of the flesh reap corruption; but he that soweth to the Spirit shall of the Spirit reap life everlasting. And let us not be weary in well doing: for in due season we shall reap, if we faint not." (Galatians 6:7–9.)

As can be seen from NDErs' life-review experiences, these scriptural teachings may be more literal than we have traditionally imagined. Undoubtedly there are other aspects of this law of restoration, some of which we have already discussed, and this law will continue to operate flawlessly from the moment we enter the spirit world throughout eternity. However, this "sneak preview" provides us with a sobering insight into the literal and profound nature of the law of restoration.

A Learning Process

During this process of self-evaluation, the being of light may continue to ask probing questions or point out important lessons to be learned. Again, the process seems to be primarily instructive rather than judgmental or punitive. "The Light showed me different things I had done, things that weren't very nice, like hurting people's feelings, and things that I could and should have done, things that I could have done nicer, could've been nicer to more people, helped more people. That type of thing. It was concerned with how I related to other people: Did I care enough? Did I help enough? To care and to take care of other people seemed to be a primary function. And yet I didn't feel that it was showing me these things to condemn me. It was more or less for the purpose of understanding." (*After the Beyond*, p. 11.)

In many cases NDErs learn not to be so hard on themselves—to forgive themselves. During her life review, Phyllis Atwater was very discouraged and disgusted with herself at first. "It was me judging me, not some heavenly St. Peter. And my judgment was critical and stern. I was not satisfied with many, many things Phyllis had done, said or thought. There was a feeling of sadness and failure, yet a growing feeling of joy when the realization came that Phyllis had always done SOMETHING. She did many things unworthy and negative, but she did something. She tried. Much of what she did was constructive and positive. She learned and grew in her learning. This was satisfying. Phyllis was okay." (As quoted in *Otherworld Journeys*, p. 131.)

George Ritchie confirmed, "I realized that it was *I* who was judging the events around us so harshly. It was I who saw them as trivial, self-centered, unimportant. No such condemnation came from the Glory shining round me. He was not blaming or reproaching. He was simply . . . loving me." (*Return from Tomorrow*, p. 54.) Barbara Harris, who had felt herself so unworthy in life, realized through her life review that her sin was a failure to love herself. "Embracing herself, forgiving herself, seemed to free her from a lifetime of self-inflicted wounds" (*Full Circle*, p. 26).

On the other hand, the experience obviously leaves an indelible impression in the minds of its percipients in relation to the changes they need to make in their lives. Some understand this themselves, while others may be helped by the "being of light." Dr. Moody quotes one penitent NDEr: "When I got back from this, I had decided I'd better change. I was very repentant. I hadn't been satisfied with the life I had led up to then, so I wanted to start doing better." (*Reflections on Life After Life*, p. 36.) Further, recall that while the motorcycle gang member introduced in the first chapter of this book felt total love and acceptance, "they [he and "God"] also apparently discussed his life experiences and what changes he would make upon his recovery" (*The Return from Silence*, p. 12).

It seems that suggested changes center around two things—love and learning. As he mediates the life assessment, the "being of light" points out that these two principles are the most important things in life.

> All through this, he kept stressing the importance of love. The places where he showed it best involved my sister; I have always been very close to her. He showed me some instances where I had been selfish to my sister, but then just as many times where I had really shown love to her and had shared with her. He pointed out to me that I should try to do things for other people, to try my best. There wasn't any accusation in any of this, though. When he came across times when I had been selfish, his attitude was only that I had been learning from them, too.
>
> He seemed very interested in things concerning knowledge, too. He kept on pointing out things that had to do with learning, and he did say that I was going to continue learning, and he said that even when he comes back for me (because by this time he had told me that I was going back) that there will always be a quest for knowledge. He said that it is a continuous process, so I got the feeling that it goes on after death. I think that he was trying to teach me, as we went through the flashbacks. (As quoted in *Life After Life*, pp. 67–68.)

Little Things Mean the Most

More specifically, those who enjoy this instructive encounter learn that it is the small, seemingly insignificant acts that are important and not the great public achievements and awards. "What I had counted in life as unimportant was my salvation and what I thought was important was nil," realized a heart attack victim (as quoted in *Heading Toward Omega*, p. 67). Another man testified,

> . . . I realized that there are things that every person is sent to earth to realize and to learn. For instance, to share more love, . . . To discover that the most important thing is

human relationships and love and not materialistic things. And to realize that every single thing that you do in your life is recorded and that even though you pass it by not thinking at the time, it always comes up later. For instance, you may be . . . at a stoplight and you're in a hurry and the lady in front of you, when the light turns green, doesn't take right off, [she] doesn't notice the light, and you get upset and start honking your horn and telling them to hurry up. Those are the little kind of things that are recorded that you don't realize at the time are really important. One of the things that I discovered that is very important is patience toward other human beings and realizing that you yourself may be in that situation sometime. (As quoted in *Heading Toward Omega*, p. 69.)

The small, positive actions also carry great weight. Professor Howard Storm said he found the hypocrisy revealed by his life review "nauseating" to watch because of the selfish life he had lived, but found a few moments of redemption. "I got to see," he relates, "when my sister had a bad night one night, how I went into her bedroom and put my arms around her. I didn't say anything. I just lay there with my arms around her. As it turned out, that experience was one of the biggest triumphs of my life." (As quoted in *Glimpses of Eternity*, p. 281.)

Many experiencers bear witness of this principle. Perhaps this is because it is the little things—the unplanned, uncalculated, unsuspecting things we do—that reveal what we really are. What we do when no one is watching us or when we have no ulterior motives and nothing to gain is what really counts. During his earthly ministry, the Savior seemed to take particular delight in inculcating and exemplifying those quiet acts which would not earn the rewards and praise of men but would be seen and approved by the Lord (see Matthew 6:1–8). This was and is the test of sincerity and of true integrity.

The Lord Looketh upon the Heart

Thus it seems that the desires of the heart, as they may be manifested in these less spectacular moments, are the most central issue in the life judgment. Emanuel Swedenborg goes to great lengths to demonstrate that a person is judged by his desires or "ruling love" because righteous actions can often mask evil, hypocritical, or fearful hearts. By contrast, not all sin stems from an evil heart. Some bad choices are made because of ignorance, weakness, fear, and countless other complications of life. Someone once said, "We can never see where a person aims, we can only see where he hits." Actions alone do not totally represent the person. The Lord has said, "For I, the Lord, will judge all men according to their works, according to the desire of their hearts" (D&C 137:9). He has also declared that, rather than perfect actions, he "requireth the heart and a willing mind" (D&C 64:34). Notwithstanding, we will surely be expected to comply, in both works and desires, in accordance with the amount of light and understanding we have received from God. "For of him unto whom much is given much is required" (D&C 82:3).

A Greater Desire to Do Good

Do these life review experiences ever excuse sin? We have not found one single account in which the experiencer returned with the idea that he or she now had license to sin because all would be forgiven, or that wickedness doesn't really matter. On the contrary, they come back more committed to doing good and to refraining from hurting others. NDEr Dr. Raymond Babb extolled the perfect love of the light and said that he felt "1000% taken in, accepted, loved." However, he added this qualification. "That doesn't mean that you can do whatever you please in the here and now. There is no question that you should do all the good that you can." (In *Vital Signs*, vol. 1, no. 3, August–September 1992, p. 11.)

Perhaps these people are so profoundly affected by their own negative and positive actions as shown to them in their life review that they make a greater effort to treat others as they would want to be treated. The most important and inspiring influence on them, however, is unquestionably the complete acceptance and love they felt in the presence of the "light." This new-found love instills in these NDErs an overwhelming desire to please this wonderful being and serve others in his behalf. They want to share the perfect love they felt from him. As one man put it, "It is so hard to describe 'cause it's hard to realize a total surrendering-type love, a total love that kind of immerses you. The kind that no matter what he would have told me, I'd have done." (As quoted in *Heading Toward Omega*, p. 68.)

We must remember that the life review that is described so frequently in near-death research is not a final judgment of a person's righteousness or wickedness. It appears to be more instructional and customized to the needs of the individual. We cannot generalize about the final judgment—ultimate rewards or condemnation—on the basis of brief life reviews. These accounts, however, remind us of what we know assuredly from the scriptures and the testimonies of prophets: that all mankind will be held accountable for their actions, desires, thoughts, motives—and most of all for their love for God and their fellowmen.

CHAPTER 12

"Welcome Home"

Since the restoration of the gospel, Latter-day Saints have held out to the world the hope of "going home" to live with their Father in Heaven again after the resurrection, as they did before they were born into mortality. Along with this they have taught that both there and in the pre-resurrection spirit world the faithful Saints will be reunited with their friends and family members who have preceded them. Prophets, both ancient and modern, have taught that, if we have been righteous, our relationships there will be even more gratifying than they are here. "We have more friends behind the vail than on this side," acknowledged President Brigham Young, "and they will hail us more joyfully than you were ever welcomed by your parents and friends in this world; and you will rejoice more when you meet them than you ever rejoiced to see a friend in this life" (in *Journal of Discourses*, 6:349). The Prophet Joseph also looked forward to the joyful reunion with his loved ones on the other side of the veil of death. "I have a father, brothers, children, and friends who have gone to a world of spirits. They are only absent for a moment. They are in the spirit, and we shall soon meet again. . . . When we depart we shall hail our mothers, fathers, friends, and all whom we love, who have fallen asleep in Jesus. . . . It will be an eternity of felicity." (*History of the Church,* 6:316.)

While this familiar doctrine is often taken for granted by members of the Church, there are millions in the world who feel no such hope. They feel or are taught that death is the end of their existence or the beginning of some altered form of consciousness which does not allow for such earthly associations. How overjoyed a person who has passed through the portals of death must be, then, to discover that those he or she mourned as forever lost except in memory are indeed alive, well, and waiting for that loved one to join them. Meeting deceased friends and relatives is a commonly reported element of near-death experiences. Imagine the joy this elderly accountant, who is not a member of the Church, felt at meeting his parents again and seeing them well and happy. "I saw two figures walking toward me and I immediately recognized them. They were my mother and father, both had died years ago. My mother was an amputee and yet that leg was now restored! She was walking on two legs! I said to my mother, 'You and father are beautiful.' And they said to me, 'You have the same radiance and you are also beautiful.'" (As quoted in Maurice Rawlings, *Beyond Death's Door,* pp. 80–81.)

As recounted in some cases, a dying individual may meet relatives who were unknown to him or her on earth. A man who suffers from severe spastic quadriplegia had several out of body experiences in which he visited the spirit world. He was able to communicate the following incident which is consistent with LDS theology concerning the role and relationship of the extended family in the next life. "In February 1989 Stuart had his sixth out-of-body experience. He indicated he went to 'Paradise' while asleep and saw a glowing woman with a Scandinavian accent who had died a century ago. Stuart believed she was an ancestor of his, and he was thrilled at how loving she was. He also saw two deceased grandfathers who touched him, two deceased grandmothers, and two deceased stepbrothers. (His adopted mother confirmed that she had lost two sons prior to Stuart's OBE.) He also saw others there whose genders he could not determine, and indicated it was like a 'big re-union.'" (In *Journal of Near-Death Studies,* vol. 9, no. 2, Winter 1990, p. 94.)

In addition to seeing family and friends, a British man reported that he also saw people who, although not personal acquaintances, were well-known on earth. "The people I recognised whilst dead were my mother and grandmother, and although I could not have recognised them, I was aware of such giants as Peter and Paul and the founder of the Church Army, Wilson Carlisle. There were also numerous Christian people I have known in life. I especially recognised the Sunday School teacher called Frank, who influenced me a great deal and who lost his life in the Second World War. I think that I was surrounded by what I can only describe as a reception committee. Frank was one of these. Another was my saintly Roman Catholic doctor who had just previously died." (As quoted in *Return from Death,* pp. 52–53.)

A small number of experiencers, mostly children, were even greeted by family pets or other non-threatening animals that had died. Gospel teachings indeed confirm that animals have spirits just as people do, though of a lesser intelligence (see Moses 3:5; D&C 77:2). The Prophet Joseph Smith taught that animals also would be saved by the atonement of Jesus Christ and that animals in myriad forms would enjoy the eternal felicity of heaven (see *Teachings,* pp. 291–92; see also *Encyclopedia of Mormonism,* 1:42–43). Interestingly, the presence of animals seems to be a unique source of comfort for some NDErs—particularly children. This manifestation of the Lord's total love and his concern for the uniqueness of his children seems evident in Amber's near-death experience. The following took place when she was ten years old.

> Two animals also appeared to Amber while she was in this "dark place" [tunnel]. She saw a shadow of what she believed was a dog and thought it might have been the family's pet, which had been put to sleep a few years earlier. She also saw a white lamb that came near her but did not touch her. The lamb was loving and gentle, and led Amber back to her body, whereupon she regained consciousness.

None of Amber's loved ones were deceased at the time of her NDE. She had always had a love for animals, but when she was young, she developed a fear of people, especially people dressed in white. During surgery at age 2, she was permanently injured when her surgeons, who wore white, accidentally severed nerves to her left leg; she has little mobility in that limb to this day. (As quoted in *Journal of Near-Death Studies*, vol. 9, no. 1, Fall 1990, p. 34.)

Other Encounters

It is worth noting that while several accounts by Latter-day Saints mention encounters with spirits who have not yet been born, we have also found one account by someone not of that faith in which such premortal spirit beings were perceived. It may be that, without its being explicitly allowed, NDErs cannot discern any difference between pre-earth and post-earth spirits. While we have no authoritative doctrinal declaration or scriptural evidence which confirms that both premortal and postmortal spirits are ever together in the same realm, we have no doctrine that definitively declares otherwise, either. Rather, we set forth this example only as an affirmation of the teachings of the restored gospel that we lived as spirit children of our Heavenly Father, raised to maturity by him, before we were born into mortality. Dr. Melvin Morse related the report of Jamie, a little girl who "died" of bacterial meningitis. Her childish innocence lends objective credibility to her report. She expressed to Dr. Morse that she was uneasy because her near-death experience "did not match with things she had been taught in Sunday school. . . . She was taught that heaven was where people go when they die. So why had she seen people about to be born?" (*Transformed by the Light*, p. 127.)

A few NDErs and visitors to the spirit world also may report seeing children. "In the garden there was this one, big, large tree and there were children playing a game; there were seven children; . . . The children saw me and they beckoned me to come over" (*The Return from Silence*, p. 144). However, the relative absence of accounts involving children in the afterlife seems conspicuous, especially when so many conditions there reflect and magnify the same conditions found in earth life. Once again, a prophet of the Restoration offers a doctrinal clarification to this dilemma.

> The spirits of our children are immortal before they come to us, and their spirits, after bodily death, are like they were before they came. They are as they would have appeared if they had lived in the flesh, to grow to maturity, or to develop their physical bodies to the full stature of their spirits. If you see one of your children that has passed away it may appear to you in the form in which you would recognize it, the form of childhood; but if it came to you as a messenger bearing some important truth, it would perhaps come as the spirit of Bishop Edward Hunter's son (who died when a little child) came to him, in the stature of full-grown manhood, and revealed himself to his father, and said: "I am your son."
>
> Bishop Hunter did not understand it. He went to my father and said: "Hyrum, what does that mean? I buried my son when he was only a little boy, but he has come to me as a full-grown man—a noble, glorious, young man, and declared himself my son. What does it mean?"
>
> Father (Hyrum Smith, the Patriarch) told him that the Spirit of Jesus Christ was full-grown before he was born into the world; and so our children were full-grown and possessed their full stature in the spirit, before they entered mortality, and as they will also appear after the resurrection, when they shall have completed their mission. (Joseph F. Smith, *Gospel Doctrine*, p. 455.)

Indeed, some of those who had NDEs as children recount that they saw or experienced themselves as adults in that other world. Dr. Raymond Moody noted this significant phenomenon: "A surprising number . . . say that they are adults during the episode, although they can't say how they know this." He quotes one woman who recalled: "In looking back at the experience, I realize that I was fully mature when I was in his presence. As I said, I was only seven but I know I was an adult." (*The*

Light Beyond, pp. 74–76.) However, other than LDS accounts, we have found no narratives of NDErs who saw people they *knew* who had died as children but who appeared to them as adults.

From his experiences Emanuel Swedenborg propounded some fascinating ideas in relation to children that should strike a chord of familiarity to Latter-day Saints. He boldly declared the salvation of children who had died without baptism. "Some people hold the belief that only children born within the church enter heaven, not children born outside the church. The reason they give is that children within the church have been baptized." He then attempted to rectify this common misconception. "May they know, then, that every child, wherever he was born—within the church or outside it, of godly or of godless parents—every child is accepted by the Lord when he dies and is brought up in heaven. . . . Everyone who thinks rationally is capable of understanding that no one is born for hell, but everyone for heaven; and that the individual himself is at fault for entering hell, with children being incapable of guilt as yet." (*Heaven and Hell,* p. 250.)

Again, Swedenborg's words echo the singular teachings of the restored gospel. "And little children also have eternal life," taught the ancient prophet Abinadi (Mosiah 15:25). Modern revelation from the Lord has also confirmed this compelling doctrine. "But behold, I say unto you, that little children are redeemed from the foundation of the world through mine Only Begotten; wherefore, they cannot sin, for power is not given unto Satan to tempt little children, until they begin to become accountable before me" (D&C 29:46–47). And finally, Joseph Smith the Prophet testified: "Children will be enthroned in the presence of God and the Lamb" (*Teachings,* p. 200).

Swedenborg goes on to imply other familiar doctrines. It is vital to remember as we continue to examine his writings that while he seems to have had glimpses of these doctrines, he did not necessarily see the whole picture. Nonetheless, he advanced some true principles. He attested that children

> are borne into heaven and entrusted to angels of the feminine gender who during their physical life had loved children tenderly and had also loved God. Because they had in the world loved all children with a virtually maternal tender-

ness, they accept these as their own. And the children, from their inborn nature, love them as though they were their own mothers. Each woman has as many children as she wants from her spiritual parental affection. . . . Once this first stage is completed, they are transferred to another heaven where they are educated by teachers; and so the process continues. (*Heaven and Hell*, pp. 252–53.)

The Swedish philosopher goes on to describe what he perceived about how children in heaven become adults.

Understanding and wisdom constitute an angel. Just as long as children do not possess these attributes, they are with angels but are not themselves angels. But once they become understanding and wise, they become angels. Further—which surprised me—they do not then look like children, but like adults. For at that point they are no longer of a childlike nature, but of a more mature, angelic nature. This is inherent in understanding and wisdom.

The reason that children look more mature as they become more perfect in understanding and wisdom is that understanding and wisdom are spiritual nourishment itself. So the very things that nourish their minds are nourishing their bodies as well. . . . for the form of their bodies is nothing but the outward form of their more inward elements.

It is worth knowing that children in heaven do not mature beyond the beginning of young adulthood, and remain at that point to eternity. (P. 256.)

As established earlier, latter-day prophets have taught that our spirits are adult when they reach the spirit world. Could it be that Swedenborg was allowed to perceive the spirits he saw as children in order to recognize their true status, and then as adults in order that he might comprehend the teaching and growth process that takes place? Or, is it possible that he could have witnessed the rearing of resurrected children? In either case, he offers something of a witness or allusion to the principle of rearing children to spiritual and physical maturity beyond the grave.

Truly, one of the most joyous and unique doctrines of the

restored gospel taught by the Prophet Joseph is that, if we are faithful, after the resurrection we will have the privilege of rearing to maturity our offspring who died as children. President Joseph F. Smith affirmed this doctrine. "Joseph Smith declared that the mother who laid down her little child, being deprived of the privilege, the joy, and the satisfaction of bringing it up to manhood or womanhood in this world, would, after the resurrection, have all the joy, satisfaction and pleasure, and even more than it would have been possible to have had in mortality, in seeing her child grow to the full measure of the stature of its spirit" (*Gospel Doctrine*, p. 453).

Further, it would be reasonable to believe that the innocent children of wicked parents would be "adopted" and nurtured by righteous women who loved children, especially those who were unable to bear their own while in mortality. We are assured by modern prophets and apostles that those who through no fault of their own are prevented from enjoying the blessing of having children in this life will have that deficiency made up to them in the next life. Perhaps this is one possible manifestation of that principle.

It is also conceivable, though not established as doctrine, that children beyond the veil may be taught much as they are here—in school or Primary-type settings. There are two near-death accounts from members of the Church who saw children in the spirit world assembled together and being taught. We have already quoted the story of the young man who was instructed to teach the little children to read and write. Also, as a young woman Sister Ella Jensen nearly died, and she related this experience to LeRoi C. Snow, whose son she had seen in the spirit world. (He had died while she was sick, and she believed she saw him in his childhood form so that she would recognize him.) "Finally I reached the end of that long room. I opened a door and went into another room filled with children. They were all arranged in perfect order, the smallest ones first, then larger ones, according to age and size, the largest ones in the back rows all around the room. They seemed to be convened in a sort of a Primary or a Sunday School presided over by Aunt Eliza R. Snow. There were hundreds of small children." (As quoted in *Life Everlasting*, p. 85.)

Another point of interest from Swedenborg is his careful delineation about the way these little ones are taught. "Children are taught mainly by means of representations suited to their native gifts—representations so beautiful, and so filled from within with wisdom at the same time, that no one could ever believe it. In this way, step by step, an understanding is instilled into them which draws its soul from what is good." (*Heaven and Hell*, p. 253.) He then went on to describe what appears to have been a delicate portrayal of the resurrection of Christ from the tomb by means of these "representations" or portrayals, "all done with matchless care and reverence" (p. 254).

We must remember, however, that not everything has been revealed to us concerning the development and progress of spirits in the spirit world. Neither do we yet fully comprehend how children will be "reared" after the resurrection. The ideas and possibilities discussed here, however, can perhaps assist us in gaining some limited understanding as to why some NDErs perceive children in their experiences while others do not.

Feelings of Familiarity

In addition to meeting deceased family and friends and other happy and welcoming spirits, some who visit or glimpse the spirit realms enjoy a feeling of familiarity and of being "at home." As Latter-day Saints we would desire to assure them that, in an important sense, indeed they are home! Their spirits were reared and nurtured to maturity in such a spiritual kingdom. They were taught and prepared for their further schooling on earth in a similar type of glorious surroundings. They had parents and spirit brothers and sisters in that earlier life, whom they have forgotten for a short time during mortality. When they pass through the veil of death, in the spirit world they begin to sense something familiar, some echo of that perfect heavenly home the righteous will return to after resurrection. Speaking of that abode and our Heavenly Father, President Brigham Young poignantly told us: "He is the Father of our spirits; and if we could know, understand, and do His will, every soul would be prepared to return back into his presence. And when they get there, they would see that they had formerly lived there for ages, that they had previously been acquainted with every nook and corner, with the palaces, walks, and gardens; and they would embrace their Father, and He would embrace them and say, 'My son, my daughter, I have you again;' and the child would say, 'O my Father, my Father, I am here again.'" (In *Journal of Discourses*, 4:268.)

This feeling of familiarity is illustrated in several NDE accounts. A young teen-age girl was bathed in the "light" during a brush with death. Her first reaction was to say "homey home." She later learned from her family that this "is what I would say as a toddler when we had been away from our house and as we would approach our neighborhood . . . I would stand in the seat and say, . . . homey home, homey home. . . . I was back home absolutely." (Experiencers Panel Discussion Transcript, 1990 IANDS Conference, 1990, pp. 6–7.) Another person, when questioned in an interview, characterized the reaction she had to the light as a feeling of "Homecoming." "It's strange, because I never really verbalized that before. It was really like a homecoming." (*Heading Toward Omega*, p. 60.) The victim of attempted murder, referred to in previous chapters, marveled, "Everything that occurred to me while I was in this state of conscious[ness] was vastly beyond anything I had ever experienced and yet at the same time it was familiar—as if I had always known of its existence" (as quoted in *Heading Toward Omega*, p. 64). And finally, an accident victim declared, "I felt as if I was going back somewhere I belonged. There were people all around who I sensed were loving friends." (As quoted in *Return from Death*, pp. 46–47.)

Remembering

Inherent in this feeling of familiarity is a kind of remembering or rediscovering what was once known but forgotten—usually about the meaning and purpose of life. The woman referred to above who had described her feelings in the spirit world as "homey home" also related that she had received a flood of knowledge which also seemed familiar. "I was being given information," she recounted. "What is life, why we are born, universal kinds of knowledge. Profound, but there was a simplicity to it. It was like something I had known but had forgotten. . . . It was a reunion of the highest order." (As quoted in "At the Edge of Eternity," in *Life*, March 1992, p. 66.) Though referring to those who recognize the teachings of the gospel on earth, Elder Neal A. Maxwell commented on this rediscovery of the great knowledge of the universe that may be characterized as "spiritual déjà vu." "The reality of premortality responds to puzzlings which suggest we are strangers here. It is a curative for the yearnings expressed in music and poetry and literature. . . . Thus when we now say 'I know,' that realization is rediscovery; we are actually saying 'I know—again!' From long experience, His sheep know His voice and His doctrine." (In *Ensign*, November 1985, pp. 16, 18.)

Fortunately or unfortunately, as the case may be, experiencers are not allowed to retain this recognition. The woman who asked a spirit world being, "What about my sins?" also asked, "Can you tell me—what it's all about?"

> And he did tell me. And it only took two or three sentences. It was a very short explanation and I understood it perfectly. And I said again, "Of course!" And again, I knew it was something I had always known and managed to forget.
>
> And so I asked him, "Can I take all this back with me? There's so many people I want to tell all this to."
>
> And he said, "You can take the answer to your first question—which was the one about sin—but," he said, "the answer to the second question you won't be able to remember." [And she found in fact that when she returned to physical life, she could not.] (As quoted in *Heading Toward Omega*, p. 63.)

Dr. Carol Zaleski wrote that this subsequent forgetfulness after returning to earth is as common as the feeling of remembering while in "heaven." However, she reports that, "for some, a certain aura, half-phrase, or taste of the revelation remains. One near-death visionary who was told in 'four words' what life is all about, describes his frustration in trying over the years to reconstruct the message: 'The closest I can come and have any satisfaction with is "In your own image." ' " (As quoted in *Otherworld Journeys*, p. 133.)

Given our knowledge of the remarkable revelations of the

restored gospel, perhaps we have a feel for what this NDEr was trying to express, and a pretty good idea about the answers to the great questions of life which the other experiencers received. It may be that this person was trying to say "In *his* own image" or "In *thine* own image." As Latter-day Saints, we believe we are here on earth as part of our eternal journey to become like God—first gaining a body which is "in his own image." We further believe that we are here to learn to conform to "his image" spiritually, emotionally, and intellectually, and some day also in glory and power and dominion. Even if the NDEr meant "In *your* own image," we could couch the purpose of life in terms of being sent here to reach our own potential, to be all that we can, to fulfill that which we were assigned in the preexistence. While we can never know exactly what this individual meant, that is not the important point. It is fascinating, and it hints at beliefs that are familiar to us. And it demonstrates to the members of the Church what a cosmic and sublime gift we enjoy in the knowledge we have about the purpose of life and the overall plan of salvation. Like these NDErs who are made to forget again what they were allowed to remember, we too have an essential "veil of forgetfulness" imposed upon us in this life to protect the free operation of agency and thus ensure accountability. But with the restored truths of the gospel, we know that it is not nearly so thick, or dark, or heavy—it is only a veil, not a wall. (For an extensive discussion of the role of the "veil of forgetfulness" in our mortal probation, see *The Life Before*, pp. 172–75.)

Knowing

Near-death experiencers and others who have tasted the goodness and glory of the spirit realm speak of another kind of knowledge which may come to them during their journey to that other world. They tell of just "knowing" that certain things are true. They can't explain exactly how they know, they just know. One woman's comment is representative. "At this point in the act of dying, I had what I call the answer to a question I had never verbalized to anyone or even faced: Is there really a God? I can't describe it, but the totality and reality of the living

God exploded within my being and He filled every atom of my body with His glory." (As quoted in Maurice Rawlings, *Beyond Death's Door*, p. 64.) Latter-day Saints can identify with that kind of "knowing." It doesn't come from seeing or touching or any of the other physical senses. It doesn't stem from scientific proof, but from indisputable personal and spiritual evidence— the witness of the Spirit. The Lord explained this revelatory process in scripture. "Yea, behold, I will tell you in your mind and in your heart, by the Holy Ghost, which shall come upon you and which shall dwell in your heart" (D&C 8:2).

Another of the truths which many NDErs sense or know is that they are eternal—that in some way they have always existed. "Man was also in the beginning with God. Intelligence, or the light of truth, was not created or made, neither indeed can be." (D&C 93:29.) The Prophet Joseph Smith further declared, "The mind or intelligence which man possesses is [co-eternal] with God himself" (in *Teachings*, p. 353; see footnote 8). One man expressed such feelings thus: "It was eternity. It's like I was always there and I will always be there, and that my existence on earth was just a brief instant." (As quoted in *Heading Toward Omega*, p. 54.) This sounds familiar! Moreover, as mentioned in the chapter on light, NDErs sometimes sense that they are in some way one with God. "There is no doubt in my mind that it was God. God was me and I was God. I was part of the light and I was one with it. I was not separate. I am not saying that I am a supreme being. I was God, as you are, as everyone is." (As quoted in *Otherworld Journeys* p. 126.)

And some feel a oneness, not only with the light and God but also with their fellow beings. "I didn't feel apart from them at all; one of the feelings I remember most about them was the feeling of unity, of being totally a part of everything around me and about me. There was no separateness at all." (As quoted in *Return from Death*, p. 51.) Perhaps the eternal nature of intelligence is the common denominator here, since we all possess some measure of it, though God possesses infinitely more. And most of all that feeling of unity, of "being home," and of being part of God's great system stems from the fact, as revealed in the restored gospel, that we are all children of God—literally brothers and sisters within the human race.

CHAPTER 13

_____

Eternal Possibilities

While in the spirit world, some of those who temporarily experience death get a glimpse of what the future holds for them. Some come to understand that they will be the very same individual in the next life as they were in mortality. Many testify that learning and growth seem an eternal process in that realm. Some even get a preview of their future back on earth, and a few see the future of the earth itself.

We Retain the Same Spirit After Death

Many of the principles previously examined in this book support the words of Amulek which are so familiar to Latter-day Saints. "Ye cannot say, when ye are brought to that awful crisis, that I will repent, that I will return to my God. Nay, ye cannot say this; for that same spirit which doth possess your bodies at the time that ye go out of this life, that same spirit will have power to possess your body in that eternal world." (Alma 34:34.) Amulek's use of the phrase "same spirit" has been interpreted by many to mean that the same attitudes, personality traits, disposition, and desires remain an integral part of our being even after the spirit is separated from the body at death. In addition to this scriptural teaching, there are experiences or observations from NDErs which further strengthen this point. "Whatever is in a person's spirit when he leaves the body stays with him after death, for then the person lives as a spirit," Swedenborg maintained. He further attested:

> Manifold experience has witnessed to me that when a person crosses over from the natural into the spiritual world, which happens when he dies, he carries with him everything that is his, or everything belonging to his person, except his earthly body.
> . . . As before, he sees; as before, he hears and speaks, he smells and tastes; as before he feels the pressure when he is touched. He still yearns, wishes, craves, thinks, ponders, is moved, loves, and intends as before. A person who enjoyed scholarly work reads and writes as before. In a word, when a person crosses from one life to the other, or from one world to the other, it is as though he had gone from one place to another and had taken with himself all the things he possessed in his own right as a person. (*Heaven and Hell*, pp. 306, 358–59.)

Perhaps the most convincing testimonies of the continuation of the same attitudes and proclivities after death come from those who have had near-death experiences when they have attempted to commit suicide. Invariably they return with the message that ending their lives would not end their problems but, in fact, would only make them worse. Dr. Raymond Moody summarized his research with such individuals. "All of these people agree on one point: They felt their suicidal attempts solved nothing. They found that they were involved in exactly the same problems from which they had been trying to extricate themselves by suicide. Whatever difficulty they had been trying to get away from was still there on the other side, unresolved." These people return to life resolved to do their best to overcome their difficulties while on earth. Virtually all of them say they will never attempt suicide again. "No. I would not do that again," determined one man. "I will die naturally next time, because one thing I realized at that time is that our life here is just such a small period of time and there is so much which needs to be done while you're here. And, when you die it's eternity." (*Reflections on Life After Life*, pp. 45, 46.)

Harder for the Wicked to Repent

Dr. George Ritchie also witnessed the circumstances of some of those who had succeeded in taking their own lives. He saw them in the realm of those still "bound" to the earth.

> In one house a younger man followed an older one from room to room. "I'm, sorry, Pa!" he kept saying. "I didn't know what it would do to Mama! I didn't understand."
>
> But though I could hear him clearly, it was obvious that the man he was speaking to could not. The old man was carrying a tray into a room where an elderly woman sat in bed. "I'm sorry, Pa," the young man said again. "I'm sorry, Mama." Endlessly, over and over, to ears that could not hear. . . .
>
> Several times we paused before similar scenes. A boy trailing a teenaged girl through the corridors of a school. "I'm sorry, Nancy!" A middle-aged woman begging a grey-haired man to forgive her.
>
> "What are they so sorry for, Jesus?" I pleaded. "Why do they keep talking to people who can't hear them?"
>
> Then from the Light beside me came the thought: *They are suicides, chained to every consequence of their act.* (*Return from Tomorrow*, pp. 58–59.)

Another woman also testified that she "looked down into a round opening in the black void in which people were walking around in white robes. Some people remained in the void, especially if they had committed suicide." (As quoted in *Closer to the Light*, p. 138.) Dr. Raymond Moody quotes one woman who felt that, during her death from suicide, she was forced to face and deal with the same problem over and over again, like a rerun. Just when she was glad to have it over with, it would start again. (See *Reflections on Life After Life*, pp. 45–46.) While only an omnipotent God can judge the accountability of those who take their own lives (see M. Russell Ballard, "Suicide: Some Things We Know, and Some We Do Not," *Ensign*, October 1987, pp. 6–9; also George G. Ritchie, *My Life After Dying*, p. 24), it may be that both of the above phenomena are manifestations of the principle set forth by modern prophets that it is harder to change or repent in the spirit world if we have "procrastinated the day of our repentance" (Alma 34:35).

Apparently there is something about this designated period of probation and possessing a mortal body which makes it easier to mold the spirit of man. Once this opportunity is past, those who deliberately put off, refused, or tried to escape the responsibility of making the best of their mortal lives and repenting of their sins will have to put forth an even greater effort to make progress in the next life than those who made use of this temporal time to prepare to meet God (see Alma 34:32). Perhaps it is as someone has said—"It is easier to pay the price for success than the penalty for failure." Though they come from accounts of attempted suicides, the examples cited above may provide something of a general illustration of the difficulty of trying to make amends in the spirit world for deficiencies that were never overcome on earth. George Ritchie's account of the beings who were desperately craving and futilely trying to obtain cigarettes and alcohol from mortal beings is also a sobering case in point. "Although they could no longer contact the earth, [they] still had their hearts there" he observed sadly (*Return from Tomorrow*, p. 58).

Prophets of the Restoration have explained why it is important to repent while in the mortal body and why it will be more difficult to repent without one. Elder Melvin J. Ballard, a member of the Quorum of the Twelve Apostles, provided this valuable teaching:

But this life is the time in which men are to repent. Do not let any of us imagine that we can go down to the grave not having overcome the corruptions of the flesh and then lose in the grave all our sins and evil tendencies. They will be with us. They will be with the spirit when separated from the body.

It is my judgment that any man or woman can do more to conform to the laws of God in one year in this life than they could do in ten years when they are dead. The spirit only can repent and change, and then the battle has to go forward with the flesh afterwards. It is much easier to overcome and serve the Lord when both flesh and spirit are combined as one. This is the time when men are more pliable and susceptible. We will find when we are dead every desire, every feeling will be greatly intensified. When clay is pliable it is much easier to change than when it gets hard and sets. . . .

Then, every man and woman who is putting off until the next life the task of correcting and overcoming the weakness of the flesh are sentencing themselves to years of bondage, for no man or woman will come forth in the resurrection until they have completed their work, until they have overcome, until they have done as much as they can do . . . those who are complying in this life with these conditions are shortening their sentences, for every one of us will have a matter of years in that spirit state to complete and finish our salvation. ("The Three Degrees of Glory," sermon delivered in Ogden, Utah, on 22 September 1922, quoted in *Life Everlasting*, pp. 21–22.)

In light of the doctrinal teachings of Amulek in the Book of Mormon and of Elder Ballard's comments, consider this strikingly parallel assertion by Emanuel Swedenborg. "After death a person can no longer be re-formed by teaching the way he could in the world, because his lowest level [the natural level— the flesh], which is made up of natural insights and affections, is then stilled and is incapable of being opened because it is not spiritual. The more inward elements, which are proper to the person's mind or spirit, rest on this level like a house on its foundation." (*Heaven and Hell*, p. 383.)

Easier for the Righteous to Progress

On the other hand, the prophets have taught that those who have prepared to meet God in this life will no longer be tormented and tried by the temptations of the flesh. Elder Heber C. Kimball warned, "If men and women do not qualify themselves and become sanctified and purified in this life, they will go into a world of spirits where they will have a greater contest with the devils than ever you had with them here" (in *Journal of Discourses*, 3:230). President Brigham Young maintained that the converse is also true.

> When this portion of the school is out, the one in which we descend below all things and commence upon this earth to learn the first lessons for an eternal exaltation, if you have been a faithful scholar, and have overcome, if you have brought the flesh into subjection by the power of the Priesthood, if you have honored the body, when it crumbles to the earth and your spirit is freed from this home of clay, has the devil any power over it? Not a particle.
>
> This is an advantage which the faithful will gain; but while they live on earth they are subject to the buffetings of Satan. Joseph and those who have died in the faith of the Gospel are free from this; . . . Joseph and the faithful who have died have gained a victory over the power of the devil, which you and I have not yet gained. . . . When we lay [our bodies] down, if we have been faithful, we have gained the victory so far. (In *Journal of Discourses*, 3:371.)

Swedenborg referred to what he perceived as a condition of the righteous which seems somewhat akin to this principle. He claimed that most spirits were held in the "spirit world" until they had passed through certain states, including a state of preparation, before being placed in some realm of what he perceived as "heaven" or "hell." "There are however some people who do not pass through these states," he explained, "being either taken up into heaven or cast into hell immediately after death. The people who are immediately taken up into heaven are the ones who have been regenerated and thus made ready for heaven in the world. People who have been regenerated and made ready in this way need only to cast off their soiled natural elements along with their bodies, and are immediately taken into heaven by angels." (*Heaven and Hell*, p. 398.)

Thus, once again we have seen that in this realm of perfect order and perfect restoration, exactly opposing conditions exist. Here is yet one more manifestation of the Lord's perfect justice. On the one hand, it will be harder for those who have squandered their probation on earth to make up for what they have wasted or lost. On the other, the process of progression will be hastened and henceforth unhindered for those who were faithful and obedient in this life.

Eternal Progression

Indeed, some of those who report near-death episodes learned, by a variety of means, of the concept of continued learning and progression in the next life. To begin with, a few describe being almost inundated with knowledge of all kinds while in the presence of the Light. Others report being given answers to any and all questions they wanted to ask, although they were not allowed to retain some of that knowledge when they returned to mortality. Moreover, recall the individual in whose life review the being of light emphasized love and learning. The Light informed her "that there will always be a quest for knowledge. He said that is a continuous process, so I got the feeling that it goes on after death." (As quoted in *Life After Life*, p. 68.) Dr. Ritchie, after visiting the realm of beings involved in continual research, determined, "It is this realm which removes forever the concept that we stop learning or progressing in knowledge when we die" (*My Life After Dying*, p. 25).

Despite the reports of some experiencers about the ready availability of knowledge and information in the spirit world and their increased capacity to comprehend and absorb such intelligence, it is only reasonable to believe that some sort of personal effort must be exerted in order to obtain or retain what is learned. Note that even those who feel they are momentarily filled with "all knowledge" subsequently lose this understanding when they leave the presence of the Light. Though President Brigham Young and Elder Parley P. Pratt indicated that our efforts would yield unimaginably greater rewards in that world, President George Q. Cannon acknowledged: "But we shall find that knowledge and power will not come to us there as the rain that falls upon us, without any effort of ours to acquire them. We shall have to exercise ourselves and exert our powers there just as we have to here. We shall be rewarded according to our diligence and faithfulness in the exercise of our agency." (*Gospel Truth*, p. 60.)

One remarkable NDE account reflects this eternal quest for learning. A man was led by a "spirit guide" to a vast, old library "containing all the wisdom of the ages, everything ever said or written." The instruction he received there was likewise classic wisdom. ". . . My guide . . . told me I must study and learn from the infinite array of wisdom before us. I was dismayed, and said there was no way I was capable of such a task. I was told to simply make a beginning, to do the best I could, and that would always be good enough. There was plenty of time." (As quoted in "Amazing Grace: The Near-Death Experience as a Compensatory Gift," in *Journal of Near-Death Studies*, vol. 10, no. 1, Fall 1991, p. 31.)

Though some Eastern religions have subscribed to the concept of a kind of progression of the human spirit after death, through reincarnation, Latter-day Saints are unique among Judeo-Christian religions in teaching this concept of eternal progression, because its implication—that humans may eventually progress to the point of becoming gods—is viewed as heresy in most Christian denominations (see "Eternal Progression," in *Encyclopedia of Mormonism*, 2:465–66). Nonetheless, for those who know the joy of learning and progression it is a liberating and inspiring doctrine. Man's spirit is made up of eternal intelligence (see D&C 93:29, 33, 36). To cease growing, learning, and advancing would be a kind of spiritual damnation. Brigham Young looked forward to continued and enhanced education after leaving this world. "And then we shall go on from step to step, from rejoicing to rejoicing, and from one intelligence and power to another, our happiness becoming more and more exquisite and sensible as we proceed in the words and powers of life" (in *Journal of Discourses*, 6:349). As Latter-day Saints we are continually encouraged to seek "education for eternity" because we are taught that "whatever principle of intelligence we attain unto in this life, it will rise with us in the resurrection. And if a person gains more knowledge and intelligence in this life through his diligence and obedience than another, he will have so much the advantage in the world to come." (D&C 130:18–19.) In other words, nothing we learn, if it is true and edifying, is ever wasted. It is all a part of our eternal destiny.

Keeping in mind how rare this doctrine is among western religions makes Swedenborg's advancement of it all the more remarkable. With profound observation, he testifies: "Every spirit and angel keeps the amount and quality of affection he had in the world. This is later perfected by being filled, which continues to eternity. For there is nothing that cannot keep being filled to eternity; in fact, every particular thing can be diversified in an infinite number of ways and hence enriched by different elements, and thereby multiplied and made fruitful. There is no end of any good thing, because it comes from the Infinite." (*Heaven and Hell,* pp. 371–72.)

Progression in Gospel Knowledge

The most important kind of learning and progression in the next life is in the area of gospel truths. "Knowledge saves a man;" taught the Prophet Joseph, "and in the world of spirits no man can be exalted but by knowledge. So long as a man will not give heed to the commandments, he must abide without salvation. . . . But when he consents to obey the gospel, whether here or in the world of spirits, he is saved." (In *History of the Church,* 6:314.) This is one of the paramount purposes of the spirit world. Elder Parley P. Pratt spoke of the central work of that realm. "It is an intermediate state, a probation, a place of preparation, improvement, instruction, or education, where spirits are chastened and improved, and where, if found worthy, they may be taught a knowledge of the Gospel. In short, it is a place where the Gospel is preached, and where faith, repentance, hope, and charity may be exercised; a place of waiting for the resurrection or redemption of the body." (*Key to the Science of Theology,* p. 80.)

Interestingly, Swedenborg also recognized that spirits cannot progress and desire to do good until they are taught basic theological principles. "But no one can behave like this without first being taught, for example, that God exists, that heaven and hell exist, that there is a life after death, that God is to be loved above all, and the neighbor as oneself, that the contents of the Word are to be believed because the Word is Divine" (*Heaven and Hell*, p. 419). As noted in previous chapters, he apparently perceived some type of organized religious instruction taking place in the spirit realms, and also observed that "angels are constantly being perfected in wisdom and love" (p. 162).

Finally, Dr. George Ritchie was also a witness of the preeminence of spiritual knowledge over other kinds of learning. He saw the abode of selfless beings who were totally absorbed in gaining and using knowledge to help their fellow beings, and yet even they were not in the highest spiritual realm. Only those who also had a profound knowledge and understanding of Jesus Christ and the teachings of his gospel, and had chosen to emulate him at all costs, were inhabitants of the celestial city which beckoned to Dr. Ritchie, though he could not yet enter. His experience seemed to ratify the precept, "But seek ye first the kingdom of God, and his righteousness; and all these things shall be added unto you" (Matthew 6:33).

All Things Are Present Before God

Other aspects of knowledge may also be opened up to visitors to the spirit world. These may have to do with their own personal future and/or the future of the earth itself. Although the unenlightened have sought throughout history to explain away prophecy because they are stubbornly convinced that no one can know the future, the faithful and believing have always maintained that, in God's economy, this is not only possible but is standard procedure. Within the doctrines of the Restoration we learn why this is true, though in our time-constricted world we may not fully comprehend how it is so.

> The angels do not reside on a planet like this earth;
> But they reside in the presence of God, on a globe like a

sea of glass and fire, where all things for their glory are manifest, past, present, and future, and are continually before the Lord (D&C 130:6–7).

> Thus saith the Lord your God, even Jesus Christ, the Great I AM, Alpha and Omega, the beginning and the end, . . .
> The same which knoweth all things, for all things are present before mine eyes (D&C 38:2).

> He comprehendeth all things, and all things are before him, and all things are round about him; and he is above all things, and in all things, and is through all things, and is round about all things; and all things are by him, and of him, even God, forever and ever (D&C 88:41).

A previously mentioned professor, Howard Storm, who had a near-death experience, testified that those who enter the next life become cognizant of these truths. "The Near Death Experiencer knows that past, present, and future are all simultaneously one to God, and that they have experienced the 'all present now' of God in their experience of the divine" (paper presented at the International IANDS Conference, August, 16–19, 1990, p. 9). One woman, who was given a cosmic journey through the universe witnessing "glorious celestial events," surmised, "Space and time are illusions that hold us to our plane; out there [in the universe] all is present simultaneously." (As quoted in "Amazing Grace: The Near-Death Experience as a Compensatory Gift," in *Journal of Near-Death Studies*, vol. 10, no. 1, Fall 1991, p. 16. See also D&C 88:42–44; Abraham 3:4–10; 5:13. For a discussion of possible scientific correlation with this phenomenon, see *Heading Toward Omega*, pp. 207–9.)

Because of these conditions God is able, at his will, to make the past, present, and future manifest to whomever he chooses. In modern scripture we have record of prophets who have been given such visions. A few NDErs also claim to have had similar views, though, unlike the experience of the prophets, this knowledge may be subsequently hidden from them and they remember having seen the events in vision only when or shortly before they actually happen. "The being showed Rick a vision 'as if the sky had opened up and revealed to me all things of the past and present.' The experience was both overwhelming and nuministic, but Rick was brought back to his momentary reality by the being, who warned him that his peek into the future would be largely forgotten. He would only prevision the future, the being explained, just before it took place." (*The Return from Silence,* pp. 18–19.) Belle, another recipient of this type of visionary experience remarked: "At one point I had complete knowledge of everything, from the beginning of creation to the end of time . . . [but] I was told [by her guides] that I would remain unconscious for five days so that all the things I had been shown would not resurface, so they could be stored for future reference. . . . When given this information, you are given . . . the time . . . when you can speak of it. If you were to ask me a question now . . . [and] if the time wasn't for me to answer, I couldn't give you the answer." (As quoted in *Heading Toward Omega,* p. 196.)

Dr. Kenneth Ring has studied these "prophetic visions," as he calls them. He has found them to be quite consistent, though admittedly they are relatively few in number among near-death experiencers. He discovered the following general pattern which seems to be very much in agreement with revealed prophecies concerning the "end of the world" or "the destruction of the wicked" and the ushering in of the millennial reign of Christ (see Joseph Smith—Matthew 1:4; see also D&C sections 29, 45, 88, 101; also 77:12).

There is, first of all, a sense of having total knowledge, but specifically one is aware of seeing the entirety of the earth's evolution and history, from the beginning to the end of time. The future scenario, however, is usually of short duration, seldom extending much beyond the beginning of the twenty-first century. The individuals report that in this decade there will be an increasing incidence of earthquakes, volcanic activity, and generally massive geophysical changes. There will be resultant disturbances in weather patterns and food supplies. The world economic system will collapse, and the possibility of nuclear war or accident is very great (respondents are not agreed on *whether* a nuclear catastrophe will occur). All of these events are transitional rather than ultimate, however, and they will be followed by a new era in human history marked by human brotherhood, universal love, and world peace. (*Heading Toward Omega*, p. 197.)

George Ritchie was also privileged with a vision of the future, though it was couched in slightly different terms. The being of light, whom he took to be the Savior, indicated that mankind will have somewhat of a choice as to the future of this planet.

He opened a corridor through time which showed me increasing natural disasters coming upon this earth. There were more and more hurricanes and floods occurring over different areas of our planet. The earthquakes and volcanoes were increasing. We were becoming more and more selfish and self-righteous. Families were splitting, governments were breaking apart because people were thinking only of themselves. I saw armies marching on the United States from the south and explosions occurring over the entire world that were of a magnitude beyond my capacity to imagine. I realized if they continued, human life as we have known it could not continue to exist.

Suddenly this corridor was closed off and a second corridor started to open through time. At the beginning they appeared very similar but the further the second one unfolded, the more different it became. The planet grew more peaceful. Man and nature both were better. Man was not as critical of himself or others. He was not as destructive of nature and he was beginning to understand what love is. Then we stood at a place in time where we were more like the beings in the fourth and fifth realm. The Lord sent the mental message to me, "It is left to man which direction he shall choose." (*My Life After Dying*, pp. 29–30.)

In this same vein, Dr. Kenneth Ring went on to ask if the common scenario recounted by NDErs, which he summarized above, is inevitable. "The common view of the NDErs who have these [visions] is that not only is the scenario inevitable, but, properly understood (in the light of its outcome), it is desirable and necessary," answers Ring. Then he adds: "Nevertheless, few of these individuals would argue that there is anything fixed concerning the exact dates involved or specific events. Most seem convinced of the general direction of the events they feel they have glimpsed; none of them seems to have a rigid conception of the details of that unfolding pattern. Indeed, some openly admit that it can be affected to some degree by human action and an openness to God." (*Heading Toward Omega*, p. 205.)

From the teachings of the restored Church, we know that the destruction of the wicked is unavoidable, and that the Millennium is certain as well as most desirable. Perhaps what is conditional is how the righteous and the decent people of the earth will fare in this process. It may be that we can simply lie back and accept the deterioration of mankind as fate or we can stand up and do battle against evil, joining together with all of the good people of the earth to spread love and understanding and the leavening influence of the gospel of Jesus Christ. It only makes sense that the Lord would reward and bless his children for such an effort. President Spencer W. Kimball seemed to indicate that increased righteousness and faithful pleadings for protection and help could make the millennial transition easier.

> O my beloved hearers, what a world it would be if a million families in this church were to be on their knees like this every night and morning! And what a world it would be if nearly a hundred million families in this great land and other hundreds in other lands were praying for their sons and daughters twice daily! And what a world this would be if a billion families through the world were in home evenings and church activity and were on their physical knees pouring out their souls for their children, their families, their leaders, their governments!
>
> This kind of family life could bring us back toward the translation experience of righteous Enoch. The millennium would be ushered in. (*Teachings of Spencer W. Kimball*, pp. 116–17.)

Personal Glimpses

More specifically, some who experience temporary death
are given visions of their own futures, which are also generally
removed from their memories until just before or when they
happen. In fact, one woman foresaw her meeting with a man to
whom she was to relate her near-death experience—Dr. Raymond Moody.

> [This] subject had her eschatological NDE in 1971 when her
> heart and lungs failed during surgery. During her other-
> world journey she met several spiritual guides, who re-
> vealed her future. She was simultaneously shown a picture
> of Raymond Moody and told that she would eventually
> meet him to reveal her story! Remember that this incident
> took place four years before *Life After Life* was published,
> long before Raymond Moody became famous.
>
> [Dr. Moody later moved onto this woman's street in Vir-
> ginia, but she did not know it until Dr. Moody's son came
> trick-or-treating at her door in 1975.]
>
> The young man—whose mother was standing by him—
> replied, "I'm Raymond Avery Moody, the third." Hearing
> the name brought the precognitive NDE back to Belle's
> mind. She immediately turned to the boy's mother and
> said, "I need to talk to your husband."
>
> Mrs. Moody was surprised by the remark and asked,
> "Oh, did you have one of these experiences Raymond is
> writing about?"
>
> The question made little sense to Belle, and she asked
> Mrs. Moody what she meant. The upshot of the encounter
> was that Belle finally met Dr. Moody and told him her story,
> which the psychiatrist placed in his *Reflections on Life After
> Life*. The prediction given her in her NDE was thus fulfilled,
> and the events were witnessed by her husband and Dr.
> Moody's wife. (*The Return from Silence*, p. 194.)

This is only one of many examples. NDErs report the same
vividness in these life previews as they do in the life reviews.
We have many accounts in personal and family histories of
members of the Church in which individuals have had similar

types of experiences. However, there is another aspect of seeing the future among NDErs which also has a parallel in the general history of the Church. A small number relate the phenomenon of seeing the future as it *might be* if they make certain choices. Paula, a child of eight or nine who was drowning, recalls that "she found herself traveling swiftly down a road, stopping at a house. Paula could see her parents standing in the window reading the newspaper and crying. Upon closer examination, Paula realized the reason for her parents' grief: they were reading her obituary! At that moment, Paula was revived from her near-drowning and instantaneously returned to her physical body."

Another woman who had a brush with death at age four reported a similar scenario. "I asked myself, 'What would happen to my parents if I left them?' No sooner had I finished the thought than the answer was shown to me. I suddenly saw the images of my parents and grandparents right before me—about five feet away—on what resembled a wide projector screen—only this was in 3-dimensional color! They were grieving badly, and they looked absolutely drained. It was an extremely sad moving picture. I decided I couldn't let them go through that." (As quoted in "Three Near-Death Experiences with Premonitions of What Could Have Been," *Journal of Near-Death Studies,* vol. 9, no. 3, Spring, 1991, pp. 191–92.)

Could it be that these experiences are manifestations of the same instructive tool which the Lord employed at an important juncture in Church history? Recall that President Wilford Woodruff was allowed to see in vision what *would have happened* to the Latter-day Saints if they had not ceased to practice plural marriage. (See D&C Official Declaration—1, Excerpts from Three Addresses by President Wilford Woodruff Regarding the Manifesto, p. 293.) Interestingly, Emanuel Swedenborg also referred to a similar phenomenon as a means of instruction for spirits. Surely nothing is impossible for God.

Unfinished Business

While some who "die" are given a choice as to whether to return to mortality or not, many are simply told or helped to understand that they must go back because it is not their "time" and they yet have work to do on earth. This is a very strong witness of the Church's teachings on foredesignated missions in mortality. "To carry forward his own purposes among men and nations," explained Elder Bruce R. McConkie, "the Lord foreordained chosen spirit children in preexistence and assigned them to come to earth at particular times and places so that they might aid in furthering the divine will. These preexistence appointments, made 'according to the foreknowledge of God the Father' (1 Peter 1:2), simply designated certain individuals to perform missions which the Lord in his wisdom knew they had the talents and capacities to do." (*Mormon Doctrine*, p. 290. For an additional examination of the doctrine of foreordination see *The Life Before*, pp. 135–69.)

With these basic LDS precepts in mind, it is interesting to consider some of the near-death accounts of this principle by people of other faiths.

> Afterwards, I was back looking at my body, when a brilliant light shone around me and a voice said, "it is not your time yet—you must go back. You have work to do!" (*The Return from Silence*, p. 69.)

> An eminent physician who wrote . . . about an NDE that occurred after a car accident reported that he heard, telepathically, from the Light, "Don't you think you'd better go and finish your work?" (*After the Beyond*, p. 13.)

> Suddenly, a hand reached out and grabbed me. "He's a feisty rascal, isn't he," said a voice. "Well, Bill, it's not your time this time. You have a job to do." (*Closer to the Light*, p. 146.)

Some experiencers perceive a sort of physical barrier, line of demarcation, or point of no return which represents permanent entry into the spirit world. As mentioned, many are given a choice, while others are not because their work is not yet completed. One incident involved a stream of water that served as some type of boundary or point of no return. "I've almost gotten across . . . a still stream of water . . . but they seem to push me back and tell me it's not time yet. . . ." Another barrier was represented by a mountain top. "And a voice, a clear voice, said, 'You can't go yet. You have unfinished business. Fall this way, don't fall the other way.'" (As quoted in *Recollections of Death*, p. 51.) Others may be informed by relatives they meet in that realm that they must return. "I was communicated to by someone, possibly my father, that I must come back, that I could not stay, that it was not time for me, that there was much that I had to do and that I had to return." (As quoted in *Return from Death*, p. 51.)

As would be befitting the Lord's love and concern and his desire to save all of his children, he would surely have given each and every one of them a positive and meaningful mission or a purpose in life. God is never a source of evil and would never predesignate his sons and daughters to make wrong choices. President Joseph Fielding Smith taught:

> Every soul coming into this world came here with the promise that through obedience he would receive the blessings of salvation. No person was foreordained or appointed to sin or to perform a mission of evil. No person is ever predestined to salvation or damnation. Every person has free agency. Cain was promised by the Lord that if he would do well, he would be accepted. Judas had his agency and acted upon it; no pressure was brought to bear on him to cause him to betray the Lord, but he was led by Lucifer. If men were appointed to sin and betray their brethren, then justice could not demand that they be punished for sin and betrayal when they are guilty. (*Doctrines of Salvation*, 1:61.)

Nevertheless, some have misunderstood this concept, thinking that certain individuals were given missions of failure and sin in order to give others the chance to serve or bring about other of the Lord's purposes. (It is important to note that not one NDEr has maintained that he or she was to return to earth to do anything of this sort.) Rather, it is more likely that, because of our imperfect and fallen natures, we stray away from the mission the Lord sent us to fulfill. Surely we knew of the likelihood of this in premortality and the Lord made provisions for such eventualities, assigning us to help and serve each other when and if we made mistakes. (See also the statement of Joseph Smith to Brigham Young, below.)

Moreover, there are some LDS experiencers who, according to their own perceptions of the spirit world, have implied that we were allowed to choose many or all aspects of our future temporal existence, including families and missions in life. Official statements by the First Presidency of the Church have explicitly cautioned us not to advance such an idea because we have no revealed doctrine to that effect (see *The Life Before,* pp. 157–59). In addition, it seems that such a state of affairs would be totally unfeasible. "This belief has been advocated by some," stated President Joseph Fielding Smith, "and it is possible that in some instances it is true, but it would require too great a stretch of the imagination to believe it to be so in all, or even in the majority of cases. Most likely we came where those in authority decided to send us. Our agency may not have been exercised to the extent of making choice of parents and posterity." (*The Way to Perfection,* p. 44.)

Thus, while we know that our talents and capacities were taken into account in foreordaining us to earthly callings, it may be that our desires and preferences were also considered and, in some cases, granted. But, as with the earthly church, which presumably is patterned after the organization in the premortal world, it seems logical that the final designations and callings would be made by those with priesthood authority. Otherwise, chaos would reign. Perhaps *our* choice was then in whether or not to accept our callings or foreordinations. This seemed to be the pattern followed when Christ accepted his mission as Savior (see Abraham 3:27). Elder Bruce R. McConkie was more definitive on this subject. "All men are the spirit children of the Eternal Father; all dwelt in his presence, awaiting the day of their mortal probation; all have come or will come to earth at an appointed time, in a specified place, to live among a designated people. In all of this there is no chance. A divine providence rules over the nations and governs in the affairs of men. Birth and death and mortal kinship are the Lord's doings. He alone determines where and when and among what people his spirit children shall undergo their mortal probation." (*A New Witness for the Articles of Faith,* p. 512.)

The deceased Prophet Joseph Smith seemed to be referring to this perfect organization and foreordination of the earth's inhabitants by the Lord when he appeared to Brigham Young in a dream. He counseled Brigham to "be sure to tell the people to keep the Spirit of the Lord; and if they will, they will find themselves just as they were organized by our Father in Heaven before they came into the world. Our Father in Heaven organized the human family, but they are all disorganized and in great confusion." (Brigham Young, *Journal History*, February 23, 1847, as quoted in Hyrum L. Andrus, *Doctrinal Commentary on the Pearl of Great Price*, p. 122.)

Learning that we have all been organized to contribute something positive and worthwhile to life, both here and hereafter, should endow us with renewed understanding and restored vision. We comprehend that we are here not only to discover and fulfill our own previously assigned missions but also to help our spirit siblings find and complete theirs. Indeed, as we will show in the next part, this sense of mission has an unquestionably profound effect upon those who learn of their purpose in life through near-death experiences.

PART V

Impact on Mortality

CHAPTER 14

_____

Changed Lives

One of the strongest and most irrefutable evidences of the reality of near-death experiences is the remarkable transformation in the lives of its percipients. The changes in the majority of these people are so marked that researchers conclude something significant has unquestionably happened to the individual. Separate studies have even been conducted and books written on the often measurable differences between the person before the NDE and after the experience and between NDErs and the general population.

It is necessary to remember, however, that there are some exceptions to these positive transformations. As mentioned in the chapter on hell, even those who have negative experiences tend to be changed for the better. Unfortunately, a few who have NDEs, whether hellish or heavenly, may react negatively. They may feel depressed, overwhelmed, or angry from these glimpses of another life. Some may be frightened and discouraged by hellish encounters while others may fall into pride or self-righteousness, feeling "favored" by positive experiences. Though the predominant effect of NDEs and other spirit world manifestations is to lift the recipient to a higher plane of life, the experiencer is yet human and still has agency and therefore can choose how to respond to the experience.

Depression on Returning

One unpleasant side effect of these experiences appears to be fairly common, but seems to be only temporary in most cases. It is understandably difficult for some to return to the mundane and restrictive reality of mortality after having glimpsed such transcendent love, magnificence, and freedom. Apparently President Brigham Young had tasted something of this unhappy disparity between the two worlds. "I can say with regard to parting with our friends, and going ourselves, that I have been near enough to understand eternity so that I have had to exercise a great deal more faith to desire to live than I ever exercised in my whole life to live. The brightness and glory of the next apartment is inexpressible." (In *Journal of Discourses*, 14:231.) The Apostle Paul also grappled with this strange dichotomy. "For I am in a strait betwixt two," he declared, "having a desire to depart, and to be with Christ; which is far better: nevertheless to abide in the flesh is more needful for you" (Philippians 1:23–24).

Many NDErs testify of struggling against this type of almost overwhelming burden when they return to earth life. "The Light of Jesus had entered my life and filled it completely, and the idea of being separated from Him was more than I could bear," lamented Dr. George Ritchie. ". . . And strangely enough, it was the glory of that world, . . . which made my return to this life so hard. The contrast between the love of Jesus and the world in which I found myself having to go on living made the year following my illness the most difficult of my life." (*Return from Tomorrow*, pp. 74, 85.) American author Katherine Anne Porter, who had likewise experienced "temporary death" in 1918 during a bout with influenza, described the ensuing emotional battle she fought, after her revival, to stay interested in life. "I had seen my heavenly vision and the world was pretty dull after that. My mood for several years thereafter was that it was not a world worth living in. And yet one has faith, one has the inner core of strength that comes from somewhere, . . . Throughout my life there have been times during the day when I have both an intense wish to die and later an eagerness that can't wait to see the next day. In fact, if I hadn't been tough as an alley cat, I wouldn't be here today." (As quoted in *The Light Beyond*, p. 28.)

Darryl, another NDEr who did not want to return to earth, was informed by a being of light that he must go back and finish his work there. It devastated him. "What work?" he complained.

> The next thing is that in thirty years, I experienced the worst feeling I ever had. The most depressed, the most severe anxiety I've ever had was at the moment I realized I must return to this earth. That is the greatest depths of depression I personally have ever had since that time or before. It was so devastatin' that I cannot think of anything bad that has ever happened to me and put it in the same parameters—the distance is a million miles. I did not want to come back. And now that I'm back, I'm absolutely assured of the fact that I did not want to come back. . . . This [earth] is a wonderful place to live if you don't know anywhere else. I know somewhere else. (As quoted in *Heading Toward Omega*, p. 91.)

President Jedediah M. Grant, who related to President Heber C. Kimball his visits to the spirit world, lamented, "Of all the dreads that ever came across me, the worst was to have to again return to my body, though I had to do it" (in *Journal of Discourses*, 4:135). Besides depression, some who do not want to return to this life become angry. These are sobering statements for those of us who may begin to think that we, too, would like to have a near-death encounter or visit the spirit world in some way.

Apparently there are a small number who do not overcome this depression and anger and who fail to apply the significant spiritual lessons they had learned in that higher world. A few may languish in such frustration and self-pity only for a time and then determine to get on with their lives and their journey back to the light. At any rate, it seems that the majority of experiencers go on to enjoy and contribute to life more than ever before. While some positive changes can also cause disruption in the life of an NDEr and his or her family, the net result still appears to be positive.

No More Fear of Death

Revelations of the restored gospel teach us, at least conceptually, that death is nothing to be feared if we have loved and lived according to the best we knew. "And it shall come to pass that those that die in me shall not taste of death, for it shall be sweet unto them" (D&C 42:46). Indeed, it seems that death is not only nothing to be afraid of but also an event to look forward to with some anticipation. "We shall turn around and look upon it," declared President Brigham Young, speaking of death, "and think, when we have crossed it, why this is the greatest advantage of my whole existence, for I have passed from a state of sorrow, grief, mourning, woe, misery, pain, anguish and disappointment into a state of existence where I can enjoy life to the fullest extent as far as that can be done without a body" (in *Journal of Discourses*, 17:142). Like many modern-day General Authorities, Elder Francis M. Lyman, President of the Quorum of the Twelve Apostles during the administration of President Joseph F. Smith, also taught the Saints that death is nothing to be feared.

It will be alright when our time comes, when we have finished our work and accomplished what the Lord required of us. If we are prepared, we need not be afraid to go, for it will be one of the most pleasant sensations that ever comes to the soul of man, whenever he departs, if he can go with a clear conscience into the presence of the Lord. . . . We will be full of joy and happiness, and we will enter into a place of rest, of peace, of joy, rest from every sorrow. What a blessed thing that will be! We will never be tired any more. We will not get tired, for we will be in a condition that we can endure and enjoy our work; for we shall be occupied and employed on the other side as we are on this side; we shall have plenty to occupy our attention right along. (In Conference Report, October 1909, pp. 18–19.)

Despite these and numerous other prophetic reassurances from leaders of the Church, it is understandable that those of us who have never made the transition do not yet *know* this experientially. As a result, some level of trepidation may linger in our hearts. It appears that the Lord has instilled in each of us some degree of fear and anxiety about death in order to cause us to cling to life, fulfill our missions in mortality, and complete our probation.

In contrast to those of us who have never approached death and who may nervously wonder what lies beyond the veil, the vast majority of those who have died and returned testify that, at least for those who have lived decent lives, death is not only sweet but is also a magnification and perpetuation of every good and wonderful thing and the diminution and discontinuation of every evil and undesirable mortal element. "If that is what death is like," remarked one NDEr, "then I'm not afraid to go. . . . If that's any way like the hereafter is, then I'm not afraid to go at all. I have absolutely no fear at all. . . . I'm convinced. I think I had just a peek into it." (As quoted in *Life at Death*, p. 177.) Dr. Cherie Sutherland, a near-death researcher in Australia, noted: "Over three-quarters of my respondents said that they had a fear of death before the NDE, whereas not one person among my sample has a fear of death now. Many laughed at the question." ("Changes in Religious Beliefs, Attitudes, and Practices Following Near-Death Experiences: An Australian Study," in *Journal of Near-Death Studies*, vol. 9, no. 1, Fall 1990, p. 28.)

As additional illustrations of this important by-product of near-death experiences, here are some further comments from participants in the "Transformations Study" conducted by Dr. Melvin Morse.

"It's not death, it's another kind of life."

"Heaven is a nice place to go."

"Death? Not worried about it at all."

"I don't fear it. It will be like going into another dimension. Death is simply an open door. I don't mourn too much when people die."

"Death is something that our society fears, and that people learn to fear. It is too bad, because it actually is really nice." (As quoted in *Transformed by the Light*, p. 64.)

More Purpose in Life

Ironically, although these NDErs generally lose their fear of death, they also cling even more tenaciously to life—convinced that it has a great and important purpose. They tend to feel that they know why they are here and where they are going. "I was transformed from a man who was lost and wandering aimlessly, with no goal in life other than a desire for material wealth, to someone who had a deep motivation, a purpose in life, a definite direction, and an overpowering conviction that there would be a reward at the end of life similar to the pot of gold at the end of the rainbow. . . . The changes in my life were completely positive." (As quoted in *The Return from Silence*, p. 196.)

One of our greatest blessings as members of The Church of Jesus Christ of Latter-day Saints is our knowledge and understanding of the purpose of life and the plan of salvation, of which these individuals either receive or remember only an intimation. What *they* learn tends to coincide with what the gospel has always taught *us*. "Death holds little fear for me now," said one man, "and I know myself and all humankind to be spirit, clad temporarily in body, here on earth to learn and grow" (as quoted in "Amazing Grace: The Near-Death Experience as a Compensatory Gift," in *Journal of Near-Death Studies*, vol. 10, no. 1, Fall 1991, p. 33). Professor Howard Storm, quoted previously, summarized the central lessons an NDEr gleans about life from a glimpse into the other world.

Near Death Experiencers are strong advocates of the joy of life. Near Death Experiencers don't have to prove themselves to be loved by God, they know they are loved by God and they know that the only viable response is to reciprocate God's love. Near Death Experiencers understand that the creation is an expression of God's love and that we should appreciate this creation. Near Death Experiencers know that their life is a gift from a loving God, which they are to enjoy and to use for its maximum potential for good and for learning. (Transcript of a paper presented by Howard Storm at the IANDS Conference, August 16–19, 1990.)

Even though most of these NDErs have not yet had access to the more specific revelations of the gospel, such as the Word of Wisdom, those who are privileged to gain this new understanding through near-death experiences subsequently live a life-style which is very much akin to and compatible with what we espouse in Mormonism. Many seem to comprehend the importance not only of life but also of taking care of their bodies and of developing their hearts, minds, and souls. This sort of reinforcement or confirmation of the values we teach because of our understanding of the purpose of life is very gratifying.

> For instance, people who have NDEs exercise more than the "normal" population, eat more fresh fruits and vegetables, use fewer medications like aspirin and other over-the-counter remedies. They also have fewer psychosomatic complaints, miss less time from work, and have fewer years of unemployment than the control groups.
>
> Also, they have fewer hidden symptoms of depression and anxiety than any of the control groups. They spend more time alone in solitary pursuits or in meditation or quiet contemplation. . . .
>
> Those touched by the light at an early age give more of themselves to the community by performing volunteer work. They also give more of their income to charities and are often in helping professions like nursing or special education. (*Transformed by the Light*, pp. 189–90.)

Thus those who claim that the blissful views revealed in a study of near-death episodes may make others anxious to end their own lives have missed the whole point. The net effect of seeing the next life is an understanding of how it is directly dependent on this life. Mortality becomes more important than ever. No matter how miserable life may be on earth, we are responsible to "endure to the end." Perhaps near-suicide accounts best illustrate this point. One child learned this lesson at the age of seven. Severely abused by both parents, she attempted to commit suicide. She nearly succeeded. As she felt the love and comfort of the Light, she also heard a voice say, "You have made a mistake. Your life is not yours to take. You must go back." She protested, "No one cares about me." The answer that followed shocked her. "You're right. No one on this planet cares about you, including your parents. It is your job to care for yourself." Another child who tried to kill himself at eleven years of age received a similar response. "He [the Light] was kind but not very sympathetic. He said, 'Well, you'll just have to stick around and see what you can do with your life.'" (As quoted in *Closer to the Light*, pp. 159–61.) A third girl, who attempted suicide as a teen-ager, was also taught, as we are, that the body is a temple. "I was shown the beauty of my body and of every body. I was told that my body was a gift and I was supposed to take care of it, not kill it." (As quoted in *Transformed by the Light*, p. 152.) As a result of being given this direction for their lives, all of these children went on to become happy, giving, productive adults.

Therefore, NDErs add their witness to the testimony of the Latter-day Saints that life is never meaningless, no matter how pointless and lonely it may seem at times. Several claim to have learned that there is a reason for everything that happens to us, good and bad, and that we will one day see how it all fits together and makes perfect sense. For instance, a Jewish woman questioned the Light about the terrible injustices of life.

I'm sure that I asked the question that had been plaguing me since childhood about the sufferings of my people. I do remember this: there was a reason for *everything* that happened, no matter how awful it appeared in the physical realm. And within myself, as I was given the answer, my own awakening mind now responded in the same manner:

"Of course," I would think, "I already know that. How could I ever have forgotten!" Indeed it appears that all that happens is for a purpose, and that purpose is already known to our eternal self. (As quoted in "Amazing Grace: The Near-Death Experience as a Compensatory Gift," in *Journal of Near-Death Studies*, vol. 10, no. 1, Fall 1991, p. 16.)

NDErs seem to realize that this mortal probation is literally a "once in a lifetime" opportunity; a preparation for real life—eternal life. It is a gift from God to be enjoyed and magnified to the fullest.

Psychic Powers/Spiritual Gifts

Some experiencers apparently return from their encounter with the Light having retained some portion of the abilities they enjoyed while in its presence. There have been several fascinating studies documenting increased paranormal abilities in NDErs after their near-death episode. Dr. Melvin Morse's study is typical. "The Transformations study explored other mysteries of the near-death experience. Perhaps the most intriguing is the fact that psychic and precognitive events happen many times more frequently to NDErs. I find these very pronounced psychic abilities hard to believe. In fact I *would not* believe them if there were not so many of them. When I use a bar graph to compare the number of verifiable psychic experiences, the sheer number of experiences in the study group towers above those of the control group like a skyscraper over a tract home." (*Transformed by the Light*, pp. 192–93.)

Another phenomenon which some NDErs experience is increased intelligence. Not only do NDErs return with a thirst for learning but some also retain bits and pieces of the knowledge they were given while in the light. One man named Tom Sawyer, a high school graduate and manual laborer who hated to read, was imbued with "all knowledge" during a near-death experience. Not long after his recovery, words and mathematical equations previously unknown to him would pop into his mind. Through these and other remarkable experiences he was led to seek out and study the field of quantum physics. He found that much of the information was already familiar to him. Though he continued to drive heavy equipment for the city in which he lives, he went on to study quantum physics in college and become well versed in other fields as well. (For the full account, see *Heading Toward Omega*, pp. 114–19. For a similarly remarkable story, see *Transformed by the Light*, pp. 11–15.)

Interestingly, those who have had near-death episodes also tend to have increased electromagnetic fields within their bodies. Dr. Morse found that, in a significant number, "their electromagnetic signature can actually stop a watch" (*Transformed by the Light*, p. 134). As a result, many of them cannot wear watches. One female NDEr had problems with the light-sensitive street lights that line some roads. As she would approach them at night, they would turn off, as they are supposed to do when the sun becomes bright enough that they are not needed. Others may find that they interfere with electrical appliances. Dr. Morse feels that "the electrical changes are responsible for the transformations we see in near-death experiencers. In short, people who have near-death experiences are 'rewired.' " (*Transformed by the Light*, p. 134.)

It is conceivable that, to some extent, Dr. Morse could be right. Perhaps in discovering the electromagnetic field, scientists have merely found a way to detect and measure the real energy of the spirit body and the intelligence or Light of Christ which comprises it (see chapter 2). It may be that those who bask in the light of the spirit world are "recharged" by gaining and retaining increased amounts of this light and therefore of its properties. We know that it is possible and even desirable to grow brighter and brighter by receiving God's light (see D&C 50:24), which light may be not just a figurative expression but a literal enlightenment of the mind and an illumination of the spirit. "That body which is filled with light comprehendeth all things" (D&C 88:67). Could it be that the abilities that are so often characterized as paranormal or superhuman, including the increased electromagnetic fields, are indeed the scientifically measurable results of the real influence of the Light of Christ on the soul of man? Once again, as we are becoming increasingly aware, science and religion are not enemies but companions in a marriage which unites all truth.

Inwardly Spiritual Vs. Outwardly Religious

Religion also becomes a more dominant factor in the lives of those who have near-death experiences. Those who were atheists and agnostics often come to believe in a superior being. "I felt closer to a—a God. Which I had not for years. [Before] I was an agnostic, I didn't know. (*Do you now feel you know?*) I feel much closer that I know. I find myself praying sometimes to [pause] an unknown Force." (As quoted in *Life at Death*, p. 163.) Some become more active in their churches, while others may actually become less affiliated with organized religion. Yet all tend to become more inwardly religious or spiritual, praying or communing more with God and seeking to develop a very personal relationship with him.

Those who seek to express their renewed religiousness through church affiliation are less caught up in the outward observance and in the appearance of righteousness and more concerned about their inward spirituality. A Protestant woman found her faith deepened and her need to impress others lessened. "I am known as one of the most enthusiastic of Christians. *Enthusiastic* was the word used *before* my experience. The enthusiasm before was outward and since has drawn inward into a yearning to be *real* and to be the me I was created to be in yielding my own life up to preferring others before myself. Before, I wanted the world to *see* and help me and admire the beautiful walk with God I had. Now I want to love people with the love God loved me as the Light of His love ebbed through me as I dissolved in it for a moment of life-changing revelation. That love does not exploit nor call attention to itself." Another woman felt less need to convert and more need to love, which has more converting power anyway. "I don't feel a strong need to be evangelical about the work that I do. I don't feel a need to convert people in a religious sense. I feel I'm very, extremely, low-key in this respect. I do feel that this sense of divine love within me speaks for Himself, and I believe that people can sense the genuineness of my deep spirituality and I think that this speaks louder than words." (As quoted in *After the Beyond*, pp. 81, 82.)

Nancy Clark, who enjoyed a glimpse of the spirit world while speaking at a friend's funeral service and who joined a church after her experience, described a difference between religion and spirituality. Her distinction is both insightful and significant as regards understanding the real purpose of religion in the lives of God's children.

> I feel as if I was elevated to a higher level of spirituality. This manifests itself in several ways. Prior to my experience I did not attend church or have any formal religious training during my adult life. Following the experience, I joined a church and am very interested in learning about Biblical teachings, etc. However, I must stress that there is quite a difference between religion and spirituality. It seems to me that I was elevated beyond "religion." By that I mean, religion is a tool used to climb the ladder, so to speak, to reach the higher level of spirituality.
>
> In my experience so far with organized religion, it often fails to bring about this higher level of spirituality by concentrating on rules and regulations and inter-denominational conflicts. I am in no way degrading any religion as I feel they all play an important role in providing the people with spiritual nourishment. (As quoted in *Heading Toward Omega*, p. 221.)

Indeed, it seems that the majority of recipients of the near-death experience become less inclined toward organized religion. (No empirical studies have yet been conducted to examine whether this phenomenon occurs among LDS near-death experiencers, but from anecdotal evidence it does not seem to be the case. However, they may also feel more inwardly spiritual and less inclined toward the outward "show" of religiosity.) One study found that "sixty percent claimed to be neither religious nor spiritual in orientation before the NDE. . . . The remaining 40 percent were made up of those who claimed to have been religious (24 percent) and spiritual (16 percent) before the NDE. After the NDE, only 6 percent claimed to be still religious, while 76 percent now claimed to be spiritually inclined." ("Changes in Religious Beliefs, Attitudes, and Practices Following Near-Death Experiences: An Australian Study," in *Journal of Near-Death Studies,* vol. 9, no. 1, Fall 1990, p. 28.) There are generally two reasons given by NDErs for this reaction: 1) they no longer feel the need for the external trappings of religion in order to really worship God, and, 2) they believe that all Christian religions possess some degree of truth and goodness.

Dr. Kenneth Ring quoted some of those who, in his study, felt that "organized religion may either be irrelevant to or interfere with the expression of this inward sense of religiousness."

> [Before I was] fairly religious, but in a superficial way. I was more or less caught up in the *ritual* and the *trappings* of religion. And afterwards, for the short period after, I realized that the ritual and all that [pause] really meant nothing. It was the faith and the deep-down *meaning* that was of importance.

> I've always had difficulty with religions anyway. And, after this experience, as time went on, as this progression was going on, I found that the need to go to communion, confession, go to a place to pray, observe Good Friday, or any of these kinds of things, not only weren't necessary, but they were *blocking* what was really supposed to be happening. So that's why I have no affiliation. (As quoted in *Life at Death,* p. 164.)

Further, Dr. Ring found that besides the tendency to emphasize outward observance, "it is the smug sectarian quality of some religious groups to which core experiencers tend to object, not to the basics of religious worship itself" (p. 164). One man who had been studying at a theological seminary before his encounter with death learned first-hand that feeling superior to others because of religious denomination was wrong. "My doctor told me I 'died' during the surgery. But I told him that I came to life. I saw in that vision what a stuck-up [fool] I was with all that theory, looking down on everyone who wasn't a member of my denomination or didn't subscribe to the theological beliefs that I did." (As quoted in *The Light Beyond*, p. 49.)

While some abandon organized religion altogether, a few are comfortable with any religion that teaches God's love. "I feel that church is a bit of a sham. Not God but the people. They seem to fuss over stupid little things that are really just political. But I belong to a lot of churches. I play the guitar in the Roman Catholic folk group, I'm in the musical group of the Church of Christ, and I play with the Salvation Army. I'm probably Anglican but it doesn't worry me where I am—it's all God inside me." ("Changes in Religious Beliefs, Attitudes, and Practices Following Near-Death Experiences: An Australian Study," in *Journal of Near-Death Studies*, vol. 9, no. 1, Fall 1990, p. 29.) Another experiencer believed, "I know that I can go to a Catholic church, an Episcopalian church, a Baptist church, I don't care *where* you go, it's all the same. There's no difference. It's just a different word." (As quoted in *Life at Death*, p. 165.)

All of this may seem, at first glance, to pose a problem for The Church of Jesus Christ of Latter-day Saints, which claims to be the only true church possessing a fulness of the gospel of Jesus Christ. We will address this dilemma further in chapter 15, but for now we will note the areas of agreement with these statements.

First of all, we would concur that the inward spirituality and relationship with the Lord must be the source of the outward observance, otherwise that action has little or no meaning or saving power. The word *religion* derives from the same root as the word *ligament*. While a ligament is something, as in our anatomy, that ties together, a religion is that which ties us to God. But to be effective, the practices of a religion, including the LDS church, should have the goal of bringing us to love, serve, and become like God rather than being ends in themselves. If the religious observance itself were all that mattered, the Savior would not have so roundly and consistently condemned the hypocritical scribes and Pharisees who kept the letter of the law (and then some) but completely missed the spirit of it. They overlooked the intent for which the law was given, thinking themselves better than their fellowmen because of their rigid "righteousness." Dr. George Ritchie had this to say about such religionists. "To me, pseudo-religion, or, as Blake calls it, the 'Religion of Caiaphas,' acts like religious ostriches who bury their heads in the sands of tradition because they fear anything new that will bring change. They create a church full of spiritual pygmies. This pseudo-religion creates a religion of fear, hopelessness, and lies against the teaching of Jesus." (*My Life After Dying*, pp. 118–19.)

Emanuel Swedenborg likewise spoke of the futility of dogma without inner devotion. "Almost all of [those entering the spirit world] are eager to know whether they will get into heaven. Most of them believe that they will because they have led a moral and civic life in the world, without considering that evil and good people lead lives that are similar in outward aspects, do good works for other people in similar fashion, attend church in similar fashion, listen to sermons, and pray. They are wholly unaware that outward behavior and outward worship do not accomplish anything, but rather the inner elements from which the outward ones come." (*Heaven and Hell*, p. 401.)

Dr. Raymond Moody notes that many NDErs "tend to abandon religious doctrine purely for the sake of doctrine" (*The Light Beyond*, p. 49). Where doctrine is true, has meaning and gives understanding, it need not be discarded. Fortunate are those indeed who have true doctrine and true conversion. In the midst of the controversy over the necessity of circumcision in the early Church, the Apostle Paul confirmed to the Roman Saints that the token of circumcision and their traditional Jewishness were an advantage *only* to Jews who were inwardly converted to Christ and his gospel. Circumcision had no saving value alone. The Joseph Smith Translation renders this passage more understandable. "What advantage then hath the Jew over the Gentile? or what profit of circumcision, who is not a Jew from the heart? But he who is a Jew from the heart, I say hath much every way: chiefly because that unto them were committed the oracles of God." (JST Romans 3:1–2.)

As with the Jews, Latter-day Saints feel that the "oracles of God" have been committed to the Church as the official representative of the Lord and his gospel on the earth. At the risk of seeming smug to others, we maintain that we are the one church which has been entrusted with a *fulness* of the truth necessary for salvation and the responsibility of making it available to everyone (see D&C 1:30). By no means, however, do we feel that we alone will go to heaven after we die, while all others will go to hell. Nor do we assert that we alone have a corner on all truth, goodness, love, and righteousness. Though we may be accused of being narrow-minded or self-righteous because we claim to be the only true church (a position declared by the Lord himself—see Joseph Smith—History 1:19; D&C 1:30), we recognize that many members of other faiths practice selfless Christian principles and we gratefully acknowledge the truths they teach. We believe that all people who will receive it are given at least some portion of the truth and the Spirit of the Lord to help them live lives of love and goodness. Additionally, all who have ever lived or will live on this earth will have every reasonable opportunity to be taught, to understand, and to accept the doctrines and ordinances of the gospel of Jesus Christ, either here or in the next life. God has one true way, and he will make it available to all of his children, whom he loves with a perfect and divine love.

In the meantime, whatever church one belongs to, the most important thing is what kind of life one lives in relation to the two great commandments. It is easier to teach an honest-hearted, truth-loving person new doctrine than to change an evil, hateful person into a righteous one, no matter what his religion. As for Latter-day Saints, they will be held accountable for both inner spirituality and outward religiousness because of the greater light and knowledge they possess. A fuller portion of God's truth should make available to them an even deeper conversion and a greater ability to love God and serve his children. This is the intent of the gospel and the responsibility which accompanies a knowledge of it.

What Matters Most

One of the most important lessons people who have glimpsed beyond the veil of death learn is what is most important and lasting in life. It often brings a radical reordering of their priorities in life. After their experiences, they tend to abandon the meaningless pursuits that preoccupy so many of us. For one thing, they become less materialistic and less worried about the unimportant concerns of life. One man related:

> This [experience] has taken a lot of the load off me. But I still have struggles in living the faith, but I realize the grace of God takes care of all that. But in my life I have discounted a lot of trivial things I used to worry about. The Lord has allowed me through this experience to separate what is important from what is not important. That has been a terrific boon to me. . . . He made me through this experience to be able to completely put myself in the hands of the Lord and totally believe. . . . You can imagine what a boon that is to my life to be able to totally commit myself 100 percent without any reservation. . . . Most men have trouble with their pride. This has ceased to be a problem, to a great extent anyway. At least it doesn't trouble me, because I understand the Lord's grace. Also, I was born into a farm family with very, very modest circumstances, and I've always had a great desire to be real prosperous. Well, I don't think anybody would mind being prosperous, but I see how little it really does mean to my faith. I found out that some of these things are really laughable as far as importance [is concerned]. (As quoted in *Recollections of Death*, pp. 131–32.)

Another man had trouble readjusting to the banalities of mortal life. He became very sensitive toward those things which were antithetical to the world he had glimpsed.

> And, I can recall in my attempt to hold onto this feeling and to hold onto this peace, I began to bump into earthly things that you know, of course, aren't going to escape from you—they're there. My first frustrating experience was with the television. I couldn't watch television. There would be a commercial, a cosmetic commercial, I couldn't— I'd have to turn it off because it was something false, it was unnecessary, it was fake. It just didn't belong, [it was]

insignificant. Any type of violence, if there was even an old Western, an old Western movie, I'd have to turn it off because to me that was total ignorance. There was just no reason on earth to show people killing people. (As quoted in *Heading Toward Omega*, pp. 96–97.)

Others become aware of the importance of "stopping to smell the roses." They developed increased respect and awe for God's creations. "There were changes in me that are worth noting," wrote a man with a Ph.D. "It bothers me to kill anything. In our old farmhouse we have some big black woolly spiders. Nobody likes them, but I really don't want to kill them . . . I do go deer and elk hunting with my sons, but . . . I don't like killing any life form and I avoid it to a much, much higher degree than before." (As quoted in "NDEs and the Not-Close-To-Death Experience," in *Vital Signs*, vol. 1, no. 3, August–September, 1992, p. 12.) A woman gained an enhanced appreciation of nature, especially for the beauties and renewed life of springtime. "I think—I think I *noticed* it more [afterward]. I think that before—before, I used to take spring for granted. But I have the feeling that I'm *looking* more and more—and seeing life. It's really nice." (As quoted in *Life at Death*, p. 143.)

Love and Learning

Above all, these individuals learn that the only things we can take with us into the next life are what we *are* and what we *know*. Most of what is important in life may be summarized, as it was by Dr. Moody, under the categories of "learning to love other people and acquiring knowledge" (*Life After Life*, p. 65). These are also the basic principles underlying virtually all of the teachings and practices of The Church of Jesus Christ of Latter-day Saints.

While the Bible teaches the preeminence of charity, the Book of Mormon not only confirms that principle with a second witness but also clarifies what charity is. "Wherefore . . . if ye have not charity, ye are nothing, for charity never faileth. Wherefore, cleave unto charity, which is the greatest of all, for all things must fail—but charity is the pure love of Christ, and it endureth forever; and whoso is found possessed of it at the last day, it shall be well with him." (Moroni 7:46–47.) This is the charity experienced by those who bask in the light and love of the Lord's Spirit. This is the love which they seek to share with their fellow beings, and more especially with family members. "I became a better person, a better husband, a better father, a better business man. Know and trust that I'm kinder, more loving, a more sensitive human being." (As quoted in "NDEs and the Not-Close-To-Death Experience," in *Vital Signs*, vol. 1, no. 3, August–September, 1992, p.12.) The following comments are also representative.

> My joy comes from another's smile. I also notice that I reach out and touch people more . . . I seem to make people feel better. I know this—that when there's a family problem, everyone turns to me. . . . I have more insight into other people [now]. . . . It's very difficult for me to lose my temper anymore. I can see the pain in other people's eyes. That's why they hurt other people because they really don't understand. . . . The most important thing that we have are our relationships with other people. . . . It all comes down to caring and compassion and love for your fellow man . . . Love is the answer. It's the answer to everything. (As quoted in *The Return from Silence*, pp. 195–96.)

> I came out of this near-death experience with the one positive knowledge that is constantly magnified in my life, and that is that love is the innermost core of our entire being, the core of what life is really all about (p. 242).

> I gained a lot of understanding. I saw that we're moving so fast in our society, we're not taking time to look at what God has given us. We're not getting to know people, which is the essence of what it's all about. We're not here to be making millions of dollars and getting to the top of the corporate ladder. That's not what God wants us to do. We're here for people. (As quoted in *After the Beyond*, p. 88.)

Interestingly, Swedenborg made this comment about those who have learned to love. "The people who have loved a great deal, then, are the ones who are called wise; the people who have loved a little are the ones who are called simple" (*Heaven and Hell*, p. 266). And, Dr. George Ritchie deduced from his interlude in the spirit world that, "God is busy building a race of men who know how to love. I believe that the fate of the earth itself depends on the progress we make—and that the time now is very short. As for what we'll find in the next world, here too I believe that what we'll discover there depends on how well we get on with the business of loving, here and now." (*Return from Tomorrow*, p. 124.) There could be numerous other examples and statements given because this is the central message of those who return from the life beyond.

In keeping with these lessons of love learned in the spirit world, most NDErs go on to become involved in the "helping" or service-related professions or devote much of their time to volunteer work. One of the most dramatic of such changes took place in a hardened gangster who had an NDE. He left his old "job" and became committed to helping others both in and out of his new profession. "I realize there has been even more of an enormous change in myself, from then to now, in that what I'm doing is to help people; it's not for gain, monetary gain" (as quoted in *After the Beyond*, p. 42). Others have similar conversions to serving others instead of focusing so much upon themselves. Latter-day Saints, like other Christians, also consider service to be the hallmark of love for God and fellowmen. "And behold, I tell you these things that you may learn wisdom; that ye may learn that when ye are in the service of your fellow beings ye are only in the service of your God" (Mosiah 2:17). True religion, pure and undefiled, is expressed in giving service to the needy (see James 1:27).

Learning all we can is the second most important thing we can do in this life. Latter-day Saints believe that such acquisition of knowledge is required not only in preparation for earthly service but, ultimately, for godhood. "We need constant instruction," announced Brigham Young, "and our great heavenly Teacher requires of us to be diligent pupils in his school, that we may in time reach his glorified presence. If we will not lay to heart the rules of education which our Teacher gives us to study, and continue to advance from one branch of learning to another, we never can be scholars of the first class and become endowed with the science, power, excellency, brightness and glory of the heavenly hosts; and unless we are educated as they are, we cannot associate with them." (*Discourses of Brigham Young*, pp. 248–49.) Thus, God's truth encompasses all truth, and "the glory of God is intelligence, or, in other words, light and truth" (D&C 93:36). For this reason, the Lord has exhorted us to seek learning of all kinds. "Seek ye diligently and teach one another words of wisdom; yea, seek ye out of the best books words of wisdom; seek learning, even by study and also by faith" (D&C 88:118; see also vv. 78–79).

Dr. Raymond Moody reported that the quest for knowledge advocated by NDErs is partly for the benefit of mankind. To one woman who had what Dr. Moody called the "vision of knowledge" (where the person experiences "all knowledge"), he asked if it is pointless to seek knowledge here since it will all be easier to learn "there." She replied emphatically: "No! You still want to seek knowledge even after you come back here. . . . It's not silly to try to get the answers here. I sort of felt that it was part of our purpose . . . but that it wasn't just for one person, but that it was to be used for all mankind. We're always reaching out to help others with what we know." (As quoted in *Reflections on Life After Life*, p. 12.)

As we noted in the previous chapter, many NDErs also learn that education is a process that goes on for eternity, though they may not comprehend why this is so. Nancy Clark, mentioned previously, related: "I read and search out everything I can. I don't know why I seem to feel as if I'm preparing myself in some way for something greater. Knowledge seems to be very, very important but I don't know why I feel so compelled to learn." (As quoted in *Heading Toward Omega*, p. 222.) Dr. Raymond Moody explained that the NDErs he studied often "embark on new careers or take up serious courses of study." He qualifies: "None that I know of, however, have pursued knowledge for the sake of knowledge. Rather, they all feel that knowledge is important only if it contributes to the wholeness of the person." He quotes the following man who, previous to his "temporary death" experience, had little schooling and resented scholars and professors, thinking they contributed little to the world.

> But while the doctors were saying I was dead, this person I was with, this light, the Christ, showed me a dimension of knowledge, I'll call it. . . .
>
> Now that was a humbling experience for me. You can say I don't scorn professors anymore. Knowledge is important. I read everything I can get my hands on now . . . It's not that I regret taking the path I did in life, but I'm glad that I have time now for learning. History, science, literature. I'm interested in it all. My wife fusses at me about my books in our room. Some of it helps me understand my experience better. . . . All of it does, in one way or another, because, as I say, when you have one of these experiences, you see that everything is connected. (As quoted in *The Light Beyond*, pp. 44–45.)

From his experiences, Dr. Ritchie also saw the correlation of all truth. He surmised: "God wants us to search for truth in every area of life until we find it. This is not only true on the spiritual level but also in the mental and physical levels. Any time we learn a new truth in any field we are drawing closer to God." (*My Life After Dying*, p. 32.)

Finally, Emanuel Swedenborg adds his witness of the importance of acquiring knowledge in order to become more like God. "A person who is involved in that faith and in a life conformable to faith is involved in the ability and capacity to become intelligent and wise. But if he is to become intelligent and wise, he needs to keep learning many things—not just things of heaven, but things of earth as well. He needs to learn things of heaven from the Word and the church, and things of the world from the sciences." (*Heaven and Hell*, p. 267.)

True Knowledge

All of these passages imply that not all knowledge is equal. Only knowledge of the truth is of any real worth in the next life. Undoubtedly there are many learned people in the world who make a great effort to promulgate and promote their own carnal ideas, man-made theories, and false information because it lifts them up in their own eyes and, as they suppose, in the eyes of others. They are, as the Apostle Paul says, "Ever learning, and never able to come to the knowledge of the truth" (2 Timothy 3:7). They scoff at the things of God. However, such worldly wisdom is foolishness in the next world, where only God's truth endures. "O the vainness, and the frailties, and the foolishness of men!" lamented Jacob. "When they are learned they think they are wise, and they hearken not unto the counsel of God, for they set it aside, supposing they know of themselves, wherefore, their wisdom is foolishness and it profiteth them not. And they shall perish. But to be learned is good if they hearken unto the counsels of God." (2 Nephi 9:28–29.) The Apostle Paul also warned that "the natural man receiveth not the things of the Spirit of God: for they are foolishness unto him: neither can he know them, because they are spiritually discerned" (1 Corinthians 2:14).

Swedenborg claimed to have encountered such worldly-wise individuals in spirit world experiences and to have seen this very principle in operation in regard to them. He went to great lengths to explain just why their learning was "foolishness" in that realm. "False intelligence and wisdom are every kind that is devoid of a recognition of what is Divine. In fact, all people who do not recognize what is Divine, but rather recognize nature instead of what is Divine, do their thinking on a physical sense basis and are wholly sense-oriented, no matter how scholarly or learned people believe they are. Their scholarship rises no higher than the kind of material that is visible to their physical sight in the world, which they keep in their [physical] memories. He further taught:

> I have been allowed to talk with many scholars after their departure from this world, with some who had been most prominent, renowned in the learned world. . . .
>
> The ones who denied the Divine at heart, no matter how much lip service they gave it, had become so senseless that they could scarcely grasp a civic truth, let alone a spiritual one. You could tell and even see that the more inward

reaches of their minds were so closed off that they seemed black (phenomena like this are presented visually in the spiritual world), and of such nature that they could not stand any heavenly light or receive any inflow from heaven.

This blackness that appeared around their more inward reaches was greater and more widespread in people who had justified themselves in denying the Divine by means of the data of their scholarship. . . .

We may determine that these people are like this in the spiritual world when they arrive there after death, simply from this: all the things that are in the natural memory and are directly bonded to the physical senses . . . become inactive. . . . (*Heaven and Hell*, pp. 269–70, 271–72.)

Some of those who are exposed to the truth during their near-death or other spiritual encounter learn to discern truth and distinguish it from falsehood. "The knowledge flows through my consciousness instinctively and I am able to recognize what is true and what is not," explains Nancy Clark. "I did not feel this way prior to the experience." (As quoted in *Heading Toward Omega*, p. 221.) Again, we know that such discernment is a gift of the light of Christ. "Whatsoever is truth is light, and whatsoever is light is Spirit, even the Spirit of Jesus Christ" (D&C 84:45).

Indeed, though they are still every bit as human as others, the lives of those who survive these transcendent occurrences seem to be more filled with the Spirit of the Lord. Because of this, they manifest the "fruits of the spirit"—"love, joy, peace, longsuffering, gentleness, goodness, faith, meekness, temperance" (Galatians 5:22–23). These fruits extend to many other positive changes besides those we have mentioned. Though they don't suddenly become perfect, some stop drinking and "partying." Some stop their cussing and use of foul language. Others spend more time with family members. The list is endless, because it is different for each individual. Suffice it to say that all of these changes seem to be not only compatible with the teachings of the restored gospel, but central to them. They partake of some characteristics of the "rebirth" that takes place in those who are converted to the gospel. As should be the case with a truly converted Latter-day Saint, the lives of those who enjoy this experience become a witness to the world of life after death and of the profound love and life-enhancing influence of the Spirit of the Lord Jesus Christ.

CHAPTER 15

What Does This Mean to Latter-day Saints?

This book has not been written to make members of the Church feel superior to others in the world because we are already privileged to possess much of the knowledge and understanding gained by those who get a glimpse of the spirit world. Rather, we as Latter-day Saints should feel overwhelmed and humbled at the transcendent treasure which has been entrusted to us. It is gratifying but humbling to have so many of our doctrines and beliefs confirmed in these other-faith NDEs and other similar experiences—especially since as a people we have been persecuted and ridiculed throughout the generations for teaching some of these precepts. While all this may prove little or nothing to the world, to us it is a thrilling external affirmation of our faith.

Further, it is humbling to realize how much we can learn, not only from these experiences but also from all truth wherever and from whomever we can find it. "One of the grand fundamental principles of 'Mormonism,'" declared the Prophet Joseph Smith, "is to receive truth, let it come from whence it may" (*Teachings*, p. 313). And lastly, it is *very* humbling to realize the profound responsibility which has been placed upon us because of the momentous gift we have been given. "For of him unto whom much is given much is required" (D&C 82:3).

Near-Death Experiences and the True Church

If near-death, out-of-body, or other spirit world experiences so strongly affirm the doctrines and teachings of what we testify is "the only true and living church upon the face of the whole earth" (D&C 1:30), why aren't the recipients of these encounters led or directed to it? At first consideration such a result might be considered most logical and desirable, but after examining the implications of such we conclude there may be several reasons why this seldom happens.

First, it is true that some have been led to the Church through near-death and other similar experiences. However, there are also a few who have been led to other churches. In any case, the NDErs are rarely if ever told by the being of light or others they encounter, "This is the true Church," or "You will find happiness at this church." Almost invariably they are shown or told something symbolic which only comes to have full meaning to them after they have put forth the effort to find the answers. The Lord still requires each individual to exercise faith and exert personal effort and desire to find and obey the truth, and being told—in a short, unique visit that required no effort of mind or faith—which was the true Church would be inconsistent with this principle. As we have learned, each discovers the truth only as he or she is ready to accept and live it.

This leads us to the second possible reason why NDErs don't automatically come back knowing about the true Church. It may be that the spirits (other than the being of light) whom many contact during their exposure to the spirit world do not yet know this themselves. We have demonstrated that the process of teaching the gospel in the spirit world proceeds much as it does here on earth, though it may be more successful and proceed somewhat faster. However, there are many billions more people to reach on that side of the veil, and each must be taught in his or her own time.

The preaching of the gospel in the spirit world, in turn, brings to mind another possible reason why most experiencers may not be led to the true church after their NDE, but merely to live good lives of love, service, and integrity. Not all of Heavenly Father's children were designated in premortality to receive the gospel in this life. Apparently most, for a variety of reasons—some known only to the Lord—will receive it in the next life rather than here. While we know that each person's mission or foreordination is different, we know that everyone will have a full opportunity to learn and accept the gospel of Jesus Christ and its ordinances.

Why a True Church?

Some members of the Church may wonder, "If all of the above is true—if what matters most is what is in your heart, and if all of God's loving children are welcomed into the spirit world, seemingly with the same joyous reward, why do I need to belong to this church?" The authors have been aware that near-death experiences may cause some to struggle with this question. We have pondered this carefully and have come to recognize some very important answers.

First and foremost: *most of these individuals must die or nearly die to get just an inkling or an intimation of the knowledge and understanding we have available to us every day through the restored gospel of Jesus Christ!* Even then, when they return to mortality, many of the pieces of the puzzle are missing and some of the insights gained there are forgotten. By virtue of modern revelation, the guidance of latter-day prophets, and the gift of the Holy Ghost—which is a higher and fuller manifestation of the Light of Christ possessed by all people—members of The Church of Jesus Christ of Latter-day Saints have a distinct advantage in this life as well as in the life to come. They already have within their grasp, sometimes from childhood, an understanding of the purpose of life which can lead them to the happier, healthier, more meaningful and peaceful life that most NDErs often passionately pursue after their enlightenment. Even more important, it prepares them for the next life better than does any other religion on earth. They "will have so much the advantage in the world to come" (D&C 130:18–19).

Along with this advantage, of course, comes responsibility. While religious affiliation and doctrine may not yet matter for some, for those of us who have been called to establish and promote the Lord's true kingdom and authority on the earth it matters very much. Apparently not every one of the Father's children on earth will be a member of his Church *before* the Savior's second coming, but it is imperative that the Lord's government, his priesthood, and his holy temples be organized, functioning, and prepared to receive him and continue his monumental work during the Millennium. Shortly after the restoration of his Church in the latter days, the Lord referred to the responsibilities and blessings of being called to such a work: "Verily, I say unto you that ye are chosen out of the world to declare my gospel with the sound of rejoicing, as with the voice of a trump. Lift up your hearts and be glad, for I am in your midst, and am your advocate with the Father; and it is his good will to give you the kingdom." (D&C 29:4–5.) And in another revelation:

> He that is ordained of God and sent forth, the same is appointed to be the greatest, notwithstanding he is the least and the servant of all.
>
> Wherefore, he is possessor of all things; for all things are subject unto him, both in heaven and on the earth, the life and the light, the Spirit and the power, sent forth by the will of the Father through Jesus Christ, his Son.
>
> But no man is possessor of all things except he be purified and cleansed from all sin. (D&C 50:26–28.)

In more recent years, Elder John A. Widtsoe further explained what it means to be foreordained to this trust. This is the ultimate reason why we cannot turn away from our covenants to be the Lord's instruments on earth.

> In our preexistent state, in the day of the great council, we made a certain agreement with the Almighty. The Lord proposed a plan, conceived by him. We accepted it. Since

the plan is intended for all men, we became parties to the salvation of every person under that plan. We agreed, right then and there, to be not only saviors for ourselves but measurably, saviors for the whole human family. We went into a partnership with the Lord. The working of the plan became not merely the Father's work, and the Saviors work, but also our work. ("The Worth of Souls," *Utah Genealogical and Historical Magazine*, October 1934, pp. 189–90; quoted in Brent L. Top, *The Life Before*, pp. 192–93.)

What We Can Learn from Near-Death Experiences

Sometimes, like many people who are members of a church which claims to be "the only true church," we may fall into the trap of thinking we have a corner on all truth and righteousness. We may suppose that we are above learning spiritual truths from those outside the Church, since they couldn't possibly be more inspired than we are or have access to any truth that we don't. However, as pointed out above by the Prophet Joseph Smith, we are to be open to truth wherever it may be found.

There are, consequently, many things that we can learn from near-death-type experiences that help us to understand more fully the literal nature of some of our own doctrines and how we should live them. The paramount lesson we should learn from NDEs and, hopefully, from this book, is that of *the supremacy of love in heaven and on earth*. We have seen endless evidence that love is the source and the motivation for all genuine goodness and truth—and, as Jesus declared, that all commandments literally do stem from the first two commandments of love (see Matthew 22:36–40). Yet as Latter-day Saints we often find ourselves putting greater emphasis on lesser commandments, especially those which differentiate us from others, or, as some of us may think, put us above others. One Mormon near-death experiencer learned this lesson for himself.

I was raised as a Mormon. I was raised thinking, maybe, that God loved certain individuals more than others. Or that he cared about certain individuals more than others depending upon how they lived. I didn't find that to be true.

I found that his love was extended to everyone, all the time. And that he understood why we are what we are, and why we are going through what we are going through. . . .

After the experience I went through, I had to read everything I could find on Mormonism, and the Bible, and everything else, to find out if it was true or not. I found that the teachings were true, from the Bible through the Book of Mormon, and the Doctrine and Covenants; but too many times our priorities are mixed up. We forget the teachings of the New Testament—to love our neighbor, and to do all the other positive things written there. (As quoted in Arvin S. Gibson, *Glimpses of Eternity,* pp. 188–90.)

Without compromising our standards or diluting our unique doctrines, we should put more effort into searching for common ground with our fellowmen. We have seen how the Lord loves his children with a perfect love. If we claim to be members of his church, it is for us to exhibit this same kind of love toward our brothers and sisters on earth. If we have not charity, even if we belong to the true church, we are nothing. Shortly before his death, the Savior taught his disciples that godly love of one another is the mark of true discipleship (see John 13:34–35).

Moreover, the accounts about the personage or "being of light," who seems to be the Lord's representative to those entering the spirit world, can teach us not only about love but also about mercy and righteous judgment. Though this being apparently has great power and knows virtually everything about the person whose review passes before him or her, still he refrains from condemnation. He gives love, support, and guidance but never denigrates, demeans, or humiliates the experiencer. Not only does this teach us to refrain from criticizing and censuring others, whose hearts we cannot see, but it also teaches us the profound truth that love has greater power to change lives for the better than fear, anger, coercion, or any of the many other negative tools we mortals tend to resort to in seeking to influence or change others. It seems a great irony that we can do more to get people to repent by loving and accepting them (not their sins) as they are. As we do this, they begin to feel lovable and worthwhile even in their imperfect state (as we all want to feel). This also inspires them to love themselves and instills in them a desire to please the One who loves them so completely. Most NDErs who have this wonderful experience with the light go back to earth and change their lives for the better, not because they fear condemnation, but because of the overwhelming desire they have to once again bask in such infinite love. Although we cannot equate this feeling of divine love with ultimate forgiveness, this love can powerfully affect a person's attitude *and* behavior. One person said:

> So many times, fundamentalists think the NDE takes away from the judgmental aspect depicted in the Bible. But when you go into this Light, you realize the injustices that you as a person have created in the lives of other people. For me, it was *feeling* those injustices. I felt the pain I had caused. You *feel* your iniquities, your shortcomings. You feel it all. You feel yourself judged. But at the same time, you feel loved and forgiven.
>
> The questions also come up about whether or not the NDE does away with the consequences of living a bad life: criminals, that type of person. Going in that Light is a beautiful feeling in that you feel love and forgiveness. To not be able to stay in that realm of heavenly love would *be* hell. To experience it, to know that it's there, and not be able to partake of it: That's hell.
>
> Every experiencer tells me the same thing I felt and experienced. Not all of them *saw* anything, but they *felt* it. (As quoted in *After the Beyond*, p. 83.)

Cited earlier in this book are the accounts of Elders Orson Pratt, George F. Richards, and Melvin J. Ballard, who saw the Savior in dream or vision and who said they would do anything within their power to once again be in his presence and feel the love that they then felt. Indeed, those who know how to love as Christ loves are the most powerful of all people.

Inward Spirituality
as the Source of Outward Observance

We pointed out earlier that most of those who have near-death experiences come back more inwardly converted to the Lord, but often are less concerned about outward rituals and actions which, in and of themselves, seem to them meaningless. This is also an important lesson for us. In a religion which requires observance in all aspects of life, some Latter-day Saints, like the ancient Jews under the Mosaic Law, may become obsessed with outward performances of the commandments and forget the spiritual purposes for which they are given—to help them love God, above all, then neighbor and self. Like the New Testament scribes and Pharisees whom Christ condemned, we may make the mistake of measuring our worthiness and the worthiness of others by how well we fulfill the letter of the law. There are those who become almost neurotic about the gospel and drive themselves to emotional collapse trying to be outwardly perfect because they think this is what God requires or because they are so worried about what others may think about them.

Dr. George Ritchie acknowledged that "sociologists, psychiatrists, psychologists and ministers have estimated that from 55% to as much as 85% of mental illness stems not from genetic or biochemical factors but from erroneous teachings and/or misunderstanding of the doctrines of Judaism and Christianity" (*My Life After Dying*, p. 113).

The gospel of Jesus Christ is first and foremost a gospel of love, joy, and peace. If we are living the gospel out of fear—of God or of others—we have missed the whole point; we have looked "beyond the mark" (see Jacob 4:14). Perhaps, like NDErs, we need to have a new view of what is important and what is not. Outward ordinances and performances are important and indispensible for Latter-day Saints, who have been blessed with an understanding of their meaning and power. Yet we have learned from life reviews that such observances must reflect what is in the heart. For this reason, we should never condemn ourselves, our loved ones, or others solely on the basis of behavior. If our hearts are right, if we love the Lord with all of our being, given a proper diligence on our part we will be able to perform the necessary and important outward actions the Lord requires of us personally and feel at peace about it all. Then the outward observance will originate from inward devotion.

Our Responsibilities

The restored gospel, with all of its blessings and advantages, is not a religion of ease and repose, but rather one of effort and responsibility. While it may provide us with *inspiration* it also requires our *perspiration*. The Lord's work must become our work. Because of the knowledge we possess of the afterlife and the plan of salvation, we have been given numerous opportunities and responsibilities to serve and love our Father in Heaven and our fellowmen. First and foremost we must each seek, like many near-death experiencers, to complete the missions we were sent to fulfill on earth. As one experiencer put it: "I *knew* that I had a second chance at life and that God had given it to me. . . . I think at the time I thought it was because he wanted me to raise my children. As I get older, and I hope a little wiser, I have a feeling that each one of us has a *little* something to do, to pass on, that God wants us to do. It may not even register in our minds and it may even be very insignificant. But it *definitely* is part of what God wants us to do. And I feel that that's what I *have* to do. He gave me my chance, because *I* have to *do* something." (As quoted in *Life at Death*, p. 147.)

Next, we must proclaim the gospel to the world—making it available to all those who are foreordained to receive it in this life, so that they too may complete their missions upon the earth and, consequently, that the Lord's purposes may be fulfilled. Elder Hyrum M. Smith, a member of the Quorum of the Twelve and son of President Joseph F. Smith, implored the members of the Church: "You Latter-day Saints ought to praise God; but in your thankfulness for the greater blessings which you enjoy, you ought not to denounce others because they have not so much good as you have. . . . We should go forth among them with the sole desire of our hearts to manifest unto them that which God has revealed unto us, and carry to them that which has made us happy, and which has made us in very deed the Church and people of God. That should be the feeling of the Latter-day Saints." (In Conference Report, October 1903, pp. 70–71.)

Additionally, we must do our genealogical research and become "saviors on Mount Zion" by being willing proxies in the temples, thus making the ordinances of salvation available for those who have not enjoyed that wonderful privilege, as we do, while on earth. President Gordon B. Hinckley asserted that this service we can render to mankind, temple work on behalf of the dead, "more nearly approaches the vicarious sacrifice of the Son of God in behalf of all mankind than any other work of which I am aware. . . . It is a service which is of the very essence of selflessness." (*Ensign*, March 1993, p. 5.)

For those who have not received the full blessings of the gospel, and perhaps will not do so in mortality, we must provide help and encouragement through our love, service, and personal examples of righteousness, assisting them to fulfill the earthly missions they have been given. For them, religious affiliation may not now be as important as what is in their hearts. Therefore, we should join with the good and decent people of the world to "bring to pass much righteousness" (see D&C 58:27). We should support truth and goodness in all religions and in all people. The Prophet Joseph always advocated this.

The inquiry is frequently made of me, "Wherein do you differ from others in your religious views?" In reality and essence we do not differ so far in our religious views, but that we could all drink into one principle of love. . . .

If I esteem mankind to be in error, shall I bear them down? No. I will lift them up, and in their own way too, if I cannot persuade them my way is better; and I will not seek to compel any man to believe as I do, only by the force of reasoning, for truth will cut its own way. Do you believe in Jesus Christ and the Gospel of salvation which He revealed? So do I. Christians should cease wrangling and contending with each other, and cultivate the principles of union and friendship in their midst; and they will do it before the millennium can be ushered in and Christ takes possession of His kingdom. (*Teachings*, p. 313.)

Accordingly, the Prophet cautioned that we must never look down on others because of their beliefs. "We ought always to be aware of those prejudices which sometimes so strangely present themselves, and are so congenial to human nature, against our friends, neighbors, and brethren of the world, who choose to differ from us in opinion and in matters of faith. Our religion is between us and our God. Their religion is between them and their God." (*Teachings*, pp. 146–47.)

Thus we must "press forward with a steadfastness in Christ, having a perfect brightness of hope, and a love of God and of all men" (2 Nephi 31:20). We must do everything we can to encourage and foster love and hope in the world. Knowing what we know, and understanding what we understand, we should act like a leaven of love to the human race. The Prophet Joseph declared: "There is a love from God that should be exercised toward those of our faith, who walk uprightly, which is peculiar to itself, but it is without prejudice; it also gives scope to the mind, which enables us to conduct ourselves with greater liberality towards all that are not of our faith, than what they exercise towards one another" (*Teachings*, p. 147). Elder Neal A. Maxwell also elaborated on this principle. "You and I are believers, and preachers of a glorious gospel which can deepen all human relationships now as well as projecting all relationships into eternity," he reminded us: "We, more than others, should not only carry jumper and tow cables in our cars but in our hearts by which means we can send the needed boost or charge of encouragement or the added momentum to mortal neighbors. . . . Service keeps us from forgetting the Lord our God, because being among and serving our brothers and sisters reminds us that Father is ever there and is pleased when we serve, for while the recipients of our service are our neighbors—they are His children." ("When the Heat of the Sun Cometh," unpublished address delivered at Young Adult fireside, Salt Lake Tabernacle, May 20, 1979, quoted in *The Life Before*, p. 197.)

Finally, it seems fitting that we should include one last account of a non-LDS near-death experiencer. Like so many of the witnesses and statements we have explored in this book, this testimony could be paralleled by that of myriad Latter-day Saints. One woman who was given a higher understanding through her NDE spoke movingly of the desire it gave her to lift her fellow beings, regardless of personal sacrifice.

> The most important goal in my life is to use my experience in a positive meaningful way to help others. My greatest problem is determining in what capacity I can best serve. It is my sincere hope that I will be able to link up with someone who will be able to advise and help me. There is no doubt in my mind that I will accomplish my mission on this earth. I firmly believe that this experience was given as a gift to me to be shared with others. I WILL make a meaningful contribution to the research and the application of the life after death phenomenon regardless of the skepticism I shall encounter from those I reach out to. This work is far too important for my own personal feelings to be considered.
>
> I am motivated only by the gratitude I feel in being a recipient of this experience. For giving me a glimpse for a few moments of a life beyond the present one, I owe it to my fellow man to lovingly share this great truth with them.
>
> When I ultimately make my transition to the next world and meet Him again I'll say, "Lord, for the precious gift you gave to me while I lived on the earth, I did my very best work for you. This is MY gift in return to you." (As quoted in *Heading Toward Omega*, pp. 222–23.)

As the authors of this book we add our witness of the existence of a loving God, whose children we all are. Because of his infinite love for us he has provided a means whereby we can continue to live and learn and love beyond death's door. Our lives become our token of appreciation for that divine gift. We have not come to that assurance through a near-death experience or a glimpse of the spirit realm. Our knowledge, though enhanced and validated by the numerous experiences we have cited in this book, has come to us in a different manner. Just as a person need not travel to the Holy Land to "walk where Jesus walked," or kneel in the Garden of Gethsemane to know the reality of his atoning sacrifice that occurred there, one need not have an NDE or a vision of the spirit world to know with absolute surety of the reality of life after death. Such knowledge may be obtained in the doctrines of the restored gospel— through the scriptures, the words of the living prophets, and the witness of the Holy Ghost. This is the assurance we have received—a knowledge that "passeth all understanding."

This spiritual knowledge motivates us to prepare ourselves to joyfully pass beyond death's door and step into eternity. The experiences we have so frequently quoted in this book only validate and illustrate that which the scriptures teach and of which the Spirit also testifies: "The grave hath no victory, and the sting of death is swallowed up in Christ. He is the light and the life of the world; yea, a light that is endless, that can never be darkened; yea, and also a life which is endless, that there can be no more death." (Mosiah 16:8–9.) Of this we gratefully and humbly bear testimony.

Bibliography

Atwater, P. M. H. *Coming Back to Life*. New York: Dodd, Mead & Co., 1988.

Benson, Ezra Taft. *The Teachings of Ezra Taft Benson*. Salt Lake City: Bookcraft, 1988.

Cannon, George Q. *Gospel Truth*. Two volumes in one. Compiled by Jerreld L. Newquist. Salt Lake City: Deseret Book, 1987.

Conference Report. Salt Lake City: The Church of Jesus Christ of Latter-day Saints.

Crowther, Duane S. *Life Everlasting*. Salt Lake City: Bookcraft, 1967.

Dahl, Larry E. "The Concept of Hell." In *Doctrines of the Book of Mormon*. Edited by Bruce A. Van Orden and Brent L. Top. Salt Lake City: Deseret Book, 1992.

Encyclopedia of Mormonism. Edited by Daniel H. Ludlow. 5 vols. New York: Macmillan Publishing Co., 1992.

Flynn, Charles P. *After the Beyond*. Englewood Cliffs, NJ: Prentice-Hall, 1986.

Gibson, Arvin S. *Glimpses of Eternity*. Bountiful, UT: Horizon Publishers, 1992.

Grey, Margot. *Return from Death*. London: Arkana, 1987.

Greyson, Bruce, and Charles P. Flynn. *The Near-Death Experience*. Springfield, IL: Charles C. Thomas, 1984.

Harris, Barbara, and Lionel C. Bascom. *Full Circle*. New York: Pocket Books, 1990.

Hartshorn, Leon W. *Exceptional Stories From the Lives of Our Apostles.* Salt Lake City: Deseret Book, 1972.

Heinerman, Joseph. *Spirit World Manifestations.* Salt Lake City: Joseph Lyon & Associates, 1978.

————. *Temple Manifestations.* Manti, UT: Mountain Valley Publishers, 1974.

Journal of Discourses. 26 vols. Liverpool: F. D. Richards & Sons, 1851–86.

Journal of Near-Death Studies. Quarterly Publication of the International Association of Near-Death Studies. New York: Human Sciences Press.

Kimball, Spencer W. *The Teachings of Spencer W. Kimball.* Edited by Edward L. Kimball. Salt Lake City: Bookcraft, 1982.

Klinkenborg, Verlyn. "At the Edge of Eternity." *Life.* March 1992.

Lee, Harold B. *Stand Ye in Holy Places.* Salt Lake City: Deseret Book, 1974.

————. *Ye Are the Light of the World.* Salt Lake City: Deseret Book, 1974.

McConkie, Bruce R. *A New Witness for the Articles of Faith.* Salt Lake City: Deseret Book, 1985.

————. *Mormon Doctrine.* 2nd edition. Salt Lake City: Bookcraft, 1966.

————. "Our Relationship with the Lord." *1981–82 Brigham Young University Devotional and Fireside Speeches.* Provo, UT: BYU Press, 1982.

McConkie, Oscar, W., Jr. *Angels.* Salt Lake City: Deseret Book, 1975.

Melvin J. Ballard: Crusader for Righteousness. Salt Lake City: Bookcraft, 1966.

Millet, Robert L., and Joseph Fielding McConkie. *The Life Beyond.* Salt Lake City: Bookcraft, 1986.

Moody, Raymond A., Jr. *Life After Life.* New York: Bantam Books, 1976.

————. *Reflections on Life After Life.* New York: Bantam Books, 1977.

————. *The Light Beyond.* New York: Bantam Books, 1989.

Morse, Melvin, with Paul Perry. *Closer to the Light.* New York: Villard Books, 1990.

————. *Transformed by the Light.* New York: Villard Books, 1992.

Nelson, Lee. *Beyond the Veil.* 3 vols. Orem, UT: Cedar Fort, 1988–90.

Osis, Karlis, and Erlendur Haraldsson. *At the Hour of Death.* New York: Hastings House, 1986.

Packer, Boyd K. "A Dedication—To Faith." *Speeches of the Year*. Provo, UT: BYU, 29 April 1969.

————. *Teach Ye Diligently*. Salt Lake City: Deseret Book, 1975.

Peale, Norman Vincent. "There Is No Death." *Plus: The Magazine of Positive Thinking*. March 1991.

Pratt, Orson. *The Seer*. Washington, D.C. vol. 1. no. 10, October 1853.

Pratt, Parley P. *Key to the Science of Theology*. Salt Lake City: Deseret Book, 1979.

Rawlings, Maurice. *Beyond Death's Door*. New York: Bantam Books, 1979.

Ring, Kenneth. *Heading Toward Omega*. New York: Quill, 1985.

————. *Life at Death*. New York: Quill, 1982.

Ritchie, George G., Jr. *My Life After Dying*. Norfolk, VA: Hampton Roads Publishing Co., 1991.

————. *Return from Tomorrow*. Old Tappan, NJ: Spire Books, Fleming H. Revell Co., 1978.

Rogo, D. Scott. *The Return from Silence*. Northhamptonshire, England: The Aquarian Press, 1989.

Sabom, Michael B. *Recollections of Death*. New York: Harper & Row, 1982.

Smith, Joseph, Jr. *History of The Church of Jesus Christ of Latter-day Saints*. Edited by B. H. Roberts. 7 vols. Salt Lake City: The Church of Jesus Christ of Latter-day Saints, 1932–51.

————. *Teachings of the Prophet Joseph Smith*. Compiled by Joseph Fielding Smith. Salt Lake City: Deseret Book, 1976.

————. *The Personal Writings of Joseph Smith*. Compiled by Dean C. Jessee. Salt Lake City: Deseret Book, 1984.

Smith, Joseph F. *Gospel Doctrine*. Salt Lake City: Deseret Book, 1939.

Smith, Joseph Fielding. *Church History and Modern Revelation*. 2 vols. Salt Lake City: Deseret Book, 1953.

————. *Doctrines of Salvation*. 3 vols. Compiled by Bruce R. McConkie. Salt Lake City: Bookcraft, 1954–56.

————. *The Way to Perfection*. Salt Lake City: Deseret Book, 1970.

Snow, Lorenzo. *The Teachings of Lorenzo Snow*. Compiled by Clyde J. Williams. Salt Lake City: Bookcraft, 1984.

Sorenson, Michele R., and David R. Willmore. *The Journey Beyond Life*. Orem, UT: Family Affair Books, 1988.

Swedenborg, Emanuel. *Heaven and Hell*. Translated by George F. Dole. 58th printing. New York: Swedenborg Foundation, 1990.

Top, Brent L. *The Life Before*. Salt Lake City: Bookcraft, 1988.

Vital Signs (formerly entitled *Revitalized Signs*) Monthly Newsletter of the International Association for Near-Death Studies. Hartford, CT.

Woodruff, Wilford. *Discourses of Wilford Woodruff*. Compiled by G. Homer Durham. Salt Lake City: Bookcraft, 1946.

Whitney, Orson F. *The Life of Heber C. Kimball*. 1888. Reprint. Salt Lake City: Bookcraft, 1967.

Young, Brigham. *Discourses of Brigham Young*. Compiled by John A. Widtsoe. Salt Lake City, 1977.

Zaleski, Carol. *Otherworld Journeys*. New York: Oxford University Press, 1987.

Index